ASIAN STUDIES ASSOCIATION OF AUSTRALIA
Southeast Asia Publications Series

**FRAGMENTS OF THE PRESENT**

# FRAGMENTS OF THE PRESENT

Searching for modernity in Vietnam's South

**PHILIP TAYLOR**

Asian Studies Association of Australia
in association with

ALLEN & UNWIN
and
UNIVERSITY OF HAWAI'I PRESS
HONOLULU

First published in 2001

Published in Australia by
Allen & Unwin
83 Alexander Street
Crows Nest NSW 2065
Australia

Published in North America by
University of Hawai'i Press
2840 Kolowalu Street
Honolulu, Hawai'i 96822

National Library of Australia
Cataloguing-in-Publication entry:

Taylor, Philip, 1962– .
Fragments of the present: searching for modernity in Vietnam's south.

Bibliography
Includes index.
ISBN 1 86508 383 6.

1. Vietnam—Intellectual life—20th century. 2. Vietnam—Civilization—20th century.
3. Vietnam—History—1975– .
I. Title.

959.7044

Library of Congress Cataloging-in-Publication Data

Taylor, Philip.
Fragments of the present: searching for modernity in Vietnam's south /
Philip Taylor.
p. cm. — (Southeast Asia publications series)

Includes bibliographical references and index.
ISBN 0-8248-2417-2 (alk. paper)

1. Vietnam, Southern—History. 2. Vietnam, Southern—Social conditions.
3. Vietnam, Southern—Economic conditions. 4. Vietnam—Politics and
government—1975– . I. Title. II

DS559.92.S68 S39 2000
959.7—dc21                                                                          00-060762

Set in 10/11 Times by DOCUPRO, Sydney
Printed by SRM Production Services Sdn Bhd, Malaysia

10 9 8 7 6 5 4 3 2 1

# Contents

*v*

# Maps and illustrations

# Abbreviations

| | |
|---|---|
| AP | Associated Press |
| ARVN | Army of the Republic of Vietnam |
| ASEAN | Association of South East Asian Nations |
| BBC | British Broadcasting Corporation |
| DRV | Democratic Republic of Vietnam |
| *FEER* | *Far Eastern Economic Review* |
| GATT | General Agreement on Tariff and Trade |
| HCMC | Ho Chi Minh City |
| ICP | Indochinese Communist Party |
| IMF | International Monetary Fund |
| JPRS | Joint Publications Research Service |
| NLF | National Liberation Front (of South Vietnam) |
| PRC | People's Republic of China |
| PRG | Provisional Revolutionary Government (of South Vietnam) |
| RVN | Republic of Vietnam |
| SRVN | Socialist Republic of Vietnam |
| VCP | Vietnamese Communist Party |

# Preface

This book is about the idea of the Vietnamese South. In a country where nationalism runs deep, which has been divided politically and has experienced devastating military conflicts, the question of regional identities is controversial and illuminating. Making regional comparisons is a common practice among Vietnamese people. In the post-war years, after the country was politically unified, southern identity became a critical topic for discussion. Encountering this debate while in Vietnam in the early 1990s, I found the identity of many features associated with the region such as its popular music, markets, commodities, urbanised lifestyles and historical sequence of regimes, to be hotly contested. There were great discrepancies in power between the protagonists, whose views I discuss here, some having the power to silence or overwhelm the voices of others. As a participant of sorts in this debate, my own treatment of southern identity as plural unavoidably assails the authority of any given position. Regarding Vietnam as a complex country with a vigorous intellectual scene I have attended to disputes as much as unexpected convergences of thinking. These plural voices are a vivid point of entry into southern Vietnam's turbulent post-war history, the social history of ideas, shifts in state ideology, the impact of political and economic changes and the contrasting fortunes of urban and rural communities. They also indicate that beyond the issue of regional identity lies fruitful terrain for future research into local histories and other particularist identities.

This work began life as an anthropological project at a time when the concept of alternative modernities had become popular in social theory. This was the idea that the dominant forms of contemporary global society, economics, politics and subjectivity, which some have glossed as 'modernity', are not singular but have been localised in a variety of ways not only by countries such as Vietnam, but also by different state projects, religions, ethnic groups, classes and genders. I became interested in this body of theory and yet departed from its central tenets as a result of spending more than two years residing in southern Vietnam. I found that the function of the 'anthropologist' as classifier of societies had been amply superseded by Vietnamese people themselves, who have produced a plenitude of written and oral commentary on their society's relationship to modernity. I also found disagreement on this topic within the Vietnamese world to be rife. It seemed that to describe this ferment would be a valuable project, as interesting as any cumulative or objective conclusions an 'outsider' might draw on the subject of southern Vietnam's 'modernity'. I believe the Vietnamese debate has produced important departures which those interested in social theory will find significant. My response to it is this book which reflects my partial exposure to Vietnamese society and attempts to compare positions in a meaningful way so that one might learn something about the society from the dissension within it. It is hoped this account of a conversation about southern Vietnam and disagreements about its identity as 'modern', will both contribute to the understanding of Vietnam and be accessible enough to allow comparison for those engaged in like debates in other societies.

This book is a revision of a PhD thesis in Anthropology undertaken at the Australian National University (ANU). Book manuscript revisions were completed while a visiting fellow in the Research School of Pacific and Asian Studies, which is one of the most exciting places to be involved in the study of contemporary Vietnam. I learnt much from the ANU's community of Vietnam specialists including David Marr, Ben Kerkvliet, Li Tana, Nola Cooke, Thaveeporn Vasavakul, Mandy Thomas, Do My Thien and Carl Thayer. I am most grateful for their support and attentive readings. This work was inspired and given generous assistance by Geremie Barme, Sonia Ryang, Kathryn Robinson, James Fox, Gehan Wijeyewardene, Michael Young, Anthony Reid, Craig Reynolds, Rey Ileto, Melanie Beresford, Patrick Guinness, Christine Helliwell, Francesca Merlan, Alan Rumsey, Don Gardner, Ria Van de Zandt, Fay Castles, Oanh Collins and Pham Thu Thuy. I am deeply indebted to Geremie Barme, Grant Evans and Mark Seldon for their encouragement and assistance in getting my manuscript published. Perceptive comments by external reviewers have helped me strengthen my argument and delivery. Anthony Milner, Linda Poskitt and Christa Munns have helped make this book a reality.

I am grateful to my Vietnamese language teachers at the Centre for Southeast Asian Studies, Ho Chi Minh City University. The University was my official sponsor throughout my stay in Vietnam and I am thankful to its administrators for infallibly coming up with the right form to fit my unusual research requirements. I am indebted to Dr Nguyen Van Lich, Dr Dinh Le Thu and Dr Bui Khanh The for advice and assistance in negotiating the paperwork necessary to allow my official metamorphosis from language student into field researcher. My thanks for assistance with securing a research site and for many interesting discussions are warmly extended to Professor Do Thai Dong, formerly of the Institute of Social Sciences, Ho Chi Minh City.

Numerous other debts of gratitude are owed to those who helped me in my research including Professor Mac Duong, Nguyen Thi Hoa, Le Thanh Sang, Nguyen Thu Sa, Chi Lan, Phan Ngoc Chien, Huynh Ngoc Trang, Le Van Nam and other members of Ho Chi Minh City's Institute of Social Sciences. I thank Son Nam, Phan Thanh Van, Phi Hung and numerous other musicians, writers and artists who were my guides to southern Vietnam's world of arts and letters. Thanks also go to Anh Hai of the So Thuy Loi, to Nam Chau and Anh Vu of the Tien Giang party school and to Anh Thuy of Minh Hai TV station.

In the village of Vinh Kim I am deeply indebted to my host, 'Chu' Nam. I am afraid that my short but disruptive stay must have given someone with his social and administrative commitments and pressing economic responsibilities an unwelcome added burden, but he and his family made it their highest priority to show me hospitality and escort me around the village in conformity with official requirements. I would like to thank my various other anonymous interlocutors (to whom I have given pseudonyms in the book) for graciously making their time available and indulging my persistent questioning about their lives. My thanks also go to Professor Tran Van Khe, professor of musicology at the Sorbonne and by many villagers' reckonings Vinh Kim's most famous living son, for his prompt and detailed response to my letter.

Special thanks for their unwaivering support and their interest in this project go to my mother and to my family. I also owe sincere thanks for their friendship to To Kim Anh Tran, my first guide to the Vietnamese world, to Phuc Tien for his warm hospitality, to Dung Hanh for her valuable insights to Sam Korsmoe, to Phan Ngoc Chien and, finally, to Dat, Binh and their family, for being a family to me in Vietnam.

Fieldwork for this book was conducted in Vietnam between October 1992 and March 1994. A one-month return trip was undertaken in May 1995. Funding for these periods of fieldwork was provided by the Australian Department of Education (Australian Award for Research in Asia) and a PhD scholarship and field grant from the Department of Anthropology in the Research School of Pacific and Asian Studies at the ANU. On subsequent trips undertaken in 1998 and 1999, I was able to confirm or rethink some of my earlier findings.

Some of the discussion on music in Chapter 1 is forthcoming in 'Music as a "neocolonial poison" in post-war Southern Vietnam',

*Crossroads, An Interdisciplinary Journal of Southeast Asian Studies* (vol. 14:1). Part of Chapter 3 has appeared in 'Indigenizing colonial modernity in *Nam Bo*', *East Asian History* 1998 (vol. 15–16: 97–128).

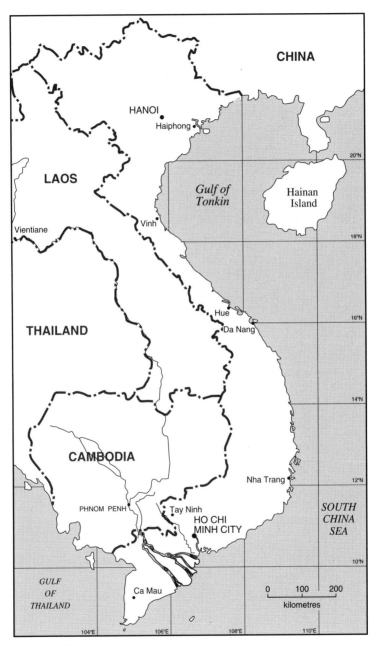

**Map 1  Vietnam**

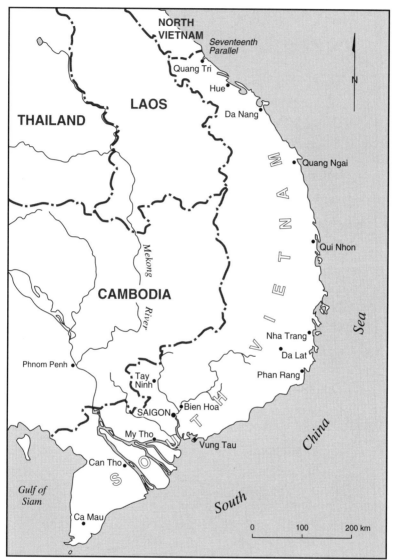

**Map 2   The Republic of Vietnam 1955–75**

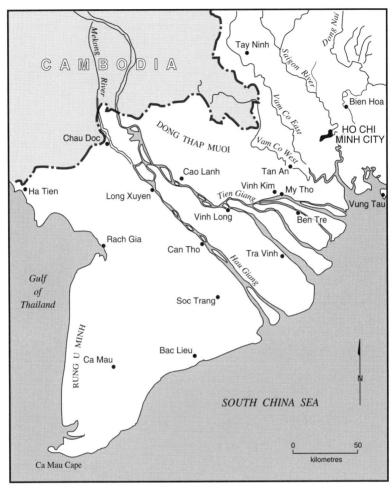

**Map 3  Major rivers and towns of the *Nam Bo* plain**

# Introduction

## VIETNAM'S PASSAGE TO MODERNITY

Gazing out the window, I wondered what flying into the field on a 727 might have in common with the outbound journeys of my disciplinary forebears. It was 1992. Cabin service, air-conditioning and a selection of the day's newspapers in a variety of languages did little to evoke the privations and unfamiliarity often associated with ethnographic fieldwork.

Once across Vietnam's territorial limits, we would be breaching the perimeter of the capitalist world. The US-imposed trade embargo was still in force. Until its withdrawal from Cambodia, all of Vietnam's land borders had been with socialist countries. The stretch of sea below was Vietnam's approximation of the Iron Curtain. Passing across it would be to confront the West's other 'Orient': the Eastern bloc. I hardly expected to be greeted with open arms. I had been told to expect surveillance of my activities. I had been granted a student visa but was not sure if a permit to do fieldwork would be granted.

Flights such as the one I was on were becoming more frequent, carrying waves of foreign investors, trade negotiators and consultants investigating possibilities of doing business in Vietnam. In 1988 the *Far Eastern Economic Review* was still speaking of 'socialist stag-nation' and 'floundering' private enterprise (*FEER* 28 July 1988:20). However by 1991 ASEAN investment was helping to 'buoy Vietnam's economy' (*FEER* 27 June 1991:52) and by 1992 the country was experiencing a 'rice glut' (*FEER* 14 May 1992a:57). Talk abounded that Vietnam had the potential to turn into a breakaway tiger-cub economy. Waves of investors were turning into floods, streams of

*1*

**The luxury class 'Floating Hotel', on the Saigon River, which was a prestigious symbol of Vietnam's global re-engagement in the early 1990s**

applicants for investment licences were swelling. Simultaneously, in the early 1990s, Vietnam was becoming the hot new destination for independent travellers. Jaded overland travellers in Bangkok's Khao San Road were raving about the freshness and spontaneity of travel in Vietnam, interactions with locals 'unspoilt' by mutual cynicism. A note of urgency could be detected in some reports. Vietnam would soon succumb to a flood of Westernisation, the latest victim of the capitalist juggernaut. Travellers should get there soon, before its traditional way of life gave way to modern culture. Like the sea below, history was surging relentlessly towards the Vietnamese shore.[1]

As the time-space co-ordinates of my passage to fieldwork began to resolve in this way, I thought of steamers depositing anthropologists on tropical islands with instructions to return a couple of years later. Agents in the high tide of colonialism or salvagers of wrecked traditions, the journeys of my professional forebears were framed against the global expansion and consolidation of the imagined 'deluge' of modernity (Marcus 1986:165). Marx, one of the nineteenth century's great modernists, had captured the liquefying properties of capital expansion in a phrase: 'all that is solid melts into air'. The meaning of the present moment was being rendered in the same way. The dam between East and West had just been breached. Crowds of Germans poured ecstatically through gaps in the Berlin Wall mingling with each other after decades of separation. Marshall Berman, referring in part to the revolutions of the former Eastern bloc dubbed 1989 'a great modernist year' (Berman 1990:55). It seemed inevitable that ripples of change would continue around the world, washing aside the political legacies of the cold war. In that year Vietnam was described as moving 'against the tide' of political reform (*FEER* 14 September 1989:29). Nonetheless, under policies referred to as *doi moi* or 'renovation', dramatic steps towards bureaucratic decentralisation, privatisation and the commercialisation of everyday life were occurring.

Encapsulated in such fluid imagery, Vietnam thus appeared to be entering a condition that social scientists were contemporaneously describing as the global condition of 'modernity'. The fall of the wall produced an exceptional moment of consensus on the identity of the present moment as modern or even as 'postmodern'. This was a chorus with rich textures. 'Modernity' signified different things to its burgeoning number of theorists: ceaseless dynamism, order, rationality, secularisation, self-consciousness, industrialisation and capitalism, to name but a few of its denotations. Moreover, the timing was not agreed on: the characteristic processes of modernity were purported to have begun as early as the fourth century (Kroker and Cook 1988) but also variously with the discovery of America, the Renaissance, the Reformation, the Enlightenment, the Industrial Revolution and as late as the Russian Revolutions (Lefebvre 1995:228). Its original geographical denotations were also variable, including Europe, America, the North Atlantic, the 'West', and colonial metropoles such as Japan. Through a variety of processes of diffusion, such as imperialism, globalisation, and time-space compression, the condition of modernity had spread and now, with the fall of the wall, traversed the earth. Loosely defined, and subject to endless improvisation, the 'modern' had become a compelling symbol of global temporal unity. Time had come to an end. The world had become one. If the sociologist Anthony Giddens was right in thinking that we were now in a situation 'of modernity coming to understand itself' (1990:48), there was little more to do but to join in this festival of published self-congratulation, staged by, and on behalf of, this sublime condition.

On the other hand, anthropology as a discipline had been distinctive for its focus on the description of human difference. In a world considered modern, what could the anthropological study of societies such as Vietnam offer? Would the spread of 'modernity' erase human differences and eventually render anthropology irrelevant? These questions were addressed by a number of anthropologists who attempted to transcend the unilinealist assumptions of much sociological theory by decentring modernity. Although accepted as a global phenomenon, modernity was seen to have been plurally indigenised in a manner initially associated with Japan, one of the first 'non-western' nations to have been admitted into the 'modern' club (Clammer 1995). Various versions of 'alternative modernity' were sketched out: Brazilian modernity (Rabinow 1992), East Asian modernity (Tu Wei-ming 1996), Congolese modernity (Friedman 1992:351), Trinidadian modernity (Miller 1994) as well as French and other European modernities (Rabinow 1989; Pred 1995). Modernity had been 'indigenised' (Sahlins 1993), 'localised' (Miller 1995) 'encompassed' (Friedman 1992:351) and 'consumed' (Breckenridge 1995). This spate of ethnography made a plausible case for an enduringly heterogeneous world of multiple modernities.

Responding in such ways, it appeared these anthropologists had pulled off something of a coup. While recognising the ties and inter-dependencies that make up the world, they had preserved a sense of its human diversity. They had factored in the effects of new constellations of global power, while allowing that the societies they studied retained power to influence their own histories. They had transcended the logic that binds others to a temporally inferior status when terms like 'tradition' and 'backwardness' are used and they had recognised these places as 'in history', contemporaneous with the societies of the 'developed' or 'modern' world. Thus they imagined those places as implicated in 'modernity' not external to it, part of its development, not anterior to it (Piot 1999). This was an antidote to Orientalism, a view of the ethnographic other as out of time (Said 1978). It was a corrective to anthropology's past practices of 'allochronism', the rendering of otherness in terms of temporal difference (Fabian 1983). The solution was to render others in the now.

Yet this approach made the discipline's focus of study subject to the politics that invariably surrounds the now in centres of academic production. It rendered the subjects of anthropological study vulnerable to such shifts, and reduced their temporal condition to an effect of powerful nations' struggles over the meaning of their times. For example, in the 1990s, when the victorious states of the capitalist order celebrated their 'modernity', anthropologists began to construe other societies as equivalently 'modern'. The clear danger in hyphenating human diversity to the 'modern' in such ways is the effect of ongoing disagreements over its meaning, periodisation and location. As the meaning of 'our' times shifts in debates staged in privileged centres of learning, the positioning of other societies, in time and space, continues to shift and fracture accordingly.[2] The way Vietnam has been represented in academic scholarship affords examples of this peril. Scholars of Vietnam have described this country as one profoundly implicated in the events of the 'modern' world. However disagreements over the advent, the meaning and the location of modernity in Vietnam have left that country in a kind of classificatory limbo.

## AS 'MODERNITY' MELTS INTO AIR

Vietnam, the land of the 'television war', had first come to my youthful attention in the late 1970s, through graphic TV images of the boat people exodus. After peace returned to their troubled land, more than one million Vietnamese had fled the country. I recalled stories of repression I had heard from Vietnamese-Australian friends in Cabramatta, Sydney's 'Little Saigon'. The brother of a close friend had gone mad in a 're-education' camp. Others had told of discrimination at school, the confiscation of houses, forcible relocations and hunger. Several had tried to dissuade me from doing field research. They told me that in Vietnam I would hear only communist propaganda or the lies of people whose hearts and minds had been corrupted by decades of misrule. The film *Cyclo*, made in 1995 by Vietnamese French director Tran Anh Hung, similarly conveyed a vision of contemporary Vietnam as a society blighted by cruelty and savagery. According to one Vietnamese-Australian acquaintance, 'there are no good people left in Vietnam. Even if you meet people who retain a flicker of conscience, they will be too terrified to speak to you.'

Former regime affiliates in influential positions in overseas Vietnamese community organisations have helped keep alive the memory of the old South Vietnam as a valid, if flawed, post-colonial alternative to its nemesis, communist North Vietnam.[3] According to this view, once subscribed to by the US State Department and influential scholars writing in the 1950s and 1960s, the foundation of the Republic of Vietnam (RVN) in 1955 had spelt a decisive break with colonialism and was represented by some as the dawn of Vietnamese modernity.[4] Many overseas Vietnamese of southern origin (and most of the two-million-person Vietnamese diaspora is from the South) subscribed to this view and to its corollary, that the demise of the RVN on 30 April 1975 represented the dusk of political pluralism, independent critique and free speech in Vietnam. In contrast with those who would frame the 1990s as modernity's new Vietnamese episode, this view saw modernity as a visitor, which for two decades, had graced the southern half of Vietnam with its presence before being rudely evicted by the 'barbaric' communists. Throughout the 1990s a growing number of Internet sites operated by Vietnamese émigrés passed on this view of 1975 as the dusk of Vietnamese freedoms to a generation of Vietnamese born on foreign soil. At the same time former observers of the US involvement in Vietnam were to assert that 'new' developments in 1990s Vietnam could indeed be traced to the pre-liberation South.[5]

However, there appeared to be clear challenges to such assumptions. From the air, the astonishing Cartesian geometry of the Mekong delta's canal system is readily apparent. The hydraulic engineering of the delta bears the imprimatur of French colonialism. Sight of this ambitious watery grid, linking Vietnam to the rest of the world, was to displace ideas of the *doi moi*, or earlier RVN eras, as having constituted Vietnam's rendezvous with modernity. During almost a century of colonial rule, this region's engagement with the wider capitalist world had been more intense than in any other part of the country. Southern Vietnam had been the first part of Southeast Asia to be colonised by France in the mid-nineteenth century. Named Cochinchina, it had been the only one of France's Indochinese possessions to be ruled directly. French chroniclers of this era informed the world that France had entirely transformed the face of its colony with the development of thousands of kilometres of canals, a fourfold extension of cultivable land and the promotion of large-scale commercial production of rice and rubber (Robequain 1941). Back in the 1930s Cochinchina had been one of the world's major rice exporters. In the late 1980s, when Vietnam had dramatically returned from food scarcity to become once again one of the world's top rice exporting nations, the former French colony had returned to outperforming the rest of the country in rice production. Such results pointed to developments in the colonial era as the key to understanding this region's fluid re-integration with the capitalist world in the *doi moi* era. In the context of Vietnam's renewal in the 1990s Lockhart and Jamieson followed the literary traces of modernity's arrival in Vietnam, which was dated to the colonial era (Lockhart 1996; Jamieson 1993). Nguyen Thi Dieu (1999) reaffirmed that the French had transformed Vietnam's lower Mekong delta from scarcely populated swamp to a bustling heartland of commercial export agriculture.

Yet there were problems with rendering the French colonial period as the inception of Vietnamese modernity. From the air, one could see that the fertile green checkerboard of the delta was scarred by archipelagos of silvery pockmarks. Clustered around residential concentrations and lining the canals like track-marks up a vein, were thousands of water-filled bomb craters, dating from the US war in Vietnam. In the name of defending the 'Free World' from the march of communism, which had secured a foothold in Vietnam, the US military unleashed a torrent of violence on Vietnam's green land. The immense and seemingly pointless destruction wreaked in the name of 'modernisation' (Rostow 1961; Huntington 1968:652) had spurred many witnesses into a critical rejection of the legacy of Western intervention in Vietnam.[6] Many downplayed the achievements of French colonialism, investing their belief in the survival of Vietnamese tradition in Vietnam's most successful anti-colonial organisation, the Vietnamese Communist Party. Critical of what they described as the destructive legacy of modernity in Vietnam, some considered the Communist Party as expressive of Vietnamese tradition. James Scott (1976) depicted the Communist-led Depression rebellions of the 1930s as informed by the traditional value system of the peasantry, who he argued were motivated to revolt against the colonial order by its violation of a pre-colonial subsistence ethic.

Alexander Woodside (1976), Nguyen Khac Vien (1974) and Hy Van Luong (1992) similarly depicted Vietnam's Communist Party founders as perpetuating the traditional concerns of that country's rural scholars, their leadership of anti-colonial resistance filling the moral void bequeathed by colonialism and capitalism.

Others dated such a challenge to Vietnamese tradition much later, during the massive US intervention,[7] and yet a number were again to consider tradition perpetuated in the form of the NLF—the Vietnamese Communist Party's front organisation in the South. Fitzgerald (1972) for instance, saw the NLF as the expression of traditional Vietnamese village social relations in post-colonial South Vietnam. She described its role vis-à-vis what she saw as the depredations of US modernity as restorative and reintegrative of damaged traditions. Eric Wolf (1969) thought that the NLF offered a viable organisational framework and ideology 'for an atomized society striving to gain greater social cohesion' (Wolf 1969:207). Similarly, David Hunt (1982) argued that despite the secular, rationalist world view of many NLF militants, their movement kept alive the feeble pulse of traditional village culture in a South Vietnamese countryside ravaged by the bombs of the enemy. The success of the Vietnamese communists in the war against the French, the US and the RVN might thus be regarded as having institutionalised tradition as political ontology in post-war Vietnam.

On the other hand, America's rain of violence was to precipitate an equally critical, but more inclusive, appreciation of the Vietnamese Communist Party's revolutionary project by Western commentators. According to Marr (1981) and Turley (1993), French colonialism had comprehensively restructured Vietnamese society, creating few winners and many losers and leading to the emergence of new social and economic interests. These theorists equated the rise of the Communist Party in Vietnam with the political representation of these interests. Not only had the party wrested power from the French but it had successfully competed for national power with its domestic rivals. In *Vietnamese Tradition on Trial, 1920–1945*, David Marr (1981) equated the political success of the then Indochinese Communist Party (ICP) with the emergence of a new sensibility among the intelligentsia, a class formed in colonial times. He argued that this group's evolving relationship to tradition went from a 'talismanic' embrace of the promise of the modern to an instrumental evaluation of traditional knowledge and practices (1981:9–12). This intellectual evolution culminated for many in membership of the ICP. With its consummate political and military capabilities, the party represented the expression of a new consciousness in Vietnam. Marr's narrative concluded with a portrayal of the party's 1975 victory in the South: an event signifying the

**Mekong delta rice in Vinh Long, en route to the world**

unification of this condition in Vietnam. William Turley similarly associated Vietnamese modernity with communism's fortunes, arguing that from the 1920s and 1930s onward, 'it was the Vietnam Communist Party that defined the terms of Vietnam's entry into the modern world' (Turley 1993:342). The party's policies of post-war liberalisation, commonly referred to under the label of *doi moi*, or 'renovation', were described as continuous with its history of responding to the needs of the people.

There was little to dispute the responsiveness of the southern region and its busiest metropolis to the Vietnamese government's reform policies. In the 1990s rice, Vietnam's main export, followed the same pathways that it had in the 1930s, when Mekong delta rice similarly fed the world. Yet even in pre-colonial times, according to material assembled by Li Tana and Anthony Reid, this region had been a thriving hub of regional commerce, a major exporter of rice and a place where merchant ships clustered in search of profitable cargo (Li Tana and Reid 1993). Occupied by Vietnamese only three or so centuries ago, southern Vietnam was a frontier region. The southern flow of settlers was predicated on the displacement of two neighbouring civilisations, the Cham and the Khmer. Home to a multi-ethnic, ever-changing population, connected by water to the rest of the world and thereby open to the exchange of people, objects and ideas, the ecological distinctiveness of this region, according to Pierre Brocheux, represented a factor of largely unrecognised importance in understanding the events of colonial history (Brocheux 1995). He suggested that the pre-colonial history of this region was marked by features such as a plural society, previously considered by others as products of the modern colonial era. Put more abstractly, his argument re-situated such traits of 'modernity' as indigenous to the region. Native and chronicler of this same sub-region, Brocheux decried the grandiose and 'inflexible' schemes of social engineering imposed upon it by post-war 'urban intellectuals'. Acting in the name of modernity, they had been unequal to capturing the essence of the region or harnessing its potential (Brocheux 1995:212).

The southern plain's liquid geography offers a source of visual cues for rehearsing theories about Vietnam's relationship to modernity. Yet as can be seen, this body of work entails a great range of assumptions. Describing the country's relationship with the wider world over time as one of perennial confrontation between 'tradition' and 'modernity', such scholarship has been analytically non-cumulative and has put Vietnam into an assortment of time frames. Tradition is forever renewing itself, while 'modernity' is always just arriving in Vietnam. Time is ambushed and meaning eroded in a rhetorical tradition which offers the reader less of a fix on Vietnam's place in the world than a readout of different theorists' imagined relation to it.

## THE LOCAL TERRAIN OF THEORY

That countries such as Vietnam risk being assigned a new time on each occasion an armchair theorist speaks is an effect of a global concentration of the power to define time. It reflects inequalities in the power to speak or make oneself heard. This is the bind confronting the anthropology of plural modernities. Indeed the diverse societies of the world have been unified temporally but at the cost of being understood within a Euro-American time frame: that is, difference is assigned contemporeneity by its points of reference to the presumed heartland of modernity. Although motivated by the critical concerns of Said and Fabian, the anthropological literature pluralising modernity arguably has continued to function as an ideology expressing and endorsing geopolitical inequalities in terms of time. Such theories have been articulated in centres of concentrated information, capital and power. Those resources are funnelled into designating the rest of the world as beholden to these places for their contemporeneity. Remarkably little has changed since political inequalities were considered temporal deficits, a view by which half the world was colonised.

Such solutions to the problem of assigning time to place have overlooked the simple question: is this the way those whom they describe would render their world? In various theories of indigenised modernity only seldom does one encounter a discussion of the self-perceptions of one's subjects as 'modern'.[8] In their concern to update and unify disciplinary theory, anthropologists may have momentarily stopped listening to others. Similarly, these anthropologists may have taken to the study of other societies the a priori assumption of their own identity as modern, imagining themselves as agents or emblems of modernity. Here, one is up against the problem that others who they represent may not be in agreement with anthropologists' self-perceptions.

There seems little need for anthropology, a discipline based on fieldwork, to be transfixed by the unitary world proposed in the post-cold war explosion of writing on modernity. The challenge for anthropology is whether its symbolic constructions are sufficient to render the complexity of our world or, if they are not complicit in the denial of difference, the collapsing of time and the silencing of voices. There is an urgent need to seek out alternative sites than the ones from which social theory is enunciated, to enquire whether existence is articulated in such ways. Indeed, many societies are characterised by their members as 'developing', 'backward', 'civilised' or involved in processes of 'modernisation', or alternatively, construed as encumbered by, or proudly maintaining, their 'traditions'. In so doing, they often appear to position themselves in a universal time frame, in contrast to those who would pluralise modernity. However, the net effect of listening to these dispersed voices explodes the unitary assumptions of this trend in social theory. Indeed, because a unitary vision of time is endorsed, the multiplication of referents against which such views are enunciated shatters the impression of global historical time as ontology and replaces it unmistakably as a discourse, or a language game: a tool by which to orient oneself in time or in space.[9]

My alternative project is to listen to the statements about time made by those removed from privileged sites of discourse. This is to understand the concept of modernity, whenever it is used, as an imagined condition[10] rather than an objective reality, a symbolic resource as distinct from a constituted event, an epistemology rather than an ontology of temporal difference and an ideology rather than an objective process. Anthropology, a discipline motivated by the plurality of visions as to what it means to be human, is a suitable vehicle to explore variation in the use of temporal schema: an attribute of the ongoing process of decolonising the world. In this it joins company with the comparative study of intellectual history which has investigated trajectories of thought in different local contexts. The field for study opened up by such a fusion of methods is broad and offers great comparative scope. In the nineteenth century the global expansion of European power saw versions of the ideologies of 'civilisation', 'progress' and 'modernisation', spread far and wide, attached to a variety of political and economic projects.[11] In their wake, local actors of every political hue were to engage with these schema, appropriating them to address their own concerns. Their counter-readings of identity were in turn challenged, as well as evolving to fit changed circumstances. This clearly was the case in Vietnam, which illustrates that the appropriation of colonial categories of time was not singular, but multiple, shifting and contradictory.

Arriving in Vietnam scarcely allowed me to leave the theorising of modernity behind as an ephemeral and moreover inconclusive concern of armchair theorists. Touching down in 'the field' was to ground me in new co-ordinates of theorising. I was to find the plotting of Vietnam's condition relative to 'modernity' to be very much a concern of Vietnamese themselves. Disagreements over its referents were commonplace. Dissension was nowhere greater than in the country's southernmost region.

## MODERNITY AS A VIETNAMESE IDEA

One of the practices I found most noticeable during my stay in Vietnam was the widespread use of temporal categories to rank social or cultural differences. People frequently referred to their condition, to society, customs and ideas, variously as 'progressive' (*tien bo*), 'developed' (*phat trien*), 'civilised' or 'modern' (*van minh/hien dai*)[12] or, alternatively, as 'backward' (*lac hau*), 'undeveloped' (*chua phat trien*) or 'traditional' (*truyen thong*). Ubiquitous billboards erected by the state displayed images of electrification, factories and vast orderly rural fields ploughed by tractors as exemplifying 'civilisation/modernity' (*van minh*), and they caricatured as 'uncivilised' (*khong van minh*) and 'backward', phenomena such as gambling, superstition, drinking and large families. Such terms were common in everyday use and they were distinctive to an ear trained to accord equivalence to human variation. Urbanites looked at my photographs of thatched cottages and clucked in sympathy at the 'backwardness' of their rural countryfolk. Southerners told me jokes about 'uncivilised' northern hicks. Religious practices were either evaluated positively as 'traditional' (*truyen thong*) or as 'backward' and 'superstitious' (*me tin*). Some foreigners were thought to have arrived from 'civilised' or 'modern' (*van minh*) nations. Russians, French, Americans, Japanese and Taiwanese were often included in these designations. Others, for example Cambodians, Lao and Vietnam's mountainous minority peoples, were sometimes described as 'backward' (*lac hau*) or even 'primitive' (*nguyen thuy*).

Vietnamese people have not always ranked social systems by such temporal schema. Before French colonialist ideology achieved dominance, the political order in Vietnam had been undergirded by a neo-Confucian philosophy that ranked societies according to their grasp and exemplification of the principles of right understanding and self-cultivation.[13] The Vietnamese court conceived of the social good in terms of Confucian ethics, whereby knowledge and self-cultivation led to proper family regulation which induced state order, which promoted universal peace (Marr 1981:103). Geopolitics was understood in such terms. Many Vietnamese elites looked to China for the political philosophy that underlay local institutions. Other bordering countries such as Cambodia were sometimes regarded as 'barbarian' *phien* or *man* (designations drawn from the Chinese appellation of border tribes) and it was expected that they should pay tribute to the Vietnamese court. As Woodside observed, included in the list of Vietnamese vassals were not only the neighbouring polities of Cambodia, Laos and the highland societies, but also England and France (Woodside 1971:237). He argued that in the nineteenth century, Vietnamese elites, internalising Chinese geography, situated themselves at the centre of a moral spatial order as the 'middle kingdom'. This official view was frequently challenged even at the level of the political centre[14] and certainly at the margins of the kingdom by a mix of old and new ideologies, which ordered space and social collectivities in non-orthodox ways, with varying degrees of success at deflecting or hijacking the centralising tendencies of the court.

French colonisation brought a distinct way of ranking societies in space, according to the notion of civilisation or progress in historical time. Transferred to France's Indochinese possessions in the nineteenth century, as an ideology of colonial rule, 'universal time'[15] became one of the central underpinnings of the new political order. The Vietnamese bureaucratic order, although founded on qualities such as literacy, order and self-regulation, was described as 'backward' by the French. The violent unseating of the king and the replacement of the imperial system by 'advanced' forms of administration was done in the name of 'progress'. In 1886 French Resident-General Paul Bert justified the French colonisation of Vietnam to accomplished man of letters, Truong Vinh Ky, in terms of the colonial power's 'already refined civilization, advanced arts and sciences, strongly organized social hierarchy and an admirable moral code' (De Francis 1977:121).[16] France's semi-theological *'mission civilisatrice'*, the bringing of progress, enlightenment and modernisation to Vietnam, was to remain the key justification of the colonial political order until the middle of the next century.

It was the most ideological variant of this conception of time, Social Darwinism, which naturalised differentials of power as evolutionary outcomes, that achieved the biggest impact among Vietnamese thinkers. Social Darwinism arrived in Vietnam around the end of the nineteenth century, via Chinese writings which emphasised national rather than social struggles for survival. It was less a fatalistic doctrine of the strong crushing the weak, than a doctrine outlining the terrain and the rules of the game by which nations who sought to survive had to play (Shiraishi Masaya 1988:59). In the hands of Vietnamese anti-colonial activists, it was to leave a major and enduring intellectual legacy. Phan Boi Chau (1867–1940) might have been the first Vietnamese to internalise this ideology, situating Vietnam within a linear narrative of world time. In *Viet Nam Su Khao* (1908), Phan Boi Chau, citing Western ethnologists' theories, stated that all human societies were following a linear path of development, 'from the stage of animals (*dong vat*), through those of barbarians (*da man*) and the civilizing process (*khai hoa*), to the stage of civilization (*van minh*)' (Shiraishi Masaya 1988:63). Phan considered Vietnam a 'backward' (*lac hau*) country, Western Europe and Japan had attained the stage of 'civilization' (*van minh*). For Phan, Japan's Meiji restoration represented a model for Vietnam to advance according to this scheme. He founded the *Duy Tan Hoi*, an association to secure the modernisation of Vietnam[17] and he instigated the 'Travel East' (*Dong Du*) movement, in which Vietnamese students would study in Japan and learn from it the secrets that would allow Vietnam to achieve independence from France. In an inversion of Hegelian spatial ranking, this eastward movement was conceptualised as a journey forward in time. Phan wrote: 'The Japan of the present day is the Vietnam of tomorrow' (Vinh Sinh 1988:128).

Phan Chu Trinh (1872–1926), an anti-colonialist reformer of similar stature, was equally influenced by Social Darwinism. Unlike Phan Boi Chau, who sought Vietnam's emancipation by violent means, Phan Chu Trinh emphasised education and the reform of customs and institutions, delivering stinging critiques of 'tradition' as a deadweight to 'progress'. To propagate his vision for the modernisation of Vietnamese society, he helped found the Dong Kinh Nghia Thuc school in Hanoi in 1907, and contributed to its curriculum. Phan Chu Trinh was to tirelessly promote *van minh* as a process of self-improvement, according to which the achievements of Europe and Japan were considered exemplary. His *Van Minh Tan Hoc Sach* (*Civilization and New Learning* 1907), borrowing the metaphors of Chinese reformist writer Liang Qichao, characterised Vietnam's backward status in the world struggle for survival as an 'illness'. Civilised nations' pursuit of science, commerce and industry were contrasted with the Vietnamese predilection for witchcraft, leisurely games and music. In the minds of these activists, Europe or Japan had replaced Imperial China as the exemplary political order. Coinciding with the internalisation of ideas of unilineal world time, this placed Vietnam into temporal deficit in relation to the imagined modernity of France or Japan.[18]

By the eve of World War I, Governer Albert Sarrault still expressed his vision of Franco–Vietnamese collaboration as one in which France was ready to act as an 'elder brother' in transmitting to the Vietnamese the full benefits of modern civilisation (Marr 1981). However, the European civilisational ideal was badly damaged by the events of the

Great War. In its wake, religious and new political movements flourished in Vietnam as they did globally. These reflected a general questioning of a bloodstained Europe as the pinnacle of modernity towards which all societies were moving. In Vietnam, the ideal of progress, emancipation and the ideals of the French Revolution remained strong, however after the war, Vietnamese increasingly disavowed French colonialism as exemplary in this respect. Many shared the idea of Phan Boi Chau who, at his trial in 1925, disputed French colonisation was synonymous with *van minh* (Marr 1981:17). In the 1920s Vietnamese who had lived and studied in metropolitan France, such as Nguyen Anh Ninh[19] and Nhat Linh[20] voiced trenchant criticisms of colonial double standards. The success of the Russian Revolution seized the imagination of many who were seeking alternative models of political emancipation and they saw its achievements as relevant to Vietnam. Marxism arrived in Vietnam, not necessarily challenging Vietnam's place in the periodisation of world time, but suggesting a further stage beyond French imperialism: socialism, a formulation which situated the USSR at the pinnacle of modernity and displaced France from the status of historical avant-garde.

Intellectual histories of the post-World War I period in Vietnam characterise a progression in anti-colonial appropriations of the idea of modernity, from idealism and radicalism, towards sophistication and pragmatism. In the post-World War I years, as Duiker has argued, Vietnam's urban nationalists such as the Constitutionalists,[21] and Nguyen Anh Ninh, reflected the aspirations of a new class, and their understanding of colonialism greatly surpassed that of the scholar patriot generation of Phan Boi Chau and Phan Chu Trinh (Duiker 1976:183). However, they were themselves outflanked in political effectiveness by those belonging to the Indochinese Communist Party. According to Duiker the communists' ability to orchestrate the disaffection of both urbanites and the peasantry allowed them to engineer their own success (Duiker 1976; 1996:352–9). In the rise to power of the communists, Marr saw the intellectual evolution of the new Vietnamese 'intelligentsia'. This included progress from attempting to critically assess what were regarded as objective conditions such as 'tradition', to ICP thinking that the truth of the past could be manufactured. What had been conceived of as a struggle with, or through, time became a struggle over the definition of time. Voluntaristic formulations, such as a timeless 'Vietnamese spirit' or the idea of resistance as a higher form of human self-consciousness, became common fare in ICP proselytising, displacing—in public pronouncements at any rate—more candid assessments of the sometimes overwhelming odds the party faced (Marr 1981:362–5). Hue Tam Ho Tai, speaking of similar processes, argued that the Vietnamese communist movement arose from origins in Vietnamese intellectuals' anti-colonial radicalism. The 'Vietnamese Revolution', she argued, had its roots in the 1920s in spontaneous, inspired and individualistic assaults on both traditionalism and the legitimacy of colonial rule. It was to culminate, according to her Weberian routinisation narrative, in disciplined, organised revolutionary activity (Hue Tam Ho Tai 1992).

Such works allow one to appreciate Vietnam's emergence as an alternative site for the enunciation of the co-ordinates of global time. They enable one to question objectivist theory, which places the world in a unitary time frame, and they indicate the shifts in meaning and denotation of 'modernity' for Vietnamese people over time. These intellectual histories begin with initial grapplings by Vietnamese anti-colonialists with the temporal schema invoked to justify colonialism. 'Modernity's' referents were to slip, from France to the Soviet Union and thence, by self-arrogation, to the Vietnamese resistance itself. The story ends with the party's ability to produce and strategically disseminate an alternative truth. The communists' vision of self-conscious resistance removed Vietnam from the colonial time frame, multiplying time. Vietnamese were not the West's past but its coeval rivals.

The state's power to define its time in this way was clearly illustrated in the early 1990s. Ubiquitous public broadcasting speakers filled early mornings and dusks with uplifting slogans. Framed in the present tense—'fulfil quotas!', 'achieve record harvests!'—these hovered between exhortation and report. Both prescriptive and descriptive, socialist realist murals suggested that an ideal, electrified, orderly, industrialised and civilised future had already been obtained. Freshly painted billboard images, which towered high and stretched wide inevitably caught the eye and displaced more dreary backdrops especially in rural areas. However, the communist view of themselves as temporally equivalent or more advanced than France, or other nationalist groups, had the greatest impact in areas where the party could mediate perceptions, which until 1975 had been far from everywhere. What is to be said about those places which remained beyond party control? While recuperating Vietnam from the colonial time frame, the views of the communists represented only one element in the Vietnamese multiplication of colonial time.

## PLURAL VOICES IN SOUTHERN VIETNAM

One of the dangers in narrating Vietnamese intellectual history in the singular is reliance on the assumption of homogenised national space. For example, narratives of Vietnamese modernist consciousness which describe a transition from the internalisation of Social Darwinism to the ICP's selective application of Marxism, rely on dramatic and perhaps unjustifiable shifts of geographical focus. If the complex nature of space is restored, such narratives look incomplete. This can be demonstrated by focusing on the region of southern Vietnam where the idea of modernity has had a far richer history than some accounts have allowed.[22] Southern Vietnam is a somewhat obvious location for reassessing this scholarship, for it seems to exemplify many of the denotations commonly accepted for the concept of modernity and yet has stood in an awkward relationship to those who achieved power in Vietnam and who were to speak in modernity's name. It is one place to turn for alternative voices, although one could also find challenges to official perspectives from other Vietnamese groups, who are often evaluated in deficient relation to 'modernity', including ethnic minorities, women, inhabitants of rural areas or mountainous regions and religious practitioners.

The protagonists who feature at the commencement and conclusion of most narratives of the reception of the idea of modernity in Vietnam hailed from beyond the region of southern Vietnam. Phan Boi Chau and Phan Chu Trinh, with whom accounts usually begin, were natives of central Vietnam, a region formerly settled by the Chams and wrested from the Vietnamese in turn by the French. It was, like much of the northern delta, a land of harsh choices: one where harnessing one's fortunes to state power had been a vital route to survival and upward mobility. The mandarinate had long been a key employer of local sons, even under the French, who were to initially administer the region indirectly. Both Phans were scholars who had been educated in the Chinese classics in preparation for bureaucratic careers. Their reformism was mediated by Chinese reformists; their metaphors for the problems of society and the confrontation with the West were deeply influenced by the images that had evolved in a distinct Chinese context. This was a familiar mode of distinguishing themselves among local consociates and rivals: by their superior grasp and didactic wielding of esoteric foreign doctrine.[23] Phan Boi Chau's call for Vietnamese to learn lessons from Japan's Meiji Restoration arguably transferred to Japan the central and northern Vietnamese power elite's habit of recourse to external models to competitively achieve local legitimacy. Ho Chi Minh, the crucial figure associated with the importation of communist doctrine to Vietnam—a view which was to replace France with the distant USSR as a symbol of achieved modernity—was a native of the same central region of Vietnam. Like the two Phans, Ho Chi Minh had wielded this prestigious foreign ideology to excoriate domestic rivals. While the north was to become the place in Vietnam where the prestige of the Soviet Union (and later the People's Republic of China) as civilisational ideal was strongest, the use of the imagery of such distant power centres to address the problem of local legitimacy had strong precedents.[24]

The country's extreme south was a very different political space, only settled by the Vietnamese in the seventeenth century. Non-

Vietnamese settlers and sojourners, including the Khmer, southern Chinese, Malay and Europeans had established a significant local presence. Intellectually it was relatively heterogeneous. Ideologies such as Theravada, Mahayana, and Pure Land Buddhism, Islam and Christianity, along with secret societies and apocalyptic movements jostled side by side and rivalled neo-Confucianism, which never came close to establishing a hegemonic status in the region. Being geographically more amenable to the type of economic programs favoured in the course of French imperial expansion, southern Vietnam experienced the greatest impact of capitalism, commercialisation, urbanisation and a bustling traffic in new intellectual movements. Before either of the two Phans had learnt to put brush to paper, the import of French culture was being digested and explained in encyclopedic scope by accomplished local mediators such as Paulus Tinh Cua (1834–1907) and Truong Vinh (Petrus) Ky (1837–98), employing genres as diverse as dictionaries, short stories, newspaper articles, essays, textbooks and primers (Jamieson 1993:70; Nguyen Van Trung 1998). Under French direct rule, southern Vietnam continued to provide better opportunities for debate, publishing and political dissent than the other parts of the former kingdom (Hue Tam Ho Tai 1992). Whereas Phan Boi Chau had operated surreptitiously and from abroad in Japan and China, the very techniques (meetings, newspapers, speeches, fundraisers) by which his ideas were propagated in southern Vietnam, and the strong support received from the southern bourgeoisie, were indicative of the existence there of some of the very freedoms and social forms he was fighting for in his native central region (Marr 1971:143). In the 1920s and 1930s, southern Vietnam continued to be a place of undeniable intellectual ferment: a crucial site for dissemination and evaluation of the idea of modernity and divergent claims as to where it might be best exemplified. Accounts of Saigon in this era dwell on the publicised debates, the political movements, symbolic events, and the charismatic intellectual and political figures of the city. These accounts sketch a portrait of Vietnamese people seizing the terms of the debate, thinking critically about their past and their future alternatives and exposing colonialism to some of its most graphic denunciations.

Narratives which construe the rise of the Communist Party as the outcome of this process depend crucially on reference to the Saigon of the 1920s to 1940s. While its history of intellectual ferment pre-dated this era, events in Saigon during this period have been taken to demonstrate a 'stage' in the supposed evolution of anti-colonial consciousness, between the uncritical modernism of the earlier scholar patriots and the more sophisticated politics of Communist Party cadres. Duiker's narrative of nationalism in Vietnam shifts its focus from central Vietnam's 'scholar patriots' Phan Boi Chau and Phan Chu Trinh, to the urban south where, in the 1920s, the Saigonese 'Constitutionalists' and Nguyen Anh Ninh were representatives, for him, of 'modern' urban nationalism. While the appeal of versions of Marxism to Saigonese intellectuals in the 1930s was undeniable, the supposed culmination of urban nationalism in ICP debates about strategy is a conclusion requiring yet another shift in focus to northern Vietnam, where by 1941 the party's centre of gravity lay (Hemery 1992:187). David Marr's 1981 account also relies heavily on key southern events, personalities and ideas to evoke the intellectual ferment that he claims eventuated in many embracing ICP doctrine and organisation. In a similar way, Hue Tam Ho Tai evocatively describes the influence of southern Vietnam's distinctive history, economy and political climate on the radicalism and individualism that she argues was the catalyst of the Vietnamese Revolution. Saigon was a hotbed of radical activity and was to be Indochina's key centre for the dissemination and early organised expression of the ideas of anarchism, Leninism and Trotskyism. However, the idea that these events represented 'the experimental and most individualistic, stage of the Vietnamese Revolution' (1992:258) is diminished by the fact that by the early 1940s the locus of 'the Revolution' was to be found in the more disciplined and rule-governed social milieu of northern Vietnam.

In southern Vietnam the party's relevance as the Vietnamese antithesis to colonialism was less compelling. In the early 1940s a great many local ICP members and supporters had just been led to their deaths and imprisonment in the failed Southern Uprising of 1940. Vietnamese anti-colonial intellectuals were supposed to have become more effective and pragmatic, exemplified by their acceptance of communist organisational discipline. To the contrary, the communists in the extreme south were plagued by a series of further tactical miscalculations and political failures, such as the politically disastrous elimination of domestic rivals in the wake of the August 1945 revolution, their failure to secure an effective coalition with southern-based political and religious movements, or to secure control of Saigon during the anti-French war (1946–54). On the eve of the French withdrawal in 1954, the communists had failed to distinguish themselves as successors to colonialism in the extreme south of the country. Over the next two decades they fully exposed the political and military weaknesses of the RVN government, whose seat Saigon lay in this region, but struggled to make themselves politically relevant to the majority of the population. Ultimately their control over this region was only established in a full-scale invasion from the North: hardly an evolution in consciousness.

By contrast, southern Vietnam in the late-colonial, early postcolonial period was a place where thinking about modernity remained heterogeneous, fertile and in flux. In the early 1940s, with the party apparatus decimated, the millenarian Buddhism of the Hoa Hao and the religious universalism of the Cao Dai made rapid inroads into the southern population.[25] Saigon's cafes, bars and public spaces remained home to the reformist ideas of Phan Chu Trinh, ideas of self-reliance, neo-traditionalism, anarchism, Trotskyism and Marxism, non-communist nationalism and Japanese-influenced Pan-Asianism. During the 1945–54 war the countryside of the Mekong delta could be characterised as carved into different zones of imagined temporality, some anticipating the apocalypse leading to the Hoa Hao's *Long Hoa* festival, others experiencing the Cao Dai's Third Great Universal Religious Amnesty (*Dai Dao Tam Ky Pho Do*[26]), some 'liberated' (*giai phong*) as communist strongholds and others controlled by Catholics, the Binh Xuyen river pirates and emperor Bao Dai's French-backed State of Vietnam. In 1954 a number of those versed in Marxist voluntarism went north and a crucial injection of committed anti-communists came south. With the founding of the Republic, US 'modernisation' and 'nation-building' theory was advanced as the ideological premise of the southern-based state. Communist-led resistance to this cohered in the NLF, which attempted to co-ordinate a range of grievances and motivations in political and military opposition to the government. Meanwhile, Ngo Dinh Diem's anti-materialist philosophy of Personalism was jostled by Parisian existentialism, new-left Marxism, structuralism, non-aligned nationalism, neo-Confucian traditionalism, evangelistic Christianity, various strands of Buddhism and unabated religious eclecticism, evidenced by the synthesis effected by the Mekong delta's 'Coconut Monk'. From the late 1940s and early 1950s Indochina's largest city had been swelling as a result of the wars. Amidst the ravages of war, mourning the loss of ties to land, and in a city of refugees, foreign troops, mushrooming shanty dwellings and social upheaval, many urbanites did not affiliate with any of these alternative frameworks. Instead many of them plunged into a world of medieval romances, adventure stories and fabulous tales (Vo Phien 1992; Hoang Ngoc Thanh 1991).

These developments are yet to be given adequate attention and my sketch of them here as 'southern' phenomena simplifies an extraordinarily complex human geography. They ran parallel with the trajectory being followed by the communists who were attempting to realise their vision of a socialist modernity in the northern half of the country. To present the communist elaboration of the idea of modernity as the end point in its Vietnamese reception is to repeat the exclusions effected by the communists in the post-war years, who were to declare departures from the Democratic Republic of Vietnam (DRV) experience as invalid, displacing developments occurring in non-communist-controlled territory from the status of the modern. This repeated the 'allochronism' of colonialist ideology, which excluded much of global space from the time frame of the political centre (Fabian 1983). Yet it is unwise to endorse the new regime's conviction that these excluded identities had passed into the category of pre-communist intellectual history. The party's understanding of southern Vietnam was challenged in the post-war years as difficulties imposing its vision there mounted. In response, the prestige of the northern-based regime as the culmination of modernity was to erode and alternative interpretations began to be heard. Since reunification the idea of modernity in Vietnam has been subject to some of its most compelling reworkings and displacements, and the identity of the Vietnamese 'South' has been a focus of this rethinking. It is this history, which illustrates the value of seeing modernity as a discourse of identity, which forms the topic of this book.

## ORGANISATION

Chapter 1 deals with the way those who 'liberated' Vietnam below the 17th parallel in 1975 regarded this region's departures from the society of the northern-based DRV as expressions of US militarism. The new regime considered social relations such as markets and cultural expressions such as popular music as indexes of South Vietnam's military domination. The denial of the modernity of such phenomena excluded the territory formerly under the Republic from the accomplished modernity officially attributed to the rest of the nation.

Chapter 2 discusses the rethinking that occurred in the wake of the failure to transform the South according to the DRV blueprint. Shifts in policy in response to the nation's socio-economic crisis were paralleled by unofficial questioning of the legitimacy of party rule. Many party members expressed doubts about the modernity of Vietnam's communist legacy. This reopened the question of southern temporal difference. Within official circles some were to revalidate US-era developments in the former South Vietnam as emblematic of what Vietnamese modernity might mean.

Fifteen years after unification, thriving growth in the extreme south of the country, referred to as *Nam Bo*, exemplified for many the benefits of the nation's new market-oriented policies. Some came to see that this region possessed distinctive attributes which explained its successes. Chapter 3 charts how traits such as the commodity market, cultural dynamism and rapid social change, previously considered (positively or negatively) as effects of this region's recent collisions with the capitalist world, were accorded greater historical depth and considered perhaps indigenous to the region. While this body of theory advanced understanding of the complexity of Vietnam's pre-colonial past, the embrace of certain qualities as timeless also indicated that the legitimisation of contemporary relations was also at work.

While the first half of the book documents these shifts in state agents' ideas of 'the South', the second discusses how residents of this region, who were objectified in these ways, regarded their own identity vis-à-vis the 'modern'. Not all were advocates or beneficiaries of the kind of social relations celebrated and naturalised in the state's accounts. Chapter 4 begins by describing the perception of southern difference as an ongoing threat to the nation and it recounts the views of those antipathetical to the idea of modernity as 'essential' or 'natural' to the South. However, significant conservative reactions to rapid and unauthorised change were also to come from Ho Chi Minh City itself: supposed paragon of Vietnamese modernity. In response to the forces of change unleashed upon this southern metropolis, many southern urban intellectuals were to construe their home as a place of threatened tradition.

Chapter 5 pursues these same questions in a rural context. In the early 1990s the rural society of the Mekong delta was viewed as an emblem of 'tradition' to urbanites feeling assaulted by rapid change. This, however, was not a view espoused by all of the delta's rural inhabitants. This chapter describes how debates about identity in one Mekong delta village were themselves framed in the familiar idiom of *van minh*—'modernity' or 'civilisation'. In response to the marginalisation of their rural home a group of elderly villagers recalled a time in which their village had been at the forefront of their nation's revolutionary challenge to colonialism. Their characterisation of their home as a former cradle of cosmopolitanism and enlightened resistance highlighted the deficits of their present leaders and the marginalisation which rural areas were continuing to experience. Although they failed to publish an account of their village's history, they were successful in making known their views as to why this was so.

Tracking how 'modernity' has been allocated to, and displaced from, various places in post-war Vietnam illustrates how perspectives have shifted over time and it shows such designations to have been contested, accepted and reconfigured. This history attests to the vitality and urgency of debates about identity in Vietnam. It challenges the concept of modernity as an objective category: one hyphenating human diversity to time's Euro-American centre. The southern Vietnamese case shows 'modernity' released as an important attribute of that place, as an identity which continues to be debated by those speaking about or from within the region.[27] While it is necessary to incorporate subjective experiences of time into any discussion which broaches the temporal dimension of human life, the complex subjectivities in this one small region make one all too aware of the difficulties of determining a 'Vietnamese' stance or of establishing a nation's intellectual lineage on this question, as intellectual historians of Vietnam have attempted to do. The main difficulty and danger discussed here is the exclusion of places from time. My point in writing this book, however, is not to condemn and transcend this, but to show how prevalent it is and how negotiation over such temporalisations constitutes the stuff of change. The ontological category of time is not the preserve of the social scientist, nor the national leader, but is constantly up for grabs in the negotiation of existence. In that vein, the rich history this book explores, of excluding and retrieving the idea of southern Vietnam in relation to the time frame of modernity, is one that might be profitably explored by historians and anthropologists working elsewhere.

# 1

# Neo-colonialism as poison

## REVERBERATIONS OF A VANQUISHED PAST

Visiting Vietnam anywhere below the 17th parallel almost two decades after unification, one could not fail to notice that this region had formerly been under the control of a rival to the current regime. A marked regional preference for baseball caps was noticeable below the 17th parallel as distinct from the olive green pith helmets of People's Army issue found to its north. In most towns, one would be approached by middle aged men wanting to practise their English in a variety of US regional accents. Cafes, bars and refreshment stands could be found in profusion in most cities to the south of this line and tapered off significantly in those to its north. In all of these could be heard the luxuriant sounds of the musical outpouring of the 1955–75 Republican era. Such background music was more prevalent and significantly louder in the South than in the North. With its mixtures of tangos and ballads, translations and rearrangements of hits from the 1950s and 1960s and themes of separation and longing, this ubiquitous soundtrack reminded one constantly of the distinct historical experience of the southern half of the country.

Travelling through the South Vietnamese countryside in the early 1990s, one would hear the strains of *vong co* (yearn for the past), the haunting refrain central to *cai luong*, a reformed genre of classical opera indigenous to the Mekong delta. The genre dates from the colonial period, and its domestication (in the sense of becoming a home entertainment) was given a significant boost with the proliferation of radios as a household item under the subsequent regime. Wandering into an urban working class district, bus station or roadside stall, one couldn't miss the boisterous din of *to hai*: an assemblage of musical parodies and jokes, performed by stand-up comedians aimed at extracting cheap laughs at the expense of various forms of popular culture. In the cafes, bars and parks in urban areas one would be more likely than not to hear the slick, Orange County Sound—hits from the Republican era and post-1975 diaspora, re-recorded in California and smuggled back to Vietnam in the suitcases of overseas Vietnamese. Indeed, much of the music heard in South Vietnam in the 1990s consisted of re-recordings and rearrangements of Republican-era music. The dominance of the local music scene by the musicians of the diaspora reminded one of the dramatic socio-political rupture that had brought the Republic to an end and had sent more than a million of those affiliated with it in various ways overseas.

Deep into the maze of alleys that snaked away from Ho Chi Minh City's main streets, one might find a species of *karaoke* hell. It seemed, in some places, that every fourth house operated as a low budget *karaoke* cafe. There, one could scarcely avoid listening to several amateur performers simultaneously ventilating life experiences of considerable sorrow with the aid of powerful amplifiers. The winning combination for a *karaoke* hit appeared to be lyrical themes of separation and sorrow set against exotic and opulent foreign visual backdrops. The video images which accompanied the overseas Vietnamese (*hai ngoai*) soundtracks sung by *karaoke* adepts frequently featured well-heeled, lovesick heroes walking along windswept cityscapes, or solitary nymphettes drifting past stunning natural scenery. An important subtext appeared to be the nostalgia of the overseas Vietnamese for their 'lost' homeland and the loved ones they had left behind. Many of the heart-rending compositions which featured in such videos were of pre-1975 vintage. To a large extent the overseas Vietnamese musicians had not invented as much as selected from the musical repertoire of the Republic, those songs speaking to their contemporary condition. The ready availability of such works showed how central the themes of loss, separation and nostalgia had been to that earlier era.

In a palm frond cafe deep in the Mekong delta one could watch a smuggled video tape of a Scottish/Scandinavian-American singer performing a French love song translated into Vietnamese for a Vietnamese-American audience in California. The *Paris by Night* music video series was hugely popular in Vietnam. These were video recordings of glittering concerts staged by the overseas community in which glamorous costumes and urbane MCs strove to capture the feel of late 1960s Saigon. While nostalgic, they also had an experimental side, straining to extract novelty from combinations of new curious elements. Foreign singers such as 'Dalena', whose long blond hair and flawless Vietnamese formed an irresistible combination, were hugely popular, adding an exotic flourish. Music videos of the *Paris by Night* variety, as well as the ubiquitous translations and rearrangements of Western music, were reminiscent of the 'world music' phenomenon—the packaging of the musically exotic for mass Western consumption. By bringing different cultural traditions into the Vietnamese orbit, the overseas Vietnamese were operating as Vietnamese equivalents of Paul Simon or David Byrne. In the 1990s one could hear Western hits of months-old vintage translated into Vietnamese, rearranged, performed and produced in California, and exported for the rapidly expanding home-country market. Yet this was not an unprecedented phenomenon. The impresarios of the 1920s and 1930s who had brought Western and Chinese musical themes to the Mekong delta via the *cai luong* (reformed opera form) exercised substantially the same function. The romantic music of the pre-World War II elite, *nhac tien chien*, echoed with the strains of Montparnasse and Havana. In the 1960s the anti-war ballads of Trinh Cong Son drew influences from Bob Dylan, and the highly versatile composer Pham Duy included translations and re-arrangements of Western music in his prodigious output.

These two musical moods, of nostalgia and exoticism, serve as an apt overture to the themes of this chapter. In a venerable anthropological tradition it refers to a society that has 'disappeared' off the face of the earth, never to return. The task of understanding this society can now only be done through reconstruction, the patient collation of texts, memoirs and commentaries. Anthropology's redemptive quest has reflected nostalgia for modes of life imagined threatened by modernity's relentless progress (Marcus 1986:165). The impulse to preserve, to salvage, came precisely at that moment when a sense of the inevitable extinguishment of cultural diversity was at its most compelling. Ironically, the exotic was, to an extent, the product of the imagination or dread of global homogenisation. Yet nostalgia and exoticism had themselves been central themes of the vanished society whose traces haunted those who travelled in Vietnam south of the 17th parallel. They represented that society's two faces. A history of intense foreign engagements, economic transformation and cultural reconfiguration is reflected in the region's legacy of musical exoticism. Evidence of its people's substantial embrace of those influences is found in the musical record of translation and stylistic eclecticism. Alternatively, the strong vein of nostalgia that contemporary music inherits from that era indicates that equally, there existed imaginative rejections or escape routes from those same processes of change. Grief at the separations and bereavements of war is particularly evident in the musical record of that era. Such music was inspired by a sense of despair at intolerable ruptures and the regretful disappearance of a familiar way of life.

For an anthropology motivated by the supposedly 'modern' preoccupations of nostalgia (Robertson 1992) and exoticism, to come across such themes in the object of study could only create psychic strife. A recuperative project appeared called for, as the nostalgic strains of the music that accompanied ethnographers and other travellers on their journeys to Vietnam oriented them firmly towards a past regretfully lost to history. Yet this proved to be evidence of nothing other than a modernist sensibility, a way of life that was itself oriented between the poles of exoticism and regret. Setting about recording this evidence (a task which disciplinary logic would consider valuable and necessary, as it was 'lost', or existed now only in the minds of an ageing generation of informants), one was confronted with social data and processes of overwhelming familiarity and banality. Urbanisation, social engineering schemes, foreign development dependency, consumerism, the devastation of the countryside, were examples of the data redeemed in this anthropological project. Having opened the master program 'Modernist Disciplines' and the file 'Ethnography', into which rare ethnographic data would be recorded, one found that by some electronic equivalent of a looped tape, the data flooding uncontrollably into one's file was the modernist framework that had precipitated the quest.

The paradox of such a predicament was explained by the introduction of a third modernism—that of the Vietnamese Communist Party.[1] During the war, the party had vehemently denied the Republic of Vietnam (RVN) regime's seizure of the mantle of Vietnamese modernity.[2] After unification, the locus for the articulation of Vietnamese identity for Vietnamese south of the 17th parallel shifted dramatically northwards to the new national capital, Hanoi. The former Democratic Republic of Vietnam (DRV) became the template for the reforms prosecuted in the South in the post-war years: the 'modernisation' (*hien dai hoa*) of society through large-scale campaigns of social 'mobilisation' (*van dong*). In the immediate post-war years, at the height of this program, the North was frequently described as being two decades ahead of the South: the duration this territory had remained under the political sway of the RVN. The South was described as 'backward': host to all sorts of archaic property relations, religious creeds, 'superstitious' practices and anachronistic linguistic usages. In their impatience to sweep aside such outmoded traditions and build a brave new society, the communist unifiers of Vietnam exemplified the disposition noted by a theorist of postmodernity, Zygmunt Bauman:

> Throughout its history, communism was modernity's most devout, vigorous and gallant champion—pious to the point of simplicity. It also claimed to be its only true champion (Bauman 1992:179).

Having won power the communist successors to the RVN strove to expunge such a society, and all nostalgia for it, from the human record. In this, they had mixed results. Indeed, the RVN is deceased, never to return. However, the huge exodus and diasporic time-space rupture that followed the communist takeover was to heighten refugees' nostalgia for the past immeasurably, triggering an immense musical outpouring of rearrangements and re-recordings. The ironic result was to preserve the sensibility of nostalgia that had infused Republican society in its day. This music was to return to its homeland and, in the 1990s, it pervaded Vietnam—the lament of the unpropitiated soul of a victim of a violent and unusual death. Given the ubiquity and familiarity of these resonances from a bygone era one might question whether the taste for music had changed at all in the last thirty years. It soon became apparent, however, that a preoccupation with the music of the 1950s and 1960s was a dynamic social response to events that had transpired more recently.

## THE CRITIC AS SOCIALIST REALIST

This chapter discusses attacks on the legacy of the RVN regime advanced by the administrators of socialism in newly liberated South Vietnam during the period 1975–81. The attempt to extend North Vietnamese political culture into the unfamiliar social terrain of the southern half of the country was accompanied by a sustained critique of the way of life associated with the former regime. Such criticisms were based on the assumption that the DRV, despite having unfolded under very different circumstances, embodied an authentic model for the newly united Vietnamese people. These ideas were advanced during a period of particularly high administrative resolve. The party had just emerged victorious after years of war. The means that were employed to effect a transformation in southern society were similar to those that had brought the party to power. In particular, this involved the mobilisation of the population through various cultural forms and the use of intellectuals, familiar with the substance and forms of popular culture, as a means to advance the party's agenda to the larger public. This approach had been central to its revolutionary victory against France (Woodside 1976) and the construction of socialism in the DRV (Kim Ngoc Bao Ninh 1996). In the late 1970s, these agents were mouthpieces of the new regime in the South, their productions informed by, and popularising, the party line. The representations, issuing from the pens and typewriters of state employed intellectuals, set the co-ordinates of existence within which the population at large were to orient their lives.

Representation played a key motivational role in the regime's mobilisational approach to administration. Through a socialist realist maxim, results were always represented as being well on the way to achievement; 'the people', as agents of history, were represented as 'inevitably' overcoming the obstacles they faced. In Vietnam, socialist realism came into its own in a time of war when the morale of troops was vital and the empirical triggers to disconsolation and defeatism

**Motivational billboard: 'Bringing into play the revolutionary heroism of previous resistance, the people of Vung Tau struggle to build a prosperous, beautiful and modern city'**

were prevalent. Its depictions of muscle-bound heroes standing in stances of implacable resolve suggested inevitable victory through some process of sympathetic magic. In the years of peace which succeeded liberation, these bodily representations continued to be employed to orient the population towards challenges that remained military in conception.[3] Regime intellectuals continued to depict the pertinent issues as a struggle between a heroic population and enemy aggressors. On the new southern 'battlefield' (*chien truong*) of the construction of socialism, southerners were to become moulded into agents of history, whose dispositions were to be 'heroic' (*anh hung*), 'indomitable' (*bat khuat*), 'determined' (*cuong quyet*) and 'decisive' (*quyet dinh*). Their task was to 'sweep' away (*quet*), 'eliminate' (*bai tru*), 'attack' (*tan cong*) and 'fight' (*chong lai*) the mode of life entrenched under US occupation and to 'advance' (*tien len*) to a new life of 'socialist modernity' (*van minh xa hoi chu nghia*). The process involved 'struggle' (*dau tranh*), 'resistance' (*khang chien*), 'opposition' (*phan doi*), 'sacrifice' (*hy sinh*) and, invariably, 'victory' (*thang loi*). Accompanying such language, the erstwhile citizens of the Republic of Vietnam were introduced to the primary colours and chunky figures of socialist realist painting, and became attuned to the martial strains of PRC and Soviet-inspired military marches which were to become the soundtrack to their struggle to emulate the modern heights attained by the DRV.

When official commentators focused on the nature of the challenges such idealised heroes faced, they not surprisingly depicted them in military terms. In 1975 the complex social relations found in South Vietnam differed sharply from the collectivist and militarist ideal pursued under the DRV. These differences gave rise to much published commentary. Fields singled out for discussion and criticism included patterns of settlement, economic modes, technologies, goods, services, religious practices, ideas, lifestyles, fashions, modes of speech and artistic genres. Departures from the model presented by the DRV were understood in context of the recently concluded hostilities. The interpretation through a military lens of two of such realms—commodities and popular music—illustrates this particularly well. The market in commodities and the musical tastes of the southern population were indeed well established in the South, but were thought of as recent in origin. They were taken to symbolise anything but the product of a process of modernisation. Indeed they were considered as detrimental to that objective and in fact calculated to prevent its realisation.

## THE POISONING OF THE PEOPLE

In 1966, with hundreds of thousands of US and other foreign troops in or scheduled to arrive in South Vietnam, the war had been depicted by the DRV leadership as essentially one between the 'Vietnamese People' (*Nhan dan Viet Nam*) and 'foreign aggressors' (*xam luoc ngoai quoc*). General Vo Nguyen Giap had confidently sized up the situation in South Vietnam. The enemy represented a handful of domestic oppressors: the RVN 'militaristic clique', 'compradore bourgeoisie' and 'feudal/capitalist' landlords, abetting 'foreign troops and capitalists'. However, ranged against them was 'the people', characterised as a remarkably broad and vital movement of resistance (Vo Nguyen Giap 1966:26).[4] Giap considered them as engaged in a 'revolution', whose goals were democratic freedoms, national independence and the restoration of national unity. However, the pillar of the struggle, he argued, was the Vietnamese working class and the South Vietnamese peasantry. Characterised as the most exploited sections of society, this meant that their revolutionary will was the most resolute (Vo Nguyen Giap 1966:26).

General Giap's characterisation of revolutionary motivation in South Vietnam held that the fiercer the oppression, the clearer would be oppressed people's perceptions of reality, the purer their spirit and more steadfast their struggle:

> During the past years, the South Vietnamese people have been struggling against an extremely barbarous and ferocious enemy. They have met with difficulties and suffered losses, but on the other hand, they have seen even more clearly the cruel nature of the enemy, felt even deeper hatred for him and, with an iron will, they will fight to the end until final victory (Vo Nguyen Giap 1966:26).

General Giap's depiction of the alignment of forces in South Vietnam exploited a distinction that had been previously employed in the resistance war against the French. In 1949, Indochinese Communist Party member Hai Trieu wrote that the French colonial mercenaries were acting 'mechanically as animals', while the Viet Minh volunteers were 'sacrificing themselves self-consciously as human beings' (Marr 1981:365). The Vietnamese communist leadership acknowledged the enormous technological capacity of their new adversary, 'US neocolonialism' (*Chu nghia thuc dan moi My*) and were ever mindful of its global stature. However, it was the very efficiency of its mode of warfare that would logically prove its downfall. The more devastation its high tech weapons rained down, the clearer would be the people's self-consciousness and the fiercer their will to resist. This view celebrated war, the highest form of adversity, as forging in people the greatest possible capacity to see clearly and to experience self-determination.

On the eve of communist victory in the South, there was some official recognition of the difficulties facing the revolutionary movement. In their 1974 *Vietnamese Studies* article, 'The other war', Nguyen Khac Vien and Phong Hien noted that a sizeable proportion of the population had not been locked into fierce combat with the enemy but were caught up in the tumultuous and precarious life of the cities. They acknowledged that for many, resistance had become irrelevant. Their article traced the ills of urban alienation, rise of a consumer society, proliferation of prostitution, emergence of a materialistic urban bourgeoisie, 'addiction' to foreign films, romance novels and pornography, and the rise of drug addiction. Peasants caught up in this urban maelstrom were described as 'lost to the revolution'. The article vividly portrayed the plunge into despair of a fictional family driven by bombs out of their native village into an urban shantytown. Despite this bleak summation, the article concluded:

> neither Mr Hoa nor his children are lost forever. A PRG militant has
> only to call on him one evening to rouse in him an entire past,
> dormant ideas and feelings. Their brother has only to return from the
> maquis or a friend who takes an active part in the opposition
> movement in the cities to make contact with Mr Hoa's children and
> talk with them once or twice for the words freedom and fatherland
> gradually to find again their meaning (Nguyen Khac Vien and Phong
> Hien 1974:187).

This sobering note aside, the 1975 'liberation' of Saigon was depicted as a successful culmination of the 'national-democratic revolution' waged by the people of the South for the previous two decades. The popular nature of the South Vietnamese struggle to bring down the RVN was affirmed in official speeches, newspapers and journal articles.[5] A year later, the country was formally united and named the Socialist Republic of Vietnam. The tasks of peace were indeed as great as those faced during the war, not the least of them being to overcome the destruction wrought by decades of war. However, the leadership re-affirmed faith in the people of the South, whose heroic victory over the French and US 'aggressors' proved their capacity to overcome the most difficult of obstacles. Encouragingly, an editorial appearing in the party theoretical journal *Hoc Tap*, one year after liberation, delivered a favourable review of the 'revolution's' achievements:

> Within only a year of complete liberation, the southern revolution has progressed with great strides. How completely has the face of southern society changed. This is a great victory for compatriots in the South and throughout our country (*Hoc Tap* 16 April 1976).[6]

At formal unification in 1976, it was announced that the only effective means to secure substantive independence was for the South to immediately embark on socialist transformation. The North, whose ideology of Marxism Leninism was depicted as the 'apex of human thought', and whose socialist system, 'the inevitable development of human society' (Truong Chinh 1976:31), was prescribed as the template for the South's new revolutionary stage. Articles in *Hoc Tap*, announced the popularity of this new orientation in the South. A month following formal unification, one writer declared that the 'majority support social-ism, support proletarian democracy' (Van Tao 1976:37). It reported that 'our people from North to South are making every effort to complete the re-unification of the country and rapidly, strongly and steadily advance the entire nation to socialism' (Van Tao 1976:30). It praised 'the steadfast struggle to preserve the national culture and resist the slave culture' (*van hoa no le*) which had developed 'in the areas of South Vietnam under enemy control' (Van Tao 1976:65).

However, not long into the task of commencing the 'historically inevitable' task of constructing socialism in the South, significant qualifications began to creep into depictions of that agent of history, the 'South Vietnamese People'. More conservative assessments of the degree of support attracted by the 'anti-aggression struggle' were pub-lished. Discussions of the harmful legacies of two decades of US neo-colonialism focused on the obstacles they posed to post-war recon-struction. Far from 'inevitable', the construction of socialism in South Vietnam was considered as filled with hardship and difficulties. A *Vietnamese Studies* piece entitled 'Fostering new socialist men and women', conveyed a sense of the reconceived enormity of the task:

> In the South, American neo-colonialist capitalism had very serious effects on economic, cultural and social life. A typically American bourgeois ideology was devised and propagated as the 'national interest' and 'nationalist'; there was an Americanized culture, and for twenty years, the enemy did their best to destroy the fine cultural traditions and revolutionary spirit of our people, to destroy the souls and undermine the human dignity of our compatriots. Besides the

millions of quislings turned into mercenary soldiers, against the revolution, millions of others were ensnared in the American way of life, namely the prostitutes, hooligans, ruffians, drug-addicts, superstitious people (Ha Huy Giap 1978:17).

Commentators who questioned the spiritual resilience of the South Vietnamese population also reassessed the arsenal their former enemy had employed. Several writers pointed out that while the enemy's repressive apparatus of prisons, strategic hamlets, police, army and gruesome firepower had been able to chain or break peoples' bodies, there had been other mechanisms that could fetter or grievously incapacitate the operations of the human heart and mind. Developments such as urbanisation, the rise of mass consumer culture, the massive importation of cultural works and proliferation of educational facilities were analysed as part of a co-ordinated project of enslavement, rivalling the oppression inflicted by the enemy's purely military arsenal. Such accoutrements of the US presence were particularly dangerous because they were held to have blinded people to the truth of their oppression and eroded their will to resist.

Therefore, after unification, the 'cultural vestiges of US neo-colonialism' (*tan du van hoa thuc dan moi*) were to be treated with the same caution as was reserved for unexploded mines, toxic chemical dumps or other dangerous military ordnance. Cities, consumer life-styles, markets and pop music tapes were not viewed as indices of South Vietnam's encounter with modernity, but as dangerous threats. The new regime systematically reduced what US critics of their own government considered symbols of a pernicious, messy and counter-productive process of modernisation (Kolko 1985; Fitzgerald 1972) to the deadly and calculated potency of military weaponry.

In retrospect, far greater efficacy was attributed to the RVN than had been the case during the war. The US-backed regime was credited with having substantially neutralised resistance among those 'living in the encirclement of the enemy's morale-affecting apparatus' (Thach Phuong and Tran Huu Ta 1977:54). 'Neo-colonial poisons' (*noc doc thuc dan moi*)[7] were seen to have permeated the population of the South, extinguishing their revolutionary spirit, stifling their consciousness, dulling their scruples and ultimately effacing their humanity. The imputed anti-modernity of the republican regime and the neo-colonial system was extended retrospectively to the entire population which had lived under its influence, as implied in the *Vietnamese Studies* piece, 'Socialist fatherland: ideals and realities':

> The American imperialists . . . had considerable economic and military potential and a high scientific and technical standard; they used treachery, created a neo-colonial consumer society, and concentrated modern means of propaganda and reactionary and decadent cultural

**'Neo-colonial vestiges.' An American helicopter in a Ho Chi Minh City park 1991**

products of the 'free world' as never before for maximum impact on the mode of thinking, the psychology and life-style of the people in the South. They have soiled the souls of millions of our young people (Ha Xuan Truong 1978b:11).

## HARMFUL GOODS

The liberating troops and new communist administrators in the post-war South encountered a society flooded beyond saturation with consumer icons. Hondas and four-wheeled motor vehicles threatened to displace pedestrians and *cyclos* in the streets of Saigon. Bicycles, radios and watches were common domestic accessories. Luxury goods of all descriptions jammed shop shelves and rural market stalls. Cafes, bars and eating establishments lined the streets and clustered around markets, transport terminals and the intersections of roads and waterways. In this time of economic crisis, unemployed workers, ruined traders and former RVN soldiers filled the cafes, smoking imported cigarettes, drinking coffee, listening to taped music and furtively arranging illicit commercial transactions. Down-and-out householders dusted off or disconnected various household appliances, furniture, clothes, jewellery, books and records, bringing them to sell in a plethora of illicit open air markets that clogged traffic in the streets.

The flaunting of southern consumer wealth was very often driven by desperation on the part of unemployed southern householders (Long and Kendall 1981). However, from the perspective of the new authorities, the profusion of merchandise in the streets represented a provocation and an immense danger. Northern soldiers had been told their southern cousins were starving and decimated by disease under the tyranny of the US presence. Some had even brought humble packets of food for relatives. Now as occupying troops, they were being offered a dazzling array of unexpected luxuries that resoundingly belied official pronouncements on the North's relative prosperity.[8] Northern soldiers and administrative cadres alike were agog as the immense consumer wealth of the South was extruded into public thoroughfares, unexpectedly turning liberators into inadvertent browsers and window shoppers wherever they went about their business. Many were not long in adjusting to conditions in the South, becoming discerning buyers, adept hagglers and skilful intermediaries. Soon US, Japanese and Taiwanese goods began flowing northwards and the South became a highly sought after posting for soldiers and bureaucrats alike. The northern population's confidence in their socialist affiliations was eroded by such displays of wealth. Authorities took an aggressive line belittling the significance of such commodities. A Ho Chi Minh City newspaper ran a disparaging report a little over a year following war's end which played down the quality of the merchandise for sale in the streetside markets:

> They are from many different segments of society and I defy anyone to tell me where they all come from. The goods they display are terrible, it is stuff from the very bottom of the barrel. They have everything from once shiny hardware and art objects to old pieces of clothing hung up and dangling above them. Worse yet, some of these youths will even take off the clothes they are wearing to sell them. There is simply not enough space here to describe everything that goes on there! (Nhi Phu 1976:3).

Another piece, adopting the same tone appeared in the Hanoi newspaper *Doc Lap* a year after unification, reporting on a Hanoi journalist's first post-war trip to the South:

> We have seen people here who are proud of and who praise Saigon's period of peace and prosperity in which commodities are more plentiful, cheaper, more attractive, and more convenient than those in Paris. . . . Some people are proud that life here is a song with adequate timbres. We have listened and seen only a long string of repetitious and trite telegraphic signals—'commodities–money, commodities–money, commodities–money'—and it is like this day and night from one day to the next, from one month to the next and from one year to the next (Hoang Nhu Ma 1976).

This piece illustrated the dilemmas of being a consumer–liberator in a post-war southern Vietnamese city. The author soon shed his disparaging tone as he described the experience of consumerism:

> Actually the shops have televisions and refrigerators and there are motor vehicles everywhere and this is very convenient. But here, things are not produced in order to support people's lives and make things more convenient . . . [W]hen a new type of television or motor vehicle appears on the market, the things we are presently using suddenly become outdated, inconvenient and ugly. And we are impatient to buy the new things. Thus we run after commodities, a cross-country race with no barriers or time limits. We rush to commodities like moths rush to flames (Hoang Nhu Ma 1976).

Paragraphs later, not a trace remained of his coolly dismissive opening comments:

> The waves of commodities in this horrible ocean come in great numbers and exert a pull and people are attracted by and play in them until they are exhausted and sink. Here, commodities are really cruel; they kill people without trembling and no one can avoid their claws and teeth (Hoang Nhu Ma 1976).

At the same time that northern cadres were discovering the perils of consumerist inundation, the southern population was being introduced to the language of economic mobilisation. The papers were filled with slogans exhorting people to 'struggle' (*dau tranh*) to attain 'victory' (*thang loi*) on the new 'front' (*mat tran*) of the economy, conceptualising the economic tasks that lay ahead as military targets. In 1976 one such exhortative speech by Ho Chi Minh City People's Committee member Mai Chi Tho was reported in *Saigon Giai Phong*:

> Although we are encountering thousands of hardships and obstacles, nothing is tougher than the obstacles encountered in the last decades during the resistances against France and America and since our people had overcome them all and had won them all, our present difficulties, no matter how great they are, are only temporary (*Saigon Giai Phong* 1976b).

A month later an editorial in the same paper reported that the new stage of struggle had begun to 'score' results:

> After the brilliant spring 1975 victory, responding to the party's appeal to turn revolutionary heroism in combat into revolutionary heroism in productive labour and national construction, the southern peasants valiantly removed mines, reclaimed fallow and waste land and successively launched one irrigation campaign after another, using picks and shovels where tractors and bulldozers were not available . . . Since liberation day, the South scored three successive good crops (*Saigon Giai Phong* 1976c).

In 1977 *Nhan Dan* newspaper employed this metaphor with a heightened urgency. Its claim that only with the ending of one war could another be declared on a millennial enemy, placed its readers at the eye of a storm of violence. In tones of desperation, it urged readers to 'Press forward with the offensive on the agricultural front':

> Our nation has regained independence and freedom after struggling with perseverance for a century. Today we can concentrate our forces on defeating our 1,000-year enemy—hunger—against which only now do necessary conditions exist for us to definitively declare war. As long as the food problem remains unsolved, the living standards of our people will inevitably remain low, and hunger may occasionally occur in some places.
>     . . . Can we solve the food problem? The answer is 'yes', but only through a difficult, arduous revolutionary struggle and with a will for self-reliance and a revolutionary offensive spirit . . . The agricultural front throughout the country is seething with activity. Millions of people are rushing to the fields [words indistinct] to plow and transport on schedule and are pushing ahead with the water conservation movement in all parts of the country, resolutely advancing to solve the grain and food problem at all costs (*Nhan Dan* 8 February 1977).

Difficulties in applying this militarised economic vision, whereby a 'heroic' populace extracted value by 'attacking' an intransigent or hostile nature had begun no sooner than it was introduced to the South. The success of this model hinged on the state's ability to assume a monopoly over urban–rural trade, to command resources for use as incentives, however, the continued strength of the illegal private distribution network prevented this (Porter 1990:73). A *Sydney Morning Herald* reporter visiting Vietnam in 1977 observed that despite the threat of repression, Ho Chi Minh City was doing 'largely business as usual':

> The ordinary markets in South Vietnamese cities sell Hitachi or Sanyo electric fans, Olympic portable typewriters, Adidas sports shoes, Peugot bicycles and Michelin inner tubes. Prices are about western level, which would put them, theoretically far out of the range of any Vietnamese. But someone must be buying them (*Sydney Morning Herald* 23 April 1977).

The persistence of private markets interfered with the regime's efforts to mobilise the population in its economic 'campaigns'. Increasingly, urban markets assumed the stature of military adversaries in a struggle between the socialist and capitalist paths. In 1977 a report in the party's theoretical journal, *Tap Chi Cong San*, described Ho Chi Minh City two years after liberation as a location for the 'fortresses' of capitalism, a hub and a 'headquarters' (*bo chi huy*) of this recalcitrant and morally 'dangerous' (*nguy hiem*) commercial sector:

Formerly, this city was the largest consumer market and, at the same time, the centre of goods distribution to South Vietnam as a whole. It can be said that the fortresses (*don*) of the capitalist business forces led by the compradore bourgeoisie were mainly concentrated in this city.
. . . Through actual experience, we have found that in an economy formed by many components, the market is a hot battlefield (*chien truong*) where a struggle between the interests of the labouring people and those of the bourgeoisie takes place every day and hour (Tran Thanh 1977:41).

The new regime's administrators in the South were clearly finding it difficult to persuade urbanites of the advantages of centralised state control over the exchange and distribution of goods. Commentary in the official media focused increasingly on the population's mental shortcomings in this respect. In April 1977 the people of Ho Chi Minh City were exhorted by their local government's print media organ to 'think correctly and have a correct attitude':

Many people have made a habit of regretting the passing of the artificial glittering exterior of this city which was painted on by the old regime. It must be realized that Ho Chi Minh City cannot be a consumer and commercial city. Ho Chi Minh City must be a producing city.
Many people do not yet fully understand the great, profound, all-round revolutionary upheaval that is now taking place in our city, and do not yet realize that we are now eliminating the way of life that was dependent on the dollar and which, although there were many goods and conveniences, was a life of slavery paid for by the lives and many miseries of the people (*Saigon Giai Phong* 1977a).

Commentators began to pay attention to the effects which the goods themselves had on the capacity of the population to heed the reformist exhortations of their new leaders. A 1977 editorial in the Ho Chi Minh City newspaper *Tin Sang* identified the persistence of the private market in the city as a legacy of US military policy:

At present, there are too many peddlers in our city. Groups of them can be seen everywhere. At some places, there are more sellers than buyers. This is not, as some mistakenly think, an indication of the prosperity of a city. Rather, it is nothing more than a situation that has existed since the period of US neo-colonialism. During that period, the imperialists opened very many sources of goods in order to disorient the people and make the people forget their criminal acts (*Tin Sang* 20 October 1977:1).

The message for any who might regret the passing of South Vietnam's urbanised consumer society was that commodities were dangerous. The abundance of goods implied ongoing enslavement, not prosperity. It was no wonder people were confused. Inherent to the goods themselves were properties inhibiting thought. In *Doc Lap* news-paper, Hanoi journalist Hoang Nhu Ma reported the spiritually incarcerating and brain-numbing effects of commodities during his post-war tour to the South:

> Commodities have firmly gripped and shackled the spirit and people can no longer struggle at all. When life has been reduced to the four words 'make money, buy goods', those who still have brains think of nothing else (Hoang Nhu Ma 1976:1).

In 1978, with commercialism still rampant in South Vietnam's cities, critics sought to remind people of the wicked aims behind the US commodity aid program. Hanoi historian Tran Ngoc Dinh referred to it as a 'civilization of the dollar' (*van minh cua dong do la*) (Tran Ngoc Dinh 1978:50). US commodity aid was antithetical to humanity. By distorting conscience and consciousness it had led to pernicious results:

> Under the yoke of neo-colonial rule, American aid made many people, especially the youth, lose all character, thought, sentiment, sense of purpose—everything came down to money. People's sentiment and thought have never been razed and battered to the extent they were under the US-Puppet regime. Be they hooligans, evil-doers, scoundrels or dim-wits, all were considered respectable—providing they had money (Tran Ngoc Dinh 1978:51).

Such conceptualisations of commodities as political weapons, designed to 'take out' the human qualities of consciousness and conscience came to a crescendo in 1978, as the 'campaign to eliminate the compradore capitalists' (*chien dich bai tru tu san mai ban*), rolled into high gear. This had all the appearances, if not the efficacy, of a military operation. The identification of 'objectives', mobilisation of civilian assistants, cordoning off of premises and confiscation of assets were dramatic manifestations of state power. However, the effects on illegal marketing and private trade networks proved inconclusive. Informal commercial activity quickly returned to the norm, vitiating the effort to control resources in order to steer the population in desired directions (Dang Phong 1995).

On the other hand, the impact of these policies on southern society were dramatic. The campaign against compradore capitalists was to trigger the seaborne exodus of many ethnic Chinese, linchpins of the market economy. They were to be followed over the next few years by many hundreds of thousands of others from the former South, who found life in their new circumstances impossible. Those who had lived out the war as shopkeepers and merchants were to find that in the new society it was not commercial skills or creditworthiness but 'revolutionary merit' (*cong voi cach mang*) that gave one prospects for advancement. Displays of militancy and participation in party-led campaigns became one of the few ways to rebalance one's moral ledger, although those who did risked being referred to derogatorily as "'75 Revolutionaries' (*Cach mang '75*). Many of those who had joined the 'movement' to open new economic zones failed on this new agricultural 'front' and were to find their way from rural locations back to Ho Chi Minh City footpaths. Traders both urban and rural continued to run the gauntlet of police checks, frequently experiencing confiscation. Farmers, stifled by bureaucratic management and low prices, adulterated the produce they supplied to the state and found avenues to smuggle goods to private distribution points. The private market continued to be central to most people's basic physical survival. By the end of the 1970s it was clear that many localities were not implementing policy but it was some time before complex patterns of non-compliance emerged as a systematic shift in national orientation.

## A REVOLUTIONARY SILENCE

Accompanying the post-war attack on private markets and commodities were bans imposed upon playing the 'music of the former regime' (*am nhac cua che do cu*). This included much of the music composed in Vietnam before the consolidation of DRV rule and in the South between 1954 and 1975, as well as that from non-socialist foreign countries. Tapes, records and printed musical scores were systematically collected from private homes and commercial establishments and destroyed in campaigns to eliminate these 'cultural vestiges' (*di tich van hoa*) of the former South. Any kind of performance of such pieces was banned and could earn one serious penalties. The state took control of the broadcasting of music on television, radio and in public venues, and controlled the repertoires of public performances. Such policies remained active until the early 1980s, when a gradual relaxation was reported. In the 1990s, acquaintances still remembered the police visits, the confiscations and standard methods of evasion. However, few could illuminate the slogans in whose name the bans on music had been prosecuted. All pre-1975 southern music had been categorised as 'yellow' (*vang*). Yet few of those with whom I spoke had a clear idea of its derivation or its meaning. Most thought it was Chinese in origin. Some thought it meant 'weak', one speculated it meant 'feudal', yet another thought it meant 'sick'.

Further attempts to understand the intention behind the post-war crackdown yielded patchy results. My investigations among Ho Chi Minh City musicians and music lovers led rather inconclusively to a list of pejorative expressions they dimly remembered having been aimed at the music:

*Nhac vang*: Yellow music, connotes sickness/weakness/feudal era.
*Yeu ot*: Weak.

*Uy mi*: Weakening.
*Lang man*: Romantic (pejorative), used to designate pre-World
    War II music.
*Doi truy, Tuc tiu*: Depraved.
*Kich dam, Kich thich*: Stimulating lust/lewdness.
*Dau doc, Noc doc*: Poisonous.
*Phan dong*: Reactionary.
*Chong cong*: Anti-communist.

Acquaintances were unclear about the larger significance of such charac-terisations. One acquaintance remembered that the term *uy mi* referred to an erosion of (especially) youth's revolutionary and military spirit. Music that was *uy mi* lulled people to sleep rather than stirring them to fight. *Tinh yeu uy mi*, or weak love, implied possessive, self-indulgent love—love which weakened you. Much pre-1975 and Western music was seen to be marked by this quality. This acquaintance remem-bered that the crackdown on *uy mi* music coincided with the mobilisation for the Cambodian war. Aside from this, few of those I spoke to could help me in my quest to understand the motives of the communist reformers of southern music. It was only on consulting official news reports and commentaries in theoretical journals that these terms began to assume significance.

## ART IN THE SERVICE OF WAR

In 1981 Ho Chi Minh City party leader, Vo Van Kiet, spoke at a meeting of cadres responsible for the artistic and cultural fields in the city about the role music played in the revolutionary struggle. Vo Van Kiet told his audience that music was a debt he owed to the revolution and that it had played a vital role in the North's military victory:

> I belong to the generation which has learnt to sing and has enjoyed many songs thanks to the revolution. It is in the fire of battle that songs are written which we may all recognize as the songs of our hearts . . . Each song which wins our hearts is a prop, a zone of light, a pair of wings for the soul (Vo Van Kiet 1981:147).

In like manner during the war, depictions of the South Vietnamese resistance issued by the party had emphasised the role played by music in expressing and propagandising the anti-aggression struggle. In 1970 *Vietnamese Studies* presented an account from the NLF's domestic journal *Giai Phong*, 'by a spectator coming from Saigon', of a clandestine National Liberation Front musical performance. The performance pur-portedly had a dramatic impact on the author of the account, a jaded urbanite, who ventured a comparison:

In the towns, many shows are advertised, but they are only mongrel products, crosses of American, British or Japanese elements, which bear no relation whatsoever to what has been bequeathed to us by our ancestors. Here, looking at the scenes, colours and costumes presented by the Liberation artistes, one feels great pleasure and pride. Everything is near and dear, as if it were our ancestors' blood and flesh: nothing equivalent can be found in any mixture imported from abroad (Pham Cuong 1970:137).

The spectator's experience of these examples of 'pure' national culture had the intended effect. The author was mobilised by the music of the resistance to abandon a rootless urban existence and take part in the anti-American war effort:

You can easily imagine the patriotic feelings boiling in the hearts of those who daily see the invaders show off their weapons, planes and tanks, and who are now enjoying this charming song, 'Bamboo Spike', which makes them feel so proud of this weapon, rudimentary but dreaded by the US Imperialists. One cannot help being moved by such songs as 'Spring in the Resistance Zones' . . . What we felt that evening was beyond description. Let me say briefly that only a few days after this performance, my friends who attended it and I left for the 'maquis' ('H.B.T.') (Pham Cuong 1970:137).

Such discussions of the effects of resistance war on Vietnamese music employed General Giap's notion of the adversity of war heightening the spirit of resistance. In a 1977 article entitled 'Renaissance of Vietnamese music', Hanoi musicologist Dao Trong Tu argued that the war with America had unleashed 'a prodigious blossoming of revolutionary humanist songs':

Never before had Vietnamese songs resounded with such brilliance and vitality as during the particularly hard years of anti-US resistance. Modern imperialist war—this phrase alone expresses all the emotions one must have experienced. In this hell, however, blossomed fine songs of optimism and faith and the sweetest love songs, fruits of a rational conception of art in service of Life and of the Destiny of a nation (Dao Trong Tu 1977:125).

However, such voluntarist optimism was contradicted by other state cultural commentators in the post-war era, who saw the Republican era as having been a particularly bleak time for music. Two of these critics described a telling blow struck against the *Cai luong* opera by RVN-era commercialisation and censorship:

*Cai luong*, the most popular theatrical form in the South, had not only to abandon current social themes, [bowing to official regulations], but also to be satisfied with a stage direction adapted to the lower tastes. To satisfy the public, the artists no more thought of personifying the characters, of illuminating their personality but rather of 'bewitching' the audience by their voice and preening posture; they tried to enliven them with vulgar jokes and charm them with intrigues in which the unusual and wonderful prevailed, or give them a cold sweat with terrifying scenes, to dazzle them with sumptuous costumes and stage effects and brilliant footlights (Nguyen Khac Vien and Phong Hien 1982:119).

In his 1981 speech, Vo Van Kiet also voiced an apparently traditionalist lament on the tragic decline of traditional music by the time of liberation:

In Vietnam, after many centuries of a backward, feudal regime and a century of old and new colonialism, our fund of traditional ancestral music had sunk into oblivion, electronic music invaded our city, spread rapidly and threatened to corrupt the as-yet immature soul of our youth (Vo Van Kiet 1981:144).

These two commentaries appear to attest to the leadership's appraisal of the problem as a crisis of traditional cultural forms faced by the impact of modernity. Such an interpretation would accord with conceptualisations of the Vietnamese communist leadership as traditionalists, whose response to the ravages of modernity was informed by traditionalist reflexes (Fitzgerald 1972; Woodside 1976; Hy Van Luong 1992). Another reading is possible, however, which places more weight on the Vietnamese leadership's military experiences in shaping a distinctive habitus, a horizon of expectations and orientation towards the future (Bourdieu 1990). Throughout their discussion of the musical legacies of the US era, these same writers emphasised the operation of a neo-colonial conspiracy. The incursion of foreign musical forms was regarded not as regrettable tragedy, but as coherent strategy:

Among the cultural methods used by the neo-colonial regime, music was one of the most effective . . . to keep youth aloof from the revolutionary path by leading them to avenues of escape or to the exultation of low instincts and finally to corruption (Nguyen Khac Vien and Phong Hien 1982:123).

According to this perspective, the legacy of the neo-colonial abuse of music lingered well after liberation. In Vo Van Kiet's 1981 speech, 'youth music' (*nhac tre*)—a term for Western rock and pop-inspired compositions—was considered potentially harmful as it dissipated youths' revolutionary activity. He condemned the continued influence of rock'n'roll, underlining the deep purchase it had secured on youth's souls:

We have also seen more clearly the deep marks left on many of our youth by the old way of life. This 'yellow' and 'wandering' music with its persistent resonance was part of the enemy's 'cultural pacification process'. The whole society must be made aware of the seriousness of the question (Vo Van Kiet 1981:133).

## WHAT IS YELLOW MUSIC?

The most salient aspect of official criticism of South Vietnamese music was the politicisation of such diverse dimensions of musical expression as rhythm, melody, tempo, volume and vocal style. From 1976 a systematic critique to this effect was developed in a series of articles published in the monthly magazine *Van Hoa Nghe Thuat* (*Culture and Arts*).[9] These articles were aimed at educating the public about the dangers of the musical legacy of the Republican era, and to educate cadres, who were at the time engaged in campaigns to uncover and destroy cassettes and records of this kind, how to positively identify the harmful targets of their quest.

The first of the *Van Hoa Nghe Thuat* articles on southern music, published in May 1976, was entitled, 'What is yellow music?' (To Vu 1976). It traced the etymology of the term 'yellow music' (*nhac vang*) to Chinese communist campaigns to eliminate 'reactionary bourgeoisie musical vestiges' in Beijing and Shanghai in 1952–53. The author wondered if such a designation could be applied to the many musical cassettes from South Vietnam that had recently appeared in a number of northern cities. These included recordings of a variety of musical styles: dance music, love songs, easy listening and instrumental. He reasoned that some of the music from the South, such as songs of the Anti-US Resistance (*Nhac khang chien chong My*) were of a progressive variety. Therefore not all southern music could be considered yellow. After discussing the lyrics of a number of love songs from the South which he termed 'yellow', the author was able to identify more precisely what was 'yellow' about this music:

> The overall effect of yellow music pieces is to evoke in hapless
> listeners a gloomy, embittered, impotent and cynical mood towards
> life, an attitude negating youth's desire to be cheerful, a sensation of
> being drowned in loneliness in a withered and desolate world (To Vu
> 1976:46).

The author focused on the love songs of the Republican era, finding 'yellowness' in their 'unwholesome' (*khong lanh manh*) lyrical themes of separation, loneliness, sadness and nostalgia. 'The world of yellow music carries people into a state of suffering from love, the opposite of every thought of happiness that people seek for there' (To Vu 1976:45). A cartoon appearing in a subsequent article in *Van Hoa Nghe Thuat*'s series on the music of the RVN era illustrated the harmful property of transmitting unhappiness obtaining to 'yellow music' (see p. 44). The lyrics read 'Darling, life is crumbling!' (Tran Tan 1977:38).

To Vu asserted that a distinctive melody (*nhac dieu*) and unique expressive style (*phong cach the hien rieng*) were equally key to the identification of a song as 'yellow'. The notion of something as

— Trời ! ... Các con ốm cả hay sao thế ?

— Chúng con "đời tàn" từ lúc nghe băng nhạc vàng của bố đấy !

Tranh : Trần Tân

**—My god what's wrong, are you kids sick or what?**
**—Our 'lives have been crumbling' since listening to this yellow music tape of yours, Dad.**

seemingly innocuous as melody having a political dimension and attracting paragraphs of detailed criticism is intriguing:

> If the tunes of yellow songs of old generally exuded a harmonious, smooth, cajoling or sweet quality, then into the US-Puppet era, they became either extremely sobbing and melting or highly gloomy and desolate. They were melodies, sometimes quiet and interminable, like sad persistent drops of rain, sometimes bewailing one's lot— excruciatingly lonely like tugging flurries of wind (To Vu 1976:45).

The vocal style employed to sing such pieces could also augment their 'yellowness'. Although no names were given in this article, one can surmise that the Republican-era singer Khanh Ly, whose extraordinary voice popularised the music of composer Trinh Cong Son, might have been on this critic's mind:

> There is a factor which relatively easily helps us discover whether a piece of music is yellow, even if unable to analyze its melody or clearly hear the lyrics—that is, its rather 'original' (*doc dao*) expressive style. The most common case is the sobbing, meltingly tearful way of singing, sounding like mourning or crying which is easily recognized.

. . . Besides sobbing and moaning, yellow music singers are inclined to sing in a lingering manner, stroking each sound in a glossy or rounded way (To Vu 1976:46).

The melody and vocal styles typifying 'yellow music' were attributes urgently requiring research and publicisation. The author concluded by conspiratorially evoking the dangers inherent in these attributes. He argued that these were the most harmful aspects of this music because the way they operated was imperceptible:

> The damage done by yellow music lies not only in its negative effects but also in its mode of operation. It does not belong to that class of transparently anti-communist songs that people are on their guard against. Nor does it share the rabid frenzy of 'sensational', 'arousing' music. Yellow music slips into the heart like a shadow of the night, lulling vigilance to sleep thanks to its sweet and gentle appearance and its sonorous and honeyed harmonies. It does not roar and assault but gnaws and erodes (To Vu 1976:46).

## SLAVES TO THE 'NEO-COLONIAL' RHYTHM

Much of the critique of 'yellow music' was directed against the idea that, as an expression of 'modern' or 'civilised' urban culture, it represented a high point of human development. A cartoon accompanying the first article in *Van Hoa Nghe Thuat*'s series on South Vietnamese music linked the critique of yellow music with that contemporaneously being launched against commodities (Van Thanh 1976:44). The cartoon debunked the notion that the consumerist lifestyle (*loi song chu nghia tieu thu*) still prevalent in South Vietnam and the vogue for melancholy love songs represented a 'modern' way of life. It showed a young man equipped with the accessories of urban consumer life, snappy clothes, television, record player and coffee maker. He is depicted sprawled on his chair with one foot on it and the other on a coffee table. He has spilt some coffee and is smoking. From the record player, labelled 'yellow music', come the lyrics: 'our love is melancholy.' The young man is saying: 'How "civilised!" How can they call me uncultured?' (see p. 46) In a similar vein, an earlier piece entitled 'Several reflections on the vestiges (*tan du*) of neo-colonial culture (*van hoa thuc dan moi*) in the South today', took issue with the 'cultured' status of the arts, ideology and lifestyle imported into South Vietnam in the name of progress (Tran Quang 1976:12). Its author reflected on the differences between French and American efforts to win hearts and minds in their counter-insurgency campaigns:

> To a certain extent the cultural policies of France involved more or less cultural measures . . . America's cultural measures, while similar in some ways, were also non-cultural (*phi van hoa*). They coerced and

"Văn minh" thế này mà họ vẫn bảo mình thiếu văn hóa!!!.

### How 'civilised!' How can they call me uncultured?

> forced, rather than convinced one to follow the imperialist way.
> Crudity (*tho bao*) was the hallmark of US cultural policies, even in
> their tricks and snares . . . Although our people wanted to resist, they
> were struck from all quarters—held back and led into mistaken
> actions. America's cultural policy was to turn people into animals
> (*dong vat*) and dimwits (*u me*)—half intoxicated, half conscious (*nua
> say nua tinh*) (Tran Quang 1976:12).

According to this author, the Americans attempted to short-circuit
conscious reflection so that Vietnamese would be unaware of their
exploitation and would lose their pride and self-confidence. One of the
principal means they were held to have used was to stimulate lust, and
therefore 'animalise' the population under their control:

> No-one underestimates the harmful effects of neo-colonialist culture.
> Twenty years of US devastation created consequences arguably ten
> times more serious than those of one hundred years of French
> colonialism in a number of respects. Certainly we will need several
> years, even decades, to wash away all the harmful legacies in each of
> the areas in which neo-colonial culture, which served up germs
> (*vi trung*) and monstrosity (*quai thai*) for enjoyment and reward,

polluted (*o nhiem*) our purity (*su trong sang*). In certain groups of people, bestial depravity (*su sa doa day thu tinh*) has become a daily activity. Speaking in general, the stimulation of lust (*nhuc duc*) represents the core of neo-colonial culture (Tran Quang 1976:12).

Such an argument was picked up and applied specifically to music in the next article to appear in the *Van Hoa Nghe Thuat* series entitled 'Reactionary music'. Its author, Cuu Long Giang, contended that:

> to realize a long-term scheme of enslavement, neo-colonialism infiltrated (*du nhap*) into South Vietnam many depraved (*sa doa*) and reactionary (*phan dong*) philosophies and theories along with obscene (*dam o*) and reactionary arts and letters.
>
> Music was one important part in that system of enslaving arts and letters. There are those calling it 'yellow' music, 'arousing' music, 'unwholesome' music. Whatever else one might call it, its character was reactionary. In essence it was hostile to the forces of progress, revolution and socialism (Cuu Long Giang 1976:42).

Cuu Long Giang warned that through music, neo-colonialism had 'tried to assimilate (*dong hoa*) into society various depraved (*doi truy*) and reactionary ideas about the nation, country, love and happiness'. He mentioned 'army music' (*nhac linh*), which had tried to convince people that to fight with the Republican army was a just cause—for freedom, independence and the preservation of national dignity. Through similar lies and distortions, 'anti-communist music' (*nhac chong cong*) had tried to blacken socialism and life in the liberated zones. The author noted that such distortions were advanced in other artistic and literary mediums. The additional danger of music, as To Vu had also noted, lay in its subtle capacity to paralyse struggle through the medium of sound:

> This kind of music incited an embittered or vacuous state of mind. The way to escape this condition was to take up arms against and kill one's compatriots. Even deadlier, by various flirtatious (*ve van*) and lulling (*ru ngu*) sounds (*am thanh*), this variety of music also aimed to express a content preventing every exertion and paralyzing the energy to struggle. Or, more accurately, it prevented all exertion in a great number of people whose oppression was subtle and even tolerable! (Cuu Long Giang 1976:42).

Cuu Long Giang argued that after 1964, the former regime made greater use of 'lustful' (*nhuc cam*) and 'depraved' (*sa doa*) music. He argued that the spread of prostitution, pornography and miniskirts had been a deliberate plot to distract people from their oppression and neutralise their ethical faculties. Music had played a part in this. Deploying sensational love songs, the 'US psychological warfare apparatus' (*bo may tam ly chien My*) had turned the South Vietnamese into manipulable animals:

it is also necessary to expose the dangerous quality of psy-war music (*nhac tam ly chien*). This includes various inferior songs of romantic love with sensational titles. This music for soldiers (but actually not only for soldiers) thoroughly exploited people's instincts, heightening lustfulness and elevating it into a philosophy of life. It urged people to live for the moment and discard all responsibility for one's compatriots and nation (Cuu Long Giang 1976:44).

The musical form was ideal for the schemes of US psychological warriors. According to this critic, melody was exploited as a sensual payout in neo-colonialism's libidinal economy, whereby the regime could buy the population's political indifference or ethical neutralisation in return for melodic satiety. Moreover, the melodic dimension of music was exploited as a medium which enabled the transmission of ideas without inherent value:

> Through various cooing, contrived and ingenious melodies which sated the appetites of listeners, through pampering and caressing tricks and through ornate and intriguing lyrics—sometimes boldly reckless, sometimes confiding and intimate—music was exploited to insinuate phrases of a cheap and empty philosophy (Cuu Long Giang 1976:44).

This dangerous combination of sensuality and anti-communist ideology in music was referred to by other official critics speaking of other forms of 'neo-colonial' culture. They argued that:

> Another innovation of the anti-communist literati was to seek ways to mix poisons of reaction and decadence together in the same work. It would be very advantageous if reactionary contents could be introduced into decadent works in a certain dosage or another. That would be doubly dangerous, for it would at the same time be poisonous with regard to thought, sentiment, and the soul, or in other words both reactionary-ize (*phan dong hoa*) those who have been poisoned and animalize (*thu vat hoa*) them with regard to their souls and way of life (Thach Phuong and Tran Huu Ta 1977:48).

Cuu Long Giang associated the music of the RVN era with urban lifestyles, particularly that of Saigon, then the former seat of enemy power:

> At one time, this fashionable kind of music carried the title 'city music' as it only addressed the trivial pursuits of the city, or individual emotions and degenerate wishes (*nhung suy tu uoc le*) (Cuu Long Giang 1976:44).

He argued that a number of musical 'hacks' (*boi but*) motivated by profit had churned out inferior productions appealing to 'the evanescent tastes (*thi hieu tam thuong*) of a backward section of the urban masses'. The fleeting appeal of such works was attributed to the effects of commercialisation. However, Cuu Long Giang also attributed their faddish character to input by US psychological warfare experts who had tried to distort perceptions and memories through the manipulation of time:

> The wicked aim of the US-Puppet regime was to embellish the image of the cities and obscure the image of the countryside which was then being destroyed by the American war. Their aim was to make people forget rural desolation (*dieu tan*) and to embellish artificial urban prosperity (*phon thinh*) to attract youth to the frenzied (*dien loan*), rootless (*buong tha*) life of neo-colonialism (Cuu Long Giang 1976:44).

Cuu Long Giang was not alone in commenting on the frenetic tempo peculiar to 'neo-colonialism'. Writing about Saigon's stage and screen under the former regime, another author identified high tempo in music with the transient pleasures and short attention spans of neo-colonial society:

> In neo-colonial society, human values are reversed and discredited, people live at an hysterical tempo, art aims only at giving them transient pleasure as they follow, for instance, the intricacies of a hopeless love affair, or watch a scene of swordsmanship or some act of robbery and murder in a far off land (Nguyen Vinh Long 1978:125).

For many people, music comprised an escape route:

> this was a way of forgetting bitter reality, forgetting their wretched life. Because of this habitual relief-seeking and Westernization, most *cai luong* dramas had to be sprinkled with pop tunes and dances in *tuong* operas had to be sexy (Nguyen Vinh Long 1978:125).

This critic saw musical transience as a quality driven by audience tastes, which in turn reflected neo-colonialism, read as socio-cultural crisis. Societal hyperactivity and artistic impermanence fed each other. Such interpretations were matched by others of a more conspiratorial hue. Summing up the proceedings of a 1981 conference on neo-colonial culture, another pair of commentators warned that the rock'n'roll dance classics popular in wartime Saigon had been used as a tool by the US military to achieve domination. Rhythm had been exploited to neutralise young people's ethical faculties through sensual acceleration:

> In Saigon, crushed by the war and sinking into corruption, the psywar services as well as the record and cassette dealers knew perfectly how to use the rhythms and melodies [of rock music] to lull scruples to sleep, whilst stirring up the worst instincts. A vibrating music, added to the effects of drugs, alcohol and sexual promiscuity afforded room for the youth to lead a life at a hundred miles an hour (Nguyen Khac Vien and Phong Hien 1982:122–3).

In his next contribution to the *Van Hoa Nghe Thuat* series on music, Cuu Long Giang resumed many of these themes and continued to attack the music of the former regime. His concern in this article was to undermine its pretensions to modernity and avant-garde status, to disparage its use of new electronic technologies and its borrowing of foreign elements from Western music such as rock, folk and jazz:

> In the name of assimilating (*tiep thu*) foreign music, the music of former Saigon imported the refuse (*rac ruoi*) and cast-offs (*phe thai*) of music of foreign origin in an undiscriminating, uncritical manner. This essence was the intention of the US-Puppets: to poison (*dau doc*) and ruin (*pha hoai*) the national culture and a section of musicians either unconsciously or not, became the tools disseminating this refuse (Cuu Long Giang 1977:37).

The author attacked the commercialisation of music under the influence of the Americans and observed that need for profit had led to the vulgarisation of lyrics, the simplification of rhythm to a monotonous beat, and to music's appeal to material, sexual pleasures. This process was anathema to artistic values and indeed to the notion of a musical avant-garde:

> Using various modern means such as electric instruments, improvised forms of performance and noisy pounding under the label of the 'technological revolution', this music aimed at breaking with traditional musical sensibilities, only to open up materialism as a new sensibility (*cam thu vat chat*). People who listen to the music are temporarily inundated (*chim dam*) in a state of unawareness (*vo thuc*) and a primitive (*truy lac*), corporeal (*xac thit*) sensibility (Cuu Long Giang 1977:38).

The author was clearly unimpressed by what he characterised as the 'loud-mouthed sounds' (*am thanh to mom*) of jazz. For him its melodies were 'monotonous' (*don dieu*), its rhythms 'frenzied' (*dien loan*), or alternatively mechanical (*may moc*), improvisation was just another term for 'noisy interjections' (*su phu hoa am i*), its appeal to the audience restricted to the corporeal dimension and its arousing (*su kich thich*) performance marked by the 'shaking of buttocks and breasts' (*lac mong, lac vu*). Jazz melodies, rhythms and performative conventions 'infiltrated' (*xam nhap*) the sensibilities of Saigon's musicians and, he argued, their music was poorer for it:

> On first hearing this music, one thinks it rich for it involves many instruments, many complex melodies and arrangements; however, on analysis, it proves to be the higgledy-piggledy collection (*ket hop hon don*) of different kinds of varieties and methods . . . The principal result of this kind of music is a barbarous shrieking (*tieng gao thet man ro*) and arousal (*su kich thich*), betraying the infiltration of Jazz music— the diseased style (*phong cach benh*) marking nearly all musicians who call themselves the avant-garde (Cuu Long Giang 1977:39).

If the borrowing of foreign musical styles had been unsuccessful, the opposing trend to turn inwards to explore indigenous influences had not necessarily guaranteed an improvement:

To correspond to its depraved reactionary content, this music's artistry must make us dull-witted (*me muoi*) or aroused (*kich thich*). There are melodies which use the raw material of folk music, but in order to serve the reactionary content, composers accentuate the listless (*la luot*), and the unctuous (*mau me*) melodic aspects, stripping away the strong. The language of this kind of music combines with its lyrics to express emotional indifference, without conflict (*xung dot*), contradictions (*mau thuan*) or development (*phat trien*). The melody . . . makes our hearing dull and inspires a sensation of tiredness (Cuu Long Giang 1977:39).

As was the case for the questionably 'modern' music of the former regime, pre-liberation musicians' approach to traditional music supposedly destroyed the alertness of listeners to the reality of their oppression, either through extreme arousal or through stupefaction.

## DANGEROUS ACCOMPANIMENTS

The author of this critique concluded by reminding readers that his focus was on musical accompaniment (*phan dem*), not lyrical content. He warned that the pacification of resistance could proceed through this unexpected avenue by exploiting musical accompaniments to manipulate the senses (Cuu Long Giang 1977:39). The author argued that such arcane analysis was necessary, even now that most of the vestiges of neo-colonial ideology had been swept away, precisely because melody, tempo, rhythm and performative style remained influential. He noted that contemporary composers were still influenced by the music of the former Republic and he judged this to be a dangerous flirtation:

> Under various forms, one still sees the use of that music such as the performance of a revolutionary musical composition in the old, mannered style, or the careless setting of a revolutionary poem to music using a sad, melancholic or alternatively, boisterous melody, totally at odds with the revolutionary content and having a bad influence on the task of raising mass aesthetic aptitudes (Cuu Long Giang 1977:37).

Several years after unification, this was still considered a serious problem. In his 1981 speech, Vo Van Kiet repeated musicologist Cuu Long Giang's warnings of the problems posed by the non-lyrical dimension of 'neo-colonial musical vestiges', decrying the continued influence of Republican-era music on post-war composers. Their attraction to exciting rhythms and melodies at the expense of meaning needed to be addressed by cadres responsible for advising musicians and vetting musical output.[10] Vo Van Kiet lamented that the cultivation of genuine artistic ability was being compromised with a lingering fascination for the superficial and stagy artistry of the music of former times. He advised that rhythm and melody should cede to lyrical content: 'Music should adapt itself to the words and not necessarily become a frantic noise.' Similarly he argued that a performer's gesticulations were extraneous to the function that art should perform. Music should be stripped down to its essentials: 'Gesticulations which do not support the inner life are superfluous' (Vo Van Kiet 1981:141). Also, costumes and facial expressions were to be in keeping with the function of revolutionary art:

> 'Worker-artists' cannot copy the costumes and facial expressions of the singers and musicians of former days. They must be deeply proud of the traditional character and strong points of the Vietnamese man whom they embody (Vo Van Kiet 1981:141).

To rectify this, he recommended a return to simplicity in the performance of compositions:

> Generally speaking at the outset, we must help our artists to understand that they should give up everything extravagant and degenerate. They must retain respect for themselves and the community (Vo Van Kiet 1981:141).

A further problem he identified was the spontaneous character of the music:

> I am anxious when I try to understand the conditions of the artistic formation of some of our friends in the well-known choirs. They have a natural gift for music. Unfortunately, formerly in the performance of commercialized music, most of them got by teaching themselves. I shuddered on learning that many of them learned to sing or play music only by listening to cassettes or the radio (Vo Van Kiet 1981:142).

Spontaneous works of art were considered dangerous, for without methodical vetting of their content, performers and audiences might be exposed to harmful influences. For this reason, one music critic saw state-sponsored research into *cai luong* under the DRV as superior to the untheorised, amateur or spontaneous approaches to the form in the South:

> *Cai luong* [in the North after 1954] became a subject for serious research. It was discussed at seminars and was gradually provided with a proper theoretical basis (Hoang Nhu Mai 1987:27).

The DRV state's sponsorship and formal cultivation of this art form was seen as a great improvement over the methods by which former generations had acquired skills in it:

> Special attention was devoted to training [in *cai luong* in the North after 1954]. Unlike the older generations who had had to learn their trade the hard way, young talents could afford formal training which for the first time was available thanks to State-sponsored theatrical courses and schools (Hoang Nhu Mai 1987:27).

A billboard exhorting citizens of Minh Hai to 'preserve and develop the nation's beautiful cultural traditions' also shows images of divination—a 'backward' practice. Below the billboard are caged birds used in the 'social evil' of cockfighting

Vo Van Kiet's own view was that state training in musicianship had the virtue of eliminating any unpredictable or spontaneous exposure to non-authorised influences in music.

This pivotal speech by Ho Chi Minh City's party secretary was given at a time when the state sector was struggling to achieve some relevance in the South. The population's exposure to influences from the former regime continued to be strong and music was no exception. He attributed the blame to unreconstructed elements, profiteers and reactionaries, who exploited music for profit in market places and cafes in the city (Vo Van Kiet 1981:135). The exacting attentions of so senior a leader emphasised the magnitude of the problem. His performance might be seen as something of a last stand, for subsequent to this speech, official commentary fell largely silent on the question of neo-colonial musical vestiges. Pre-1975 music was beginning its comeback: reappearing in the cafes and restaurants of the South, spreading to the North and colonising the Eastern bloc, wherever Vietnamese guest workers toiled far from home. There was little that official commentators could do to stem this embarrassing reverse.

## IN THE END WAS THE MUSIC

The dilemma posed to the regime by these legacies of the RVN was evident in the critical concerns raised by these writers and speech-makers. Their pronouncements on commodities and music emerged in the wake of a military victory: at a time when all ends were considered attainable through military means. The consumerist lifestyle, particularly that encountered in the southern cities, was disorienting to those for whom discipline, collective privations and the fear of personal annihilation had been the overarching reality of the last decade, and it was indeed unimaginable for those who came from poor rural areas. Seen as dangerously seductive to the liberators of the South, this way of life was painstakingly disassembled, element by element, and disavowed. The commodity market and the lush offerings of popular music were systematically discredited as signifiers of 'civilisation', the 'modern' or historical progression of human society. Instead they were seen as psychological weapons that had been applied methodically to effect the extinguishment of the qualities of citizenship held as normal in the North during its time of war. These overlays were painstakingly analysed—broken down and scheduled for elimination—to enable the reactivation of the militant spirit that had been so successfully tapped in the victorious northern polity.

Yet these critics failed to achieve this result. Instead they swamped the pages of the media organs of the governing regime with detailed descriptions of the limitations of southern society. In these can be found a reproach: residents of the South were not responsive to their appeals to press forward to victories on new fronts. Although 'psy-war' or the 'battle for hearts and minds' had been a real component of the measures used against the communists, an exaggerated capability was attributed to the strategists of the enemy camp for having neutralised the southern population's agency. Commodities and the consumerist lifestyle were alleged to have stifled people's humanity, quashed their conscience and will and conditioned them not to think. Likewise, the critique of pre-1975 music attacked its non-lyrical dimensions. Every component in a musical item that did not engage literally with the intellect of the subject was to be rejected as 'poison'. The means by which the southern population remained subject to, and incorporated by, the former enemy included such attributes as melody, harmony, rhythm, tempo and vocal style. The durability of these influences was a matter of great concern and frustration to the 'thought work' cadres of the new regime. They had been outflanked by an enemy to which they attributed a diabolical proficiency in speaking directly to people's bodies.

While the disturbing implication of this critique was that southerners had been made into animals—their thought and ethical capacity short circuited—another approach is to consider these phenomena less as an enduring enemy installation than as a complex cultural response to the new opportunities, dislocations and intolerable losses of war. These were effected by people whose myriad paths through decades of war differed markedly from the version officially experienced by its victors. In the 1990s hints of this diffuse body of experience were accessible through the exoticist and nostalgic sentiments of the country's musical soundscape. In the late 1970s such musical creations were banned and drowned out by a flood of published criticism, invalidating their every non-lyrical dimension. And yet, from the yellowing pages of these obscure and now rare articles, such criticisms sound forth with a shrillness that one might read as the music critics' oblique awareness of the impending failure of their mobilisational project. The return of the music of the Republic to a central place in contemporary Vietnam provides evidence of the magnitude of their failure. Its sensual rhythms, harmonies and melodies, themes of lost love, and sultry croonings of yore now dominate the soundscape of the Vietnamese public domain. It might be apt to conclude by sketching what was, in the 1990s, a typical scene in a Mekong delta river port. Unemployed youth, traders, *cyclo* drivers and smugglers slouched in plastic chairs, sipping soft drinks. They listen to an equally saccharine melody of forsaken love, and jiggle their legs at a rate that belies the bored expressions on their faces. Behind the cafe, obscured by a pile of sugarcane stalks is an enormous billboard of workers and soldiers heroically saluting the achievement of a new production victory. Although the paint is fading, their resolute, block-like forms are clear enough to reveal traces of an alien, or just a long-lost mobilisational ideal.

# 2

# Renunciations of socialism

A REAWAKENING

From time to time I would ride through the busy streets of District Three to the offices of *Tuoi Tre* (*The Youth*) in Ho Chi Minh City to read back copies of the newspaper in the paper's reading room. Leafing through the 1975 to 1980 editions of the paper, I would plunge into a world of images which starkly contrasted with the consumerist symbolism of the city in the early 1990s and with the advertisements for foreign beer, motorbikes, elite restaurants and construction companies that filled contemporary editions of the newspaper. For hours I would read, fascinated by the socialist-realist themes of heroism, resolute defence, bold industrialisation, collectivisation of agriculture, elimination of the traces of the old society and celebrations of the national holidays of fraternal socialist nations.

The early editions of the paper were replete with references to a new 'dawn', a 'bright' new future and living 'in the light of the thought of Ho Chi Minh' (*duoi an sang cua tu tuong Ho Chi Minh*). Figures were depicted with the full radiance of the morning sun suffusing their faces. There was the unforgettable image of Nguyen Van Troi, hero of a failed assassination attempt on US Secretary of Defence Robert McNamara. Nguyen Van Troi was depicted at the moment of his execution, cut down by a hail of bullets. Out of his chest, through every bullet wound, shone a ray of light over a scene of the impending liberation of Saigon. The paper was filled with references to the former regime's 'neo-colonial culture' and contrasted living 'under the light of the party's leadership' with the pre-communist condition of darkness.

I had been at the newspaper offices for a week, imagining the assuredly profound sense of epistemological rupture southerners must have felt on reading those first editions. Sharing the room was a man who introduced himself as 'Trung', an editor of the newspaper. After several days he motioned to the article before me, on the 'movement to eradicate illiteracy' from the countryside,·and asked why on earth I was reading those early editions of his paper. I told him I was unsure what was meant by the term 'movements' (*phong trao*) mentioned in the story. His response came as a surprise:

> Don't lose sight of the fact that various Youth Federation-inspired 'movements' were not at one with reality. For example, the movement amongst youth to engage in cock-fighting was entirely beyond government sponsorship, yet very popular; so were the movements to visit pagodas and go on picnics, although the latter was later partly co-ordinated by the Federation. Then there were Federation-inspired 'movements' which failed to take hold, such as the 'movement' to visit invalids and the war-widowed (from fieldnotes).

This was an unexpected admission, coming from an official of the mass organisation in question. The Youth Federation's function had been to mobilise young people in accordance with the party's vision for society. According to Trung, its efforts had been somewhat irrelevant in the post-war years. In various respects, people had carried on regardless. The term 'movements' itself was bankrupt, more deserving of being applied to illegal activities such as cockfights than to political mobilisation. As editor of the Federation's paper, moreover, he was telling me that I was wasting my time with its account of the events of the period.

His criticism was directed at the official position reflected in the pages of the earlier editions of his newspaper rather than at me. Sitting down, his criticisms grew stronger. He told me that during the period in which I was interested, the Federation had been implicated in the party's 'period of error' (*giai doan sai lam*) which he said had lasted from the end of the war until the early 1980s. I wondered, 'should he be saying this here? Should I be listening?' I glanced around the reading room. Two or three journalists were engrossed in their writing. I reassured myself. He was one of the newspaper's editors after all.

Trung invited me back to his place for some beers and told me more about himself. A native of Vietnam's harsh central coast, he had been educated at Saigon's University of Letters. Politicised in the late 1960s, he had been imprisoned in the early 1970s for involvement in a demonstration. He had escaped and fled to the jungle in Tay Ninh. His story reminded me of Truong Nhu Tang, whose book, *A Viet Cong Memoir* (1985) recounted the participation of urban intellectuals in the communist controlled South Vietnamese Provisional Revolutionary Government (PRG) and their brief residence in the resistance bases in the jungles northwest of Saigon. Truong Nhu Tang's memoir spoke of tensions between the cosmopolitan, southern intellectuals of the PRG and the dull doctrinaire cadres who were charged with instructing them in Marxism–Leninism and of the post-war disenchantment of southern guerillas who had supported Hanoi during the war. Unlike Truong Nhu Tang, after 1975, my host had continued to work in various capacities for the Youth Federation and its newspaper. I asked whether southern resistance fighters such as himself had voiced criticisms of the imposition of central policies after the war. He set down his beer and unexpectedly dealt me a reply of a confessional nature:

> For three years after the end of the war, very little criticising went on. No-one was thinking. We were all blinded (*bi lam mu*) by Stalinism. Our problem was having been 'awakened' (*giac ngo*).
>
> You can quite easily understand how this happened. While in the jungle, political training went on for more than a year. I was isolated in a bamboo cubicle to prevent me from seeing who my fellow students were; if we were arrested, we wouldn't know who else was involved and the organisation would remain intact. I suffered from such terrible cold and cramps in that cubicle, you just can't imagine. The circulation of blood in my feet was restricted and I had to constantly massage them and light a fire to restore the blood flow. During that time, the only thing which linked me to the outside world was the voice of my instructor. Through the years following 1975, I continued to hear my instructor's voice, echoing inside my head. In 1978 I, and other southern leaders, started to have some thoughts of our own; it was the beginning of a critique of Stalinism. But then came the war with Cambodia and China and we dropped all those thoughts. We knew we needn't think any more. In 1981 a degree of stability returned and the thoughts began again. Just the faintest murmurs which grew until 1984, when they became open debate (from fieldnotes).

Trung's account engaged creatively with the imagery of illumination used by the regime to mark embrace of the communist path. He explained that the term *giac ngo* had been used by the Vietnamese communists to describe the stage in militants' lives of 'awakening to the revolution' (*giac ngo cach mang*).[1] However, he said, his 'blindness' had come from overexposure to political doctrine. With a wry grin he asked if I knew that the term was Buddhist in origin, describing the condition of awakening (often glossed in English as 'enlightenment') achieved by Buddha: the awakened one. The term was associated by the general populace with Buddhism, and was attained by only exceptional people. He concluded, 'communism was our religion. We believed we were living in a utopian paradise (*thien duong*) of Stalinism.'

Hearing a party member denounce his past practice of communism as religiously-inspired blindness raised the question: In what condition did he now imagine himself? Having admitted to years of not needing to think, and to a poor grasp of reality, his exposé of the 'true' nature of his former 'awakening' as 'blindness' was not reassuring. How could the condition in which he was now delivering his analysis be described: sceptical clear-sightedness or a reawakening? On what authority could he be so confident he had escaped his past limitations? And then I sensed my own role. The abashed and contrite mode in which his account was delivered was purgative in nature, only he had replaced his bamboo cubicle in the jungle with a well-appointed livingroom in the city. The disembodied voice of his political instructor was replaced by myself, embodying the promises of engagement with the non-socialist world. Somewhat stunned and not a little inebriated, I scarcely felt party to the clear-headed condition which, by implication, we shared. It was difficult to know what to make of his admission. Coming from a party member and former administrator of socialist reforms in the South, the editor's admission appeared to be an extraordinary confidence. Over time it dissolved into context. Underpinning his personal realignment were attempts by the regime itself to discursively recalibrate the spatio-temporal co-ordinates of its existence. Namely this involved renouncing as 'modern' its wartime orientation to administration, and, through rites of public discourse, reclaiming for itself a status in the 'now'. Trung's reorientation to the past was further shaped by many other (former) party members who, beginning in the late 1980s, were to produce a literature of dissidence that deflated the renewed modernist pretensions of the leadership. Their attack on the validity of the post-colonial path carved out by the party undermined the grounds by which parallel developments in the South had been negatively evaluated. In the wake of the *doi moi* announcements, some commentators reaffirmed that the former South had experienced 'modernisation', a view which displaced the North from its temporally 'advanced' position.

## RENOVATION AS THE COMPLETION OF MODERNITY

In the early 1990s the *doi moi* or 'renovation' reforms announced at the 6th Party Congress in 1986 featured in official rhetoric as a decisive event in the nation's history. The policies aimed to push Vietnam towards greater integration with the global economy by endorsing the existence of a non-state sector and encouraging partial privatisation and economic decentralisation. In the *doi moi* (or post-6th Party Congress) era, regime leaders discovered 'the market mechanism' (*co che thi truong*) as an engine of development and declared a 'new-found' recognition of the laws undergirding human progress. For example, in 1989 Nguyen Co Thach spoke of the need for policies to conform to 'the objective laws governing the economy', 'general development laws of the world economy', and 'universal laws of the [*sic*] commodity production' (Kolko 1995:22). The language of new-found objectivism, which was to become common after this party congress, was introduced to the public through official media outlets. In 1985 the party daily *Nhan Dan* newspaper declared: 'expanding market transactions in compliance with objective economic laws is an essential element in promoting the development of production' (*Nhan Dan* July 16 1985).

To promote the market as an 'indispensable' (*tat yeu*) and 'objective' (*khach quan*) locomotive of human progress, required that party leaders retreat from earlier positions. Their new orientation was not so much argued as embodied. Public admissions of error were the key means by which the party distanced its 'new' orientation from previous practices of centralised bureaucratic control. They inevitably accompanied the main policy pronouncements of the most senior party leaders in the latter half of the 1980s.

In 1986 the party's Secretary-General, Truong Chinh, was to announce the official policy change at the 6th Party Congress by owning up to a collective failure to defer to objective laws: 'Over the past years, we have made mistakes, developed subjectiveness and impatience, disregarded and even violated economic laws' (Truong Chinh 1986 in Kimura 1989:60).

At an address to the national party school in 1987, Truong Chinh's successor, Nguyen Van Linh shrugged off the weight of the past in a similar manner. He exhorted his audience to join with him in abjuring the past and embrace the party's new orientation:

> We must look squarely at the truth and must admit that our subjective errors are serious and protracted. We must vigorously renovate our old thinking and work style which have restrained and hampered the development of production (Nguyen Van Linh 1988:31).

The party leader who improvised most lavishly in such public admissions of error was Do Muoi, who replaced Linh as Secretary-General in 1991. His speech to a trade union congress was delivered in 1988 while he was still chairman of the council of ministers. Reportedly two hours long, it exhibited his predilection for rhetoric, for which as party leader he became notorious (Bui Tin 1995:150):

> The party and state are very distressed whenever they cannot provide food for the workers and civil servants. We realize that we have many shortcomings in dealing with cadres, workers and civil servants. These shortcomings are quite clear. Your criticisms are valid. I have served in the government for thirty years. For twenty of those years I served as deputy premier. . . . I feel heartsick listening to your criticisms. Injustice is wrong. The council of ministers bears complete responsibility. We won't try to avoid taking responsibility. I also know my responsibility. You can blame me. You can shoot me for this. I will

voluntarily accept discipline—self-conscious discipline (cited in Nguyen Ho 1988:9).[2]

In 1989 Politburo member, Dao Duy Tung, liberally deployed the European Enlightenment's opposition between backwardness and progress to lend world historical import to the mental leaps enshrined in the *doi moi* reforms. His speech was a classic of *doi moi* discourse, managing to hector his audience at the same time as abjectly bowing before objective laws and, all on behalf of 'we', confessing prejudice, blindness, subjectivism and voluntarism:

> First there exists a state of backwardness in our theoretical thinking. We are backward in many ways, especially in our understanding of socialist industrialization, of socialist transformation in production relations, of the mechanism of management and on distribution and circulation. We were prejudiced against laws of goods production and actually did not recognize their existence. We failed to correctly apply the objective laws that govern the process of transition to socialism. We acted with subjectivism and voluntarism (Dao Duy Tung 1989:22).

Comments by Trung, the *Tuoi Tre* newspaper editor, were to be understood as an improvisation on this confessional mode, popularised by the leadership as an indispensable ritual aiding passage through modernity's narrow gate. It was a position not weakened by evidence of previous failings. Quite the contrary, once the process had begun, those who most energetically demonstrated their past errors could reclaim leadership as facilitators of the new truth. This project was represented by some as a new opportunity afforded by the return of peace to the country. Once the voice of Trung's instructor subsided, he claimed, 'thinking' could recommence and debates 'open' up. According to his metaphor of the nation at war as an uncomfortable indoctrination chamber, the expediencies of war had squeezed thought into silence and confined opinion.[3]

The notion of an escape from 'error' into 'correct' (*dung*) thinking implied the existence of a canon of knowledge within which objective laws were recorded and over which hermeneutic struggles were waged. This was the canon of Marxism–Leninism, interpreted 'erroneously' in the past to conclude that markets were not consistent with socialism. Such past interpretation had been characterised by:

> simplistic and narrow thinking, meaning the desire to maintain total control over all of society's production and distribution by means of administrative directives (Nhan Dan 1985 in Kimura 1989:55).

Casting *doi moi* as a revolution in interpretation (of socialism) rather than conversion (to capitalism) paralleled the logic of the Reformation, as perhaps distinct from the European Enlightenment. In this mode, the past was not comprehensively dismissed, for the canon of

Marxist–Leninist thought was 'renewed' by more faithful interpretation. The notion of 'error' as used in the party's *doi moi* discourse referred to deviations from the correct 'path' sketched out by Marx, Lenin and even Ho Chi Minh. Reliance on the market was construed as a 'return' to a correct reading of the socialist classics. This revised socialist orientation allegedly situated the nation once again in the avant-garde of global developments. Serving the interests of constructing socialism in Vietnam, the market was held up as the infallible key to realising modernity in Vietnam.[4]

Gabriel Kolko, for one, was most sceptical of this perspective. It was beyond him 'how a ruling party could take fifty years to discover such inviolable rules in Marx's writings':

> In January 1994, after a half century of power and claiming
> infallibility throughout that time, Do Muoi confessed the errors of the
> preceding years by admitting that 'the building of socialism, however,
> is still new to us,' and that by reading Marxist 'and especially Leninist
> thoughts on new economic policy and the [*sic*] state-managed
> capitalism . . . this will help invent new forms of transition (Kolko
> 1995:22).

Kolko's denunciation of this policy flip-flop flowed from a strong expression of empathy with those Vietnamese whose pasts he considered had been invalidated by the equation of *doi moi* with faithful interpretation of the Marxist canon:

> Many thoughtful Vietnamese revolutionaries, men and women who
> made immense sacrifices, have very justifiably asked themselves
> privately and increasingly publicly whether it was worth fighting a war
> which cost millions of lives and caused immeasurable suffering to
> drive out a foreign-imposed society, only to reproduce it in a
> superficially different form and even appeal for aid from those
> Americans, French and Japanese who once tormented them (Kolko
> 1995:3).

From this perspective, Vietnam's contemporary orientation was most ironic and tragic. The ideals of anti-foreign resistance had been betrayed by an amnesia-prone leadership whose discourse of renovation as faithful interpretation masked servitude to new foreign oppressors—the IMF and World Bank:

> The Politburo's new line since 1984 . . . owed infinitely more to
> continuous International Monetary Fund advice and pressure than a
> sudden revelation from Leninist scriptures (Kolko 1995:21).

*Doi moi* discourse was not a little disconcerting in the way past thinking was summarily dismissed with the pejorative category of 'error'. And yet, by attributing this to IMF prompting, Kolko underestimated the pervasiveness of such critique in Vietnam. Indeed, the terms in which party leaders distinguished present from past practices were relatively restrained. The official construction of *doi moi*, as the inception in Vietnam of objectivism, rationality and the 'embodiment' of universal laws, coincided with a flowering of modernist discourse in Vietnam. One can chart the proliferation and mutation of this discursive orientation to the past, from official enunciation in the mid-1980s to critical epidemic threatening to wipe out the regime's own tenaciously defended claims to embody modernity.

## THE ECONOMIST AS RHETORICAL SPENDTHRIFT

No group of commentators improvised more enthusiastically within the tropes of European modernism than Vietnamese economists, who celebrated the liberal reforms of the mid-1980s as ushering in Vietnam's 'modern' age. According to this group, the dismantling of Vietnam's socialist command economy and the economic liberalisation policies had been necessary to overcome systemic limitations or 'irrationalities' in the socialist economic policies pursued prior to that time. Some sympathetic foreign observers blamed the economic stagnation of post-war Vietnam on the ravages of war, a US-imposed economic embargo, inclement weather, more wars with neighbouring countries and the burden of assimilating the non-productive economy of the former South Vietnam (Beresford 1989; Kolko 1995:8, 20). However, state-employed economists, writing at the end of the 1980s, placed far greater emphasis on internal factors. Virtually sidelining historical and environmental considerations, they engaged in self-denigration, saving their severest criticisms for the party's 'affliction' by a 'subjectivist' and 'irrational' mindset. For example, Le Hong Phuc, then a senior economist at Hanoi's Institute of World Economy, traced the post-war crisis back to the North's wartime development orientation which:

> although serving the war positively, contained many negative elements. Development of both agriculture and industry by imposed and subjective methods put a brake on all necessary and natural tendencies to develop commodity–money relationships, which was an objective and indispensable premise for developing [the] social division of labour in the countryside and indeed in the whole agricultural economy (Le Hong Phuc 1990:23).

More seriously, he argued, despite these and other deficiencies, not only had these strategies been preserved after the war had ended but they were applied to the whole country. Such application of this mode of development had been 'the main cause of the deterioration of our economy':

> The policy for development emphasized at that time was 'priority development of heavy industry in a rational way on the basis of

development of agriculture and light industry.' . . . But it did not in fact allow for the efficient and rational use of substantial new foreign aid as well as available natural resources and manpower. On the contrary, it generated new and increasingly serious imbalances (Le Hong Phuc 1990:23).

Such 'irrational' policies had been the key cause of 'an impasse in socio-economic development in 1979 and the early years of the eighties, and these were core reasons for the present day economic renewal in Vietnam' (Le Hong Phuc 1990:23). In contrast with this long history of 'subjective' thinking, the liberal reforms had supposedly reflected a clear-sighted grasp of Vietnam's 'objective' situation and equally, the 'laws of economic development' (Le Hong Phuc 1990:28).

The dichotomies used to assert a clean break with the past drew from the fund of expressions used by eighteenth-century thinkers and their intellectual heirs to denote their break with the past and their 'discovery' and mastery of the laws determining human existence. To Le Hong Phuc, 1986 represented a divide between the reign of unreason and reason, subjectivity and objectivity, the tyranny of ignorance and the understanding of nature, law and necessity. His colleague Le Duc Thuy noted that in contrast to the 'economic stagnation, waste and inefficiencies' before 1985, the 6th Party Congress had promised emancipation:

> The Congress affirmed the necessity 'of liberating all productive forces' within the society and bringing into full use the various potentials of each and every sector of the economy (Le Duc Thuy 1990:76).

Do Duc Dinh of the Institute of World Economy similarly viewed *doi moi* as a form of secularisation. He argued that prior to *doi moi*, 'socialism' had been mistakenly elevated to a 'cult' of the public sector: 'There was a time we considered the public ownership system to be an objective by itself; and that the more the public ownership system is enhanced, the more socialism is attained' (Do Duc Dinh 1991: 58). His secularist gloss of this engaged in self-ridicule: 'It could be said that for a long time we committed the error of worshipping the public sector' (1991: 56).

The pre-1986 economy was also depicted as a closed and isolated world using tropes that might have been drawn from early ethnographies of West African societies (Piot 1999:1): 'like a closed circuit', 'bogged down', 'in isolation . . . from the outside world' (Le Duc Thuy et al. 1991:183). Market relations had been 'distorted', and 'underdeveloped'. The system had been 'autarchic' and characterised by 'increasing reliance on barter trade and transactions in kind' (Le Duc Thuy et al. 1991:184). In contrast, since 1986 the market mechanism 'has been able to influence all elements of the social reproduction process' (Le Duc Thuy et al. 1991:184). Whereas the pre-1986 economy was marked by closure, isolation, self-sufficiency, and (pejoratively) by ignorance, irrationality and non-objective thinking, the post-6th Party Congress years were marked by openness, interdependence, commodity relations, high productivity and were seen (wishfully) as uniquely rationalist, enlightened and innovative. Such economists located themselves thus at the threshold of Vietnam's momentous transformation from a traditional to a modern society. Le Hong Phuc spoke explicitly of the moment as one in which a 'traditional economic structure and system of management was being replaced by another one which is more modern' (Le Hong Phuc 1990:30) as did Tran Duc Nguyen of the central economic committee of the VCP who contrasted the 'traditional socialist model' with post-reforms Vietnam (Tran Duc Nguyen 1991:29).

The depiction of present and past in such terms greatly inflated the significance of the leaderships' *doi moi* policy announcements. Vietnam's state economists were particularly extravagant in their expenditure of the tropes of European modernism to allege the break with the past effected by the policies. It was a rhetorical position shared by many non-Vietnamese economists and journalists, whose depictions of Vietnam in the early 1990s placed it on the threshold of modernity. However, while it became clear that the reforms were to be limited to the economic sphere, and not extended to the political realm, the revived modernist thinking of many Vietnamese was not to be confined to celebrating the restrictive contours of official policies.

## CONSIGNING SOCIALISM TO THE PRE-MODERN NIGHT

Exploring the party's rhetorical distancing from past practices, various writers from the late 1980s on were to criticise the 'blindness' of the past, if not necessarily embracing the clarity of the present. For others the target was the stupidity or irrationality of the past. Yet the past, criticised in this enlightenment mode, was for some, not indigenous tradition but the local application of a foreign model. In the late 1980s, as foreign investors and party leaders met together on common ground and the World Bank rated Vietnam as one of the world's most successful liberalising economies, voices could be heard criticising the party's history of compulsively embracing foreign models.

In 1987 party leader, Nguyen Van Linh, regarded as one of the architects of the liberal reforms, met with artists and writers in Hanoi to discuss the contribution they could make to the renovation process. He encouraged them to take courage and not flinch in 'exposing bad examples and practices' (Nguyen Van Linh 1988: 103). He reportedly said: 'If we should promote democracy for producers in [the] economic field, I don't see why you should not exercise your right to mastery in your domain' (Nguyen Van Linh 1988: 101). Pham Thi Hoai, whose first book *Thien Su* (*The Crystal Messenger*) was published in 1988 as a result of such a call to exercise writerly mastery, later reminisced, in an interview with an Australian newspaper, about the atmosphere of excitement that had prevailed in the wake of this announcement:

> Pham said that her book came at an important juncture in Vietnam in the late '80s when the country was opening up to the world. 'There was a policy of *coi troi* when the authorities loosened the chain on society,' she said. 'Suddenly there was a burst of critical writing after 40 years of suppression.
>
> 'There was a sort of renaissance of Vietnamese literature. There was a certain feeling and an excitement among the writers in Vietnam. Something was on fire. Something was always happening. When you went out of your house, you'd hear that someone was writing something. Then you'd jump on your bike, ride to their place, ask to see what they had written.'
>
> Pham said Vietnam's literary renaissance was sudden and brief, lasting only five or so years. But in that short time there was a plethora of writers, like Nguyen Huy Thiep, Duong Thu Huong and Bao Ninh, who weren't afraid to criticize the party and expose corruption. The most celebrated writer in this group, Nguyen Huy Thiep, said it was like waking up from 30 years of dreaming (Minh Bui 1997).[5]

One of the more notorious examples of an enthusiastic response to Secretary-General Linh's speech was the short story, *Linh Nghiem* (*The Prophecy Fulfilled*), by Hanoi author Tran Huy Quang (Tran Huy Quang 1993). Published in *Van Nghe* magazine in July 1992, the author and magazine editors attracted official criticism for overstepping the mark of acceptable criticism (Vasavakul 1995:286). The story targeted one of the party's most cherished myths—the story of Ho Chi Minh's journey abroad purportedly to search for a method to free his country from the colonial yoke. In Tran Huy Quang's story, Hinh, the young Ho Chi Minh character, 'ambitious to conquer the hearts of mankind', was introduced, longing for some magical power that would allow him to achieve this goal. After much praying, he finally achieved a kind of shamanistic state, 'ascending the nine levels of Heaven to meet the envoy of the Venerable Creator of Religions', who presented him with a scripture that would help him find what he was seeking. He read from the scripture the following nonsense directions:

> 'Thou shalt go to the South along a road flanked on one side by trees and on the other side by water, until at the end of the road there shall be a tavern selling draft beer and dog meat. Thou shalt not peer into this place of indulgence, but rather continue on slowly. Along the road there shall be a person who asks of thee, "Willya go?" And thou shalt not go. Although that person is only a laborer and not a demon sent to

**Members of the People's Committee of Ho Chi Minh City and families commemorating the 105th anniversary of Ho Chi Minh's birth**

> tempt thee, still thou must resign thyself to refusing. Upon continuing, thou shalt come upon a newspaper kiosk and thus turn left, finding before thee a small flower garden. Now, thou shalt bend down and walk very slowly, step by step, with thine eyes fastened to the ground, in order to "look for this". Continue on . . . it shall take only one moment, and thou shalt possess the world . . .'

The story continued:

> Hinh embraced the scriptures to his chest and hiccupped with emotion 'My God, this magical talisman, this oracle . . .' Ecstatic, he let loose a wild bellow (Tran Huy Quang 1993:57).

This tale unmistakably satirised the story of Ho Chi Minh's first encounter with Marxism–Leninism when, on reading Lenin's theses on imperialism, he reputedly had cried out and addressed an imaginary crowd of his countrymen saying that at last he had found the means to save them. The author Quang was on dangerous ground, taking on not only the founder of the Vietnamese state but its central theoretical underpinning, Marxism–Leninism. Pressing on with its iconoclasm, the story recounted how the young Hinh, who 'did not know what he was looking for, rather only knew absolute loyalty to his instructions', walked along, looking for 'this'. A huge multitude gathered and followed him, searching, with each follower having a different idea as to what 'this' might be. Suddenly, Hinh looked up, saw the huge crowd swarming around him, realised, with teary eyes, that the prophecy had been fulfilled and . . . went home. Despite this, the multitude continued to swell, looking fruitlessly for 'this': a devastating image of the party's sheep-like pursuit of a vacuous goal (Tran Huy Quang 1993:60).

In 1993 Lu Phuong, former party member and one of the Culture Ministry officials who had produced scathing critiques of neo-colonial culture in the early 1980s, informally circulated photocopies of a sixteen-page tract denouncing Marxism–Leninism in more explicit terms (Hiebert 1993:26).[6] Like Tran Huy Quang, Lu Phuong focused on Ho Chi Minh's adoption of socialism as a 'path' to national liberation, criticising it as a simple-minded and ignorant choice and one that had been disastrous for the development of the nation. In his essay entitled 'Questions and Answers about Marxist Socialism', he wrote:

> It (socialism) makes people afraid to look at reality and look inward to find their own thought . . . It creates the mechanism to turn the brave into cowards, the intelligent into morons, the idealistic into perverts. It drags the nation down a quagmire, paralyzed and brushed aside while the world is speeding into the future . . . Socialism is simply an 'illusion that never comes true' (Lu Phuong 1993).

As Trung of *Tuoi Tre* had held for 'Stalinism', Lu Phuong believed that the introduction of socialism to Vietnam had replaced the functioning of thought. Lu Phuong argued that Ho Chi Minh had 'chosen the socialist path' ignorant of its quality of being inherently repressive to consciousness and morality. In August 1995 biologist Nguyen Xuan Tu, writing under the pen name Ha Si Phu,[7] in an article entitled 'Farewell to Ideology' similarly attributed unconscious 'programming' powers to the doctrine of socialism itself:

> Herein lies the tragic-drama: the emissaries bringing the 'message of liberation' have ascended to the throne. On this throne, they have betrayed that very message. Aside from a number of wicked acts committed by some monsters, the betrayal, in general, was not in the beginning conscious. It had been programmed into a recipe, and even this writer, influenced by the recipe cannot emerge from the age's programming (Ha Si Phu 1996).

Like Lu Phuong, Ha Si Phu described a situation of a confinement within an ideology, from which he yearned to escape, but was hard pressed to. He argued that de-'programming', attacking the doctrine on its scientific merits, was made particularly hard because it was an historically constituted condition:

> The ideology binding us has not fallen from the sky above, and in the beginning was not prescribed by anyone. It is an historical product of mankind during the chaos (of the eighteenth and nineteenth century) along the course of civilization (Ha Si Phu 1996).

For Ha Si Phu, un-'binding' from the ideology could be achieved by attempting to objectify the doctrine as a historical product. In doing so he maintained a view of history as proceeding according to scientifically knowable laws, and having deterministically moved beyond the conditions in which Marxism–Leninism might have been appropriate. On these grounds, he was to attack Vietnam's state ideology with the secularist scorn of a Voltaire:

> The theory of Marxism–Leninism is not some far off ideal yet to be realized, but merely a perpetual dream that has been surpassed. Merely the materialistic reincarnation of a sort of feudalism left behind by history several centuries ago. It is not some spiritual force to lead the way, so full of mystery that even centuries later no person can interpret correctly, but is instead just a bunch of nonsensical predictions that will never happen (Ha Si Phu 1996).

In a 1994 paper on civil society in Vietnam, Lu Phuong argued that Marxism, a doctrine originally not intended for a country like Vietnam, had been applied in a cynically pragmatic way to build up a repressive state. Lu Phuong believed that under 'actually existing socialism', the political relations between the rulers and the ruled closely resembled those of ancient theocracies. Although Marx wrote to criticise and liquidate the old society, those who spoke in his name,

> have perfectly reproduced the outward forms of the old state with regard to society. And these forms are moulded by the influence of people with the privilege of being intermediaries between any sort of transcendental reality and the people. In the name of this transcendent reality, they bestow blessings at the same time as affectionately admonishing the masses who as naturally spontaneous, are always looked upon as backward (Lu Phuong 1994:3).

In such systems, the clear-sightedness of the leadership had become an article of faith:

> People in actually existing socialism are . . . always having to kowtow before the ranks of leaders, praising their perspicacity, and they are always having artfully to say thank you for ever and ever (Lu Phuong 1994:3).

For Lu Phuong, as for Ha Si Phu, actually existing socialism's elevation of a revolutionary theory to a monopolistic status in the political order removed it from the domain of science into sacred creed. As a result, a theory once imbued with the prestige of the 'modern' was exposed as an anachronism which left Vietnam stranded in an outmoded historical status:

> Marx's philosophical opposition to religion has been turned into a policy against monotheistic religious systems: all types of transcendental religion are suppressed and criticized in order to raise

to the status of a state creed a sort of atheistic religion, that is 'science' and 'revolution'. Here revolution and science have become modern expressions used to consolidate a state based on heavenly authority which is something history left behind long ago (Lu Phuong 1994:3).

The rhetorical escape into irony staged by these urban intellectuals, contrasted with the physical defection by Nguyen Ho,[9] one of the party's veteran soldiers and political stalwarts in Ho Chi Minh City, to the symbolic sanctuary from ideology afforded by the southern Vietnamese countryside. Nguyen Ho's 'My View and Life', circulated back in the city in 1994 as a *samizdat* publication, and recounted the personal liberation and sense of encouragement he experienced when, following his release from prison, he had resigned from the Communist Party and quit the city:

> When I left the city to live in the countryside (21.03.1990), more than ever, I felt completely free, thoroughly liberated in my mind and thought. Now my mind is no longer clamped down by the iron pincers of Marxism–Leninism, of the Communist Party. Therefore, it permits me to dare to face the truth and to dare to point out the truth, especially in light of the collapse of Eastern Europe and the Soviet Union.
>
> When I was a party member—in a way, the party's prisoner—I only spoke and thought in accordance with the way my superiors spoke and thought; but now I think freely, without any restriction, for my thought has really been liberated—it flies . . . We must confess: we have chosen the wrong ideology: communism. Because more than 60 years on this communist revolutionary road, the Vietnamese people have endured incredible sacrifice; yet achieved nothing at the end. The nation is still very poor, backward; the people are still without a comfortable, happy life, and have no freedom, no democracy. This is a shame! (Nguyen Ho 1994).

These dissident critiques of the Vietnamese application of Marxism–Leninism flowed thick and fast in the decade following the collapse of the Soviet Union, whose political and material assistance had sustained the Socialist Republic of Vietnam during the long years of the US embargo and after Vietnam's split with China in the late 1970s. Criticisms of Maoism were equally prevalent in the early 1990s. Despite the passage of time since the Sino–Vietnamese rift, the legacy of Maoism was still fresh in people's minds. To this they attributed attacks on the status of intellectuals, the valuation of 'reds' over 'experts' (*hong hon chuyen*), some very bad music, the abolition of urban commerce in the late 1970s, and the precipitous collectivisation of southern agriculture which had led to widespread shortages and hunger.

One such attack on Maoism was mounted in the memoir of a former North Vietnamese colonel and former editor of *Nhan Dan* newspaper, Bui Tin, written in exile in France where he defected in

1990. The pernicious spread of Maoism, according to Bui Tin, had begun even before the communist-led victory over the French at Dien Binh Phu in 1954:

> It could be said that the spread of Maoism after 1951 began to stultify our consciences and has caused lasting harm right up till now. We forgot our basic national values and lost our sense of pride and self-confidence. We put an end to the exciting and innocent period of respect uniting those who joined the Resistance (Bui Tin 1995:24).

Another powerful indictment of Maoism from a former party member came from the writer Duong Thu Huong, who achieved notoriety in the brief era of openness following the *doi moi* announcement.[10] Her novel, *Nhung Thien Duong Mu* (*Paradise of the Blind*) (1994) covered the period from the 1950s northern land reform era, to the market reforms of the mid-1980s, implicating Vietnam's communist reformers in Maoist excess. According to Hue Tam Ho Tai's interpretation, the heroine's cadre uncle's

> adamant devotion to rigid notions of class struggle blinds him to the obligations of kinship and even common humanity. He not only destroys his sister's happiness during the Land Reform Campaign, but he is also ready to let his children go malnourished rather than be seen to enjoy the fruits of capitalist enterprise—his sister's job as a petty trader (Hue Tam Ho Tai 1993: 89).

These critics, most of whom were party members, developed their ideas within a framework of denigrating the past provided by the party's own *doi moi* rhetoric. Yet their criticisms of ideological enslavement and the leadership's defects of vision went much further in vividness of imagery and allocation of blame. In the process, they exceeded the party's limited tolerance for criticism. Some, like Duong Thu Huong, were banned from the party or imprisoned, others, like Lu Phuong, were forced to circulate their opinions clandestinely or, like Bui Tin, defect to make their criticisms public.

Moreover, these writers' conceptions of their country's contemporary condition differed markedly from that of their leaders. The leadership purported to have escaped from the defective past into a rational and liberating universalism—the adoption of objective economic laws. Yet according to these dissident writers, the prior defect lay with the party's embrace of the universalist doctrines of Maoism and Leninism. The 'illuminating' or 'liberating' ideas of Lenin or Mao were reinterpreted as blinding, enslaving, degenerate, brutal, talismanic and foolish. On the other hand, while the regime's economists put past applications of such theories into the box of 'tradition', endorsing the regime's new modernist credentials, dissident critics of the official approach refused to regard the present in such a way, considering their country to be still enmeshed in traditional despotism.

## SOCIALISM AS IMPOTENT MODERNISM

Implicating past practices with harmful alien codes, however, did not make the stance taken by such dissident writers anti-modernist. It was not argued that the problem with 'Marxism–Leninism', 'Stalinism' and 'Maoism' had been a hostility to 'tradition'. These doctrines were judged in terms of their ability to promote emancipation from perceived defects in Vietnamese tradition. Their verdict: such programs had been impotent in the face of tradition and had even abetted the intensification of its more pernicious aspects. A poignant illustration of such modernist disappointment could be found in comparisons made between socialism and colonialism regarding their ability to transcend 'backward' traditions.

For example, in *Paradise of the Blind* Duong Thu Huong was critical of traditional patriarchy, implicating it as a force abetting the oppressive doctrinairism and greed of her times. According to Hue Tam Ho Tai's perceptive reading, a second kind of blindness to which Huong's title referred was the traditional family values which privileged men. The protagonist's mother had suffered denunciation by her cadre brother during the northern land reform campaign of the 1950s and constantly experienced his indifference to her misfortune. Yet:

> Huong's mother is equally blind. Over and over again, she forgives her brother because he is the only male in her family. She even withdraws some of her affection from her orphaned daughter and lavishes it on her ungrateful brother and his son because they, as males, will carry on her family line (Hue Tam Ho Tai 1993:89).

Duong Thu Huong saw the land reform campaign as an ideological import from China. She believed the perpetrators of harm were spared the burden of accountability by their traditional male prerogatives. The Maoist reforms of the 1950s had made few inroads on what she saw as this traditional weakness in Vietnamese society.

Various other critics of the application of socialist policy in Vietnam also stressed its failure to achieve substantive reform of what were seen as traditional rural social relations. Not only dissidents framed issues in this way. Pham Nhu Cuong[11] cited the problem of the inability of post-war collectivisation campaigns to eliminate the troublesome persistence of traditional small-scale rural production. He argued that socialist collectivisation of the South had been a failure because it had held back the development of commodity relations and encouraged the persistence or reversion to small-scale production:

> The result was that on the outside we had achieved socialism—in the form of production groups and co-operatives—yet that was merely socialism in form. The outward form was socialist yet its internal content was the restoration of elements of subsistence production of our age-old agriculture (Pham Nhu Cuong 1990:18).

Hanoi University history Professor Phan Huy Le was equally critical of his country's legacy of small-scale production as an example of traditional backwardness. He argued that the presence of this had been an obstacle in building a system of large-scale socialist production, and anticipated that only long and persistent effort would be able 'to overcome its vestiges in people's way of thinking, style of work and customs and habits' (Phan Huy Le 1989:88). While Phan Huy Le appeared to agree that socialism had been hard-pressed to eliminate the vestiges of small-scale production, he attributed the blame to French colonialism, which, according to Marx, should have prepared the ground for socialism more adequately. He cited Marx on the British colonial intervention in India: 'That intervention destroyed the small half-barbarian half-civilized communes by abolishing their economic bases and thereby carried out the greatest and indeed the sole revolution ever experienced by Asia.' Professor Le rebuked the French colonialists of Vietnam for failing to be like the British colonialists of India who, as Marx saw it, had acted as 'an unconscious instrument of history' (Phan Huy Le 1989:83).

Do Thai Dong, professor of sociology in Ho Chi Minh City, in a report criticising post-war socialist reform policies, also noted that Marx and Lenin had both accepted that the market economy had played a historically necessary role by stimulating an unprecedented growth in the strength of productive forces. He wrote:

> Despite being closely linked to the profits from imperialism and colonialism and defended by devious tricks, Marx still saw it as a necessary, unavoidable stage. For example, in 'On British rule in India', he clearly knew that it had destroyed traditional Indian society. Yet he wrote: 'The problem doesn't lie there. The problem is that only if there is a fundamental revolution in the social conditions of Asia will mankind be able to fulfil its mission. Britain, despite all her crimes has also been the unconscious tool of history in effecting that revolution' (Do Thai Dong 1993:14).

Professor Dong noted that beside this positive evaluation, 'Marx didn't revere the market' and presented the doctrine of socialism to remedy the ills of capitalism: cycles of crisis, inflation, unemployment, exploitation, class conflict etc.:

> Marx predicted a new internationalism under the appeal 'workers of the world unite' which would sweep aside capitalism, the market economy and eventually erase national boundaries as well . . . Lenin contributed the slogan 'unity of the proletariat and of the oppressed nations' (Do Thai Dong 1993:14).

Do Thai Dong's point was to critically compare these two internationalisms. On the one hand was capitalism with its strengths and evils. On the other, socialism, with its remedies to those evils but its own

**Colonial 'vestiges' .Secondary school in Soc Trang provincial capital, established in the French colonial era**

failings as well. He argued that proletarian internationalism's slogans of global solidarity had been politically well attuned to the upsurge in political movements throughout the world from the late nineteenth to the mid-twentieth century. Yet economically, the practice of central planning in socialist countries had led to stagnation, and the welfare of national economies was 'obscured behind fraternal, impartial and international principles' (Do Thai Dong 1993:14). Professor Dong clearly rated proletarian internationalism less favourably than the colonialism Marx had praised in India, in terms of its capacity to unleash productive potential and realise national wellbeing for Vietnam.

Such critics regarded the communist road to power as having failed to realise development for the country as a whole. These authors harshly judged communism's emancipatory potential, even in comparison with that of colonialism. Their comments revealed disillusionment at a universalistic promise that had amounted to little more than empty slogans, or formalistic labels masking insubstantial results.

Other critics highlighted socialism's more regressive impact on tradition. According to Bui Tin, the 'arrogance' and 'adventurism' of the post-war years was caused by the rigid application of Maoist class categories to select the nation's leadership. Cadres had been chosen on account of their classification as non-exploitative peasants and as a result, the leadership and especially the security apparatus which controlled all activities became staffed by those with inadequate vision and experience (Bui Tin 1995:26). So went the joke, 'about the foreigner who visited Vietnam and asked why the security police (*cong an*) always went round in groups of three. The reply was that one could read, another could write and the third was there to control these two intellectuals' (Bui Tin 1995:113). Bui Tin believed education was essential in a leader to promote both a sense of responsibility and to provide the capacity to do the job. He argued that the failure to select a leadership on this basis had led to the two main problems to plague post-war Vietnam, depravity and short-sightedness. The institutionalisation of peasant ignorance, attributable to Maoism, meant that after 1975, 'the leadership became lax, intoxicated and dizzy with victory':

> Few of them could resist the lure of materialism because they lacked the education which forms the basis of human dignity. Therefore there was nothing to control them and they let themselves go . . . This was the beginning of our real cultural crisis (Bui Tin 1995:98).

Bui Tin argued that Maoism's rigid class doctrines had led to the prevention of a great deal of intellectual talent from making contributions to the nation (Bui Tin 1995:98, 100). He argued that the nation's post-colonial leadership thus had extremely limited horizons:

> If they had travelled abroad, it was mostly to Communist countries. They had escaped from a feudal and colonialist society to become revolutionaries, but their conduct clearly remained Confucian, given the way they deferred to one another to preserve harmony and discipline as was done within a traditional village or family hierarchy (Bui Tin 1995:105).

'Confucian' for him denoted the leadership's intolerance of criticism, lack of practical experience and formal training—as distinct from schooling in independent and critical thought—as well as rampant nepotism and the execution of responsibilities in exchange for favours. In Bui Tin's view, the revolutionary route from colonialism taken in Vietnam eschewed modernist influences. Regressive tradition, reanimated by Maoism, ensured that in the post-war years Vietnam lurched from disaster to disaster.

These contributions adopted the regime's own 'renovating' posture to unleash an uncompromising critique of the damaging past policies of the regime itself. Whereas the party attempted to portray its reforms as the completion of modernity, the critical improvisations accompanying official discourse construed the nation as still wallowing in a pre-modern condition. If this outpouring of critical commentary was momentarily experienced by those involved as a historic breach with the past, an exciting renaissance of the role of the artist and intellectual in Vietnamese society, the potential for these participants to share the party's constitution of the present as the modern era was quickly snuffed out as their modernism touched upon the party's exclusive authority to write its history. Censored, imprisoned, placed under house arrest for expressing their views, many critics, with Bui Tin, believed that Vietnam continued to anticipate the arrival of its modern era.

## SOUTHERN MODERNITY: 'OBJECTIVE' REAPPRAISALS

At the same time as these gloomy conclusions were being drawn, more
· positive assessments were being made about Vietnam's 'other' post-
colonial experience: to which only the southern half of the country had
been exposed. After a major conference in the early 1980s, critiques
of 'neo-colonialism' south of the 17th parallel, which had filled the
pages of official publications since the end of the war, began to fade
away. By 1981 the 5th Party Congress had identified 'subjectivism' and
'haste' as two of the reasons post-war socialist transformations and
economic development in the South had not been successful. From
having invalidated all southern divergences from the northern status
quo as 'neo-colonial poisons', official publications from the early 1980s
on began to selectively resuscitate a number of developments that had
occurred during the RVN era. Cautious reappraisals of the legacies of
the Republican era began to be voiced.

In 1983 an article was published that, for foreign readers, flagged
a substantial revision of prevailing official attitudes towards the legacies
of the RVN regime. Its author was Nguyen Khac Vien, prolific inter-
preter of Vietnamese developments to foreign audiences (through his
*Vietnamese Studies* series), tireless traveller and author of a series of
articles about South Vietnam after the end of the war. His paper, entitled
'The Mekong Delta—Socio-historical Survey', was included in his
1985 collection of such writings: *South Vietnam 1975–1985*. Nguyen
Khac Vien's comments on the 'neo-colonial' RVN period contained
unmistakable praise for its achievements:

> After the fall of Ngo Dinh Diem in 1963, the Americans applied a
> new policy . . . trying to create a new stratum of rich peasants
> engaged in a capitalist-type agriculture, using new techniques and
> producing for the national and international markets . . . This policy
> partially succeeded in zones controlled by the US forces, gave an
> impetus to commercial production, created or expanded commercial
> centres which were also engaged in the transformation of agricultural
> produce and machinery repair. Part of the delta was thus modernized
> (Nguyen Khac Vien 1985:352).

This was a significant text, containing elements of a positive official
evaluation of the era of US involvement in former South Vietnam. Of
central interest was Nyugen Khac Vien's recognition of the 'modernising' effects of capitalist, or 'capitalist-type', relations in some areas
of Vietnam's southern delta. Surprisingly he implied that had it not
been for the Hanoi-backed, rural-based resistance which had impeded
US 'control', this 'modernisation' would have more completely transformed the delta.

However, Nguyen Khac Vien's text was full of reservations, suspi-
cions and condemnations of US involvement in this process. He

presumed that the commercialisation of agriculture had been designed to 'bring the Mekong delta into the orbit of US agribusiness'. He noted that commercialisation had given rise to usury and exploitation. Other technological innovations penetrating into the region, such as TV sets, had aided the propagation of 'a fierce anti-communism and the flaunting of US might'. The underlying objective of the US policies had been to create 'a strong social base in the countryside . . . for the Saigon regime'. Yet after twenty years of this regime's existence, he argued, 'cultural and sanitary conditions did not equal those of the North [Vietnamese regime]'. Illiteracy, epidemics, superstitions and a culture of living beyond one's means were rampant (Nguyen Khac Vien 1985:354).

However, Nguyen Khac Vien concluded his piece on another positive note, recognising that under the RVN regime, a transformation of rural class relations had occurred. Citing surveys done in 1976, he argued that the practical elimination of the class of 'big landowners' and reduction in the numbers of 'landless or poor peasants', had created 'an important stratum of middle peasants, constituting 70–75% of the peasant population.' Of this 'principal figure in the South Vietnamese countryside', he commented, 'draconian' agrarian reformers needed to take note:

> [The middle peasant] has enough land for all his family to work . . .
> He is capable of using new technical means: machines, chemical
> fertilizers, new rice strains and is interested in new techniques. Selling
> his products on the market, he can make economic calculations and
> adapt his production to market conditions (Nguyen Khac Vien
> 1985:358).

Nguyen Khac Vien's middle peasant was a rational actor, a figure whom Samuel Popkin (1979) also had discovered in the Mekong delta:

> The middle peasant cares not so much for the form of land property
> as for the way to increase production and his income. Unlike the poor
> peasant, who has been working for mere subsistence, the middle
> peasant is resolutely opposed to any measures that would lead to
> irrational prices that would not cover production costs and would leave
> the producer with no profit (Nguyen Khac Vien 1985:359).

During the 1980s and 1990s, cadres from the Institute of Social Sciences, Ho Chi Minh City, investigated sociological phenomena such as Nguyen Khac Vien's 'middle peasant' with a view to averting the disasters brought on by the 'subjectivist haste' of the first post-war decade. The task of investigating the many distinctive legacies of the region below the 17th parallel was seen as particularly urgent. The end of the 1980s saw the establishment of the journal, *Social Sciences Review* (*Tap Chi Khoa Hoc Xa Hoi*), issued by the Institute. In its first

edition, Nguyen Cong Binh, editor-in-chief and director of the Institute[12] announced that:

> Social Sciences Review will be a forum for researchers, teachers and
> social science workers to disseminate knowledge, primarily research on
> South Vietnamese (Mien Nam)[13] realities, contributing to the task of
> constructing socialism and developing the country's social sciences
> (Nguyen Cong Binh 1989a:1).

Early contributions to this review noted the momentous arrival of
new forces of dynamism and strength after the year 1955, that is, the
date of the establishment of the US-sponsored RVN. An article by
Nguyen Cong Binh focused on the achievements of the US-backed RVN
regime in the region under its influence. Covering many of the issues
raised approvingly by Nguyen Khac Vien, Nguyen Cong Binh's account
also alluded to America's darker motivations, but his assessment of
their 'objective' effects was devoid of negative references. His interests
were narrower than Nguyen Khac Vien's 'socio-historical' concerns, as
he focused primarily on economic development:

> American commercial aid effectively assisted America's neo-colonial
> war, but objectively speaking, it strongly stimulated South Vietnam's
> pre-existing commodity economy. It developed industry, especially
> light industry (78.2% of all industry), including many plants with
> modern equipment. It developed some industrial areas, including
> Saigon-Bien Hoa, where 80% of the industrial productive capacity was
> concentrated. Communications networks and infrastructure were
> improved. Foreign trade was bustling (kha soi dong). In 1970, Saigon
> had business relations with 43 countries. The South Vietnamese
> bourgeoisie developed quickly: a few were compradores (tu san mai
> ban), the majority were small private traders (tu san thuong loai nho).
> In 1973, there were 8,132 enterprises, 167 of which employed upwards
> of 100 workers, 1,500 of which employed from 10–100 workers
> (Nguyen Cong Binh 1989b:6).

There was little evident restraint in his evaluation of this. The RVN
era was witness to a qualitative leap in the region's productive capacity
and integration with the outside world:

> Capitalism did not achieve a monopolistic role, but encroached on
> pre-capitalist relations changing rapidly the economic and social class
> structure, stimulating the establishment of a unified market in South
> Vietnam and opening up international relations.
>     Although a multi-sectored economy had long been in evidence, it
> was only this commodity economy of large-scale production that truly
> played a dynamic role of generalized transformation (Nguyen Cong
> Binh 1989b:7).

An even more positive account was given in a contribution by Tran
Du Lich, an economic historian based in the same institute, entitled

'The characteristics of commodity production in South Vietnam from a developmental perspective':

> During the years 1955–1975 in the South, capitalist commodity production developed in a rather unique manner. Capitalist commodity production did not grow as a spontaneous development, in a 'natural process', of unselfconscious production, the way it does in many developed capitalist countries. Here US neocolonialism played a positive role in stimulating that process . . .
>
> The process of economic embourgeoisement (*tu ban hoa*) played a positive role in the liberation of productive forces . . . During nearly 100 years of French rule, there was little development of the national bourgeoisie to speak of; however, in only twenty years (1955–75), and despite war, the national bourgeoisie developed rapidly . . .
>
> In agriculture, the privatization of the farmer, 'middle-peasant-ization' of agricultural producers and embourgeoisement of the landlord class took place . . . As such, a class of entrepreneurs (*doanh nhan*) emerged in the countryside—capitalist commodity producers (*nguoi san xuat hang hoa tu ban chu nghia*). This is the group now playing a positive role in the development of agriculture and of the countryside (Tran Du Lich 1989:14, 15, 16).

Other *Social Sciences Review* articles referred to the rural class transformation that had been effected under the RVN and the emergence there of new social types. According to Nguyen Cong Binh et al., the fact that the southern Vietnamese plain (*Nam Bo*) had not experienced collectivisation as had occurred in the North under the DRV, had sped the emergence of the middle peasant as a person with new characteristics:

> The rise of middle peasantry in *Nam Bo* did not merely imply 'land to the tiller', it was linked to the commodity economy. Southern farmers do not have a disposition to hoard for future eventualities. Linked to the market, they have found ways to respond to and train themselves (*tu dao tao*) in the market. That is a style and quality of the middle peasant. The middle peasant was trained (*ren duc*) in this quality during the pre-75 years of privatization of the peasantry, and the importation of machines, fertilizers, and new rice strains (Nguyen Cong Binh et al. 1991:29).

Indeed, all peasants of the Mekong delta, possessed this familiarity with commerce:

> Mekong delta peasants usually sell rice and other agricultural produce as soon as they harvest them and buy whatever items they need when needed, including rice for personal consumption (Nguyen Cong Binh 1991:18).

The innovative capacities of southern peasants, at home with Green Revolution technology, was another frequent theme in the writings of the Institute's social scientists from the late 1980s. One writer referred to the RVN era as having ushered in a spirit of innovation among this class of farmers in the Mekong delta:

> The middle peasant emerged decisively in the years prior to 1975. Many of them played the role of avant-garde, bringing new strains of rice home to their villages and hamlets. Many became advisory 'centres' (*'trung tam' huong dan*) in the use of agricultural technology for other farmers . . . The emergence of this class of middle peasant was severely retarded in the years after 1975 (Nguyen Thu Sa 1991:33).

A tone of unqualified praise for the 'modernisation' effected under the RVN was struck in a paper presented by a Ho Chi Minh City journalist at the 1990 *Vietnam Update*, a conference held biannually at the Australian National University:

> If the now distant period of French colonialism can be dismissed as a thing of the past, the capitalist system introduced as a result of US involvement had major consequences . . . When the US government decided that it should win 'the hearts and the minds' of the Vietnamese, generally people from all walks of life benefited in one way or another from different US aid schemes, which extended to the lowest levels in society, urban as well as rural. The US-initiated 'Green Revolution' brought about radical changes in certain rural areas, enabling peasants to learn to use fertilizers and agricultural machines and to grow more highly productive varieties.
>
> For most of the period between 1961 and 1978, the US government used its economic power to construct an embryonic capitalist economy with a little of everything from a free enterprise system . . . [In the last five years of US involvement] the birth of an entrepreneurial class, trained and tried over all those years should be noted, as well as the emergence of a Western-trained corps of technocrats replacing the French-trained bureaucrats. This is the sort of 'human investment' which every developing country should strive for (Hoang Ngoc Nguyen 1991:35).

Such were the views of the US State Department in the 1960s and theorists of modernisation such as Walt Rostow.[14] At that time South Vietnam had been regarded as a crucible of modernity. It had been seen as one of the frontline states of the US-sponsored project of post-colonial nation building, the hope of the 'Free World'. The extent to which this image had ever approximated reality was questioned by many at the time. Hoang Ngoc Nguyen, who had worked as a journalist in Saigon prior to 1975, may have accepted this perspective less critically than most. However, his glowing appraisal was not so far removed from regime academics, like Nguyen Cong Binh, originally sent to the South to administer its US-era legacies out of existence, who appeared to substantially accept this perspective.

Accounts of the South Vietnamese peasant as capable entrepreneur, at home in capitalist commodity relations, represented noteworthy departures from post-war perspectives on the commodity economy in the South. The commodity economy had been identified by critics of 'neo-colonial culture' as the principal impediment to mobilising 'modernisation'. According to their critique, commodities tied one to the capitalist world and 'enslaved' one. Detracting from the spirit of sacrifice and austerity, commodities were counterproductive to the project of constructing a modern prosperous nation. They had confused the senses and had shackled the soul of the South Vietnamese, defeating their heroic 'resistance spirit'.

Notwithstanding such shifts in perspective, there were notable continuities in perceptions of the countryside as home to South Vietnam's avant-garde of modernist consciousness. During the war, the countryside, subjected to torrents of bombs, poisonous chemicals and free-fire regimes, was where party theorists had held the aggressive barbarity of neo-colonialism to be at its most intense. However, for that reason, these theorists had argued, in the countryside the consciousness of oppression was most clear-sighted and the will to resist fiercest. After the communist takeover, the cities came in for sustained criticism as places where 'neo-colonial poisons' were still found in the greatest concentrations. The lack of attention paid to the countryside in illustrating arguments about 'neo-colonial poisoning', and the occasional positive reference to the maintenance of the 'struggle spirit' in the countryside, qualified it as a relatively heroic place. Furthermore, the countryside was the place where, after the war, drug addicts, sex workers, petty traders and other 'neo-colonised' urbanites were sent to be re-'educated' and 'awakened' by purifying physical labour. In the 1980s the southern countryside came to be regarded as the site where, under US tutelage, a new modernist consciousness had emerged. As some cadres from Ho Chi Minh City's Institute of Social Sciences were to formulate it, the countryside was the birthplace of that figure of US-inspired modernity—the middle peasant—marked by a noteworthy capacity for innovation, technological nous and entrepreneurship.[15]

Despite many years of economic stagnation, hunger and mass exodus, followed by a dramatic lurch in policy, it was not hard to find those who still defended the regime's 'clear-sightedness' in designing policies that had come to terms with the 'realities' of the South.[16] However, in conversation with contributors to the *Social Sciences Review*, some argued that the regime's renovation policies themselves represented an expression of southern legacies on the national arena. According to this perspective, the 'dawning' of Vietnamese modernity might be dated not to emancipation by northern troops, nor to party-initiated renovation, but to developments in the South beginning in 1955, if not earlier, and it had taken until 1986 for the benefits of this legacy to be extended to the entire nation. Those who put this case to me most forcefully were two senior researchers, both party members, trained by the DRV and installed in the South in the wake of the communist victory.

## CELEBRATING SOUTHERN PRAGMATISM

In 1993 Professor Do Thai Dong of Ho Chi Minh City's Institute of Social Sciences produced a report on the relationship between the *doi moi* reforms and social structure, in which he argued that the nation's current reform achievements were being driven by the South:

> One half of Vietnam had the experience of operating as a market economy. From the South, the economy quickly broke out of the centralized subsidy system and became a locomotive rapidly pulling the rest of the country into renovation. People used to say that Saigon followed in Hanoi's wake: the same power cuts, the same water cuts, eating one's rice according to ration books, buying one's oil by voucher, sharing out each tube of tooth paste, studying Russian. More recently, Hanoi has followed in Saigon's wake; selling land, selling houses, struggling for a house on the main street, building hotels, opening dancing clubs, watching kung fu movies, studying English (Do Thai Dong 1993:2).

It was the South's legacy as a market economy, he argued, that had allowed Vietnam to switch to a market economy while the former Soviet Union and many countries in Eastern Europe still struggled:

> Firstly and most importantly, Vietnam consists of two regions, the South and the North, having two different economic characters. The North long had its feet planted in a socialist economy which, after 1975, did not spread to the South, despite political unification. The North is collectivist (*tap the*) in nature, while the South is still pretty much individualist (*ca the*). The relatively developed commodity economy in the South, which for many years was part of the capitalist economic order, consolidated southern society in a direction appropriate to such an economy. Post-1975 policies of commercial and agricultural reform, despite having produced great upheavals and causing great losses were unable to deeply shake southern society . . . From 1982, at the latest, the social structure of commodity production in the South began to move, finding space to emerge out of all sorts of cracks in the centralized planning and subsidy mechanism (Do Thai Dong 1993:2).

In conversation with me, Professor Dong contended that such activities were indicative of a regionally-specific style of resistance:

> The style of southern resistance to socialism was not on the plane of philosophy (*triet ly*) or of policy (*chu truong*) but of actions (*hanh*

*dong*). In this field, southerners were the first to overturn many
socialist practices (from fieldnotes).

By 'southern resistance' Professor Dong specifically excluded the activities of intellectuals, students and military personnel, whom he
contended were not significant political players. Rather, he emphasised
the role of local political leaders and their tacit sponsorship of practices
that, from the central government's perspective, had been considered
illegal and unsocialist:

> One of the most significant of these was the tacit authorization given
> by the Ho Chi Minh City leadership in the late 1970s for the Director
> of the State Food company to bypass the centralised subsidy system
> and go directly to the Mekong delta to buy rice for resale in Ho Chi
> Minh City. The local leaders closed ranks around this initiative, which
> was in contravention of national policy. Another was Long An
> provincial Party Secretary, Chin Can's decision to eliminate the
> voucher system for the purchasing of rice and meat, thereby
> authorising private individuals to buy and sell food commodities at the
> market price . . .[17]
>    Another innovation from Ho Chi Minh City allowed one's
> relatives abroad to send goods back home. At first the quantity of such
> goods was restricted, next, the limit was abolished and finally the
> sending of money was permitted. As a result of this, the market in
> gold began to grow. The city leadership allowed the opening of gold
> shops. At first these took the form of joint ventures between districts
> and individuals; however the district role was something of a
> formalism. Eventually individuals were allowed to privately own and
> operate gold shops (from fieldnotes).

These leaders were seen to have played a historically important
role as protectors of continuity in local economic practices. Their role
vis-à-vis policy was to deflect its full operation.[18] Furthermore, he
argued, the practical measures taken by southern leaders proceeded
through a process which was fundamentally different from that which
northern leaders had employed when launching reforms in the North:

> In general these measures were taken in response to a need. The
> demands of reality (*duoc thuc the nhu cau*) rather than the persuasion
> of logic (*duoc ly luan thuyet phuc*) was the key to the process of the
> dismantling of the planned economy in the South (from fieldnotes).

The 'reality' which spoke directly to southern leaders was the commodity market system (along with kung fu, dance clubs and the English
language) in which they were immersed. On the other hand, the North
was not only geographically remote from these influences but also
removed from them by a screen of logic. Professor Dong argued that
the way in which southern leaders rationalised their actions manifested
a regionally specific interpretive style. While no strangers to ideology,

southerners employed it in a contingent and opportunistic manner as opposed to northerners, whom he held to be entrapped within it in a rigid manner:

> In defending each change of practice, southern leaders made the claim that this was not in contravention of the ideology of Marxism and in no way constituted a critique of State policy. Their approach was to interpret socialism very inclusively, indeed not to suggest there had been any rupture with the principles of socialism at all! On the other hand, explanations coming out of the 6th Party Congress were couched in terms of 'errors' *(sai lam)*, that the party had committed on the path to socialism. These included an overly hasty rush to nationalise all aspects of the economy before the economic conditions were suitable for socialism. Whilst acknowledging error and endorsing the need for a period of economic liberalisation, the 6th Party Congress proclamation and all those following it, persisted in stating the end goal for Vietnam to be socialism. Moreover, the errors committed were justified by pointing out that with such a beautiful goal as socialism, party members' impatient and overly hasty rush to attain it was understandable! (from fieldnotes).

According to Do Thai Dong, the northern approach displayed an uncompromising attitude towards the notion of socialism, which was not affected by the unsuccessful efforts to realise it. The southern way displayed greater flexibility and, in its liberal definition of the notion of socialism, was undoubtedly a surer path to subverting the concept entirely.[19] He emphasised this observation in a report submitted to the National Institute of Social Sciences:

> Southerners learnt how to exploit even the vocabulary of socialism. Take, for example, the term 'co-operative'. Its connotations are most socialist, but it is the most mischievous of terms, in use all over the place. For example, the firm Minh Phung, now one of the biggest businesses in Saigon still stubbornly displays the name Minh Phung co-operative (Do Thai Dong 1993:2).[20]

Professor Dong celebrated the political nous by which southern leaders were able to maintain their course of action despite pressure to conform to ideological orthodoxy. According to him, southern pragmatism consisted of an innate relationship to one's environment, which was contingent, uncomplicated and relatively unmediated by conceptual schemes.[21]

As a result of the southern leadership's subversion of socialist reforms, the unreconstructed capitalist economy of the South was able to kick in after the *doi moi* reforms were announced, and drag the whole of the country into capitalist modernity. This formulation thus dated the inception of Vietnamese modernity in the 1950s and located its birthplace in the South. The mid-1980s brought an enlargement of its geographical scope, but entailed no qualitative transformation.

Neither, according to Do Thai Dong's schematisation, did the mid-1980s entail an 'awakening'. According to him, responsiveness to reality, political nous, tactical savvy and interpretive flexibility were dispositions already entrenched in the South and brought into play by southern leaders in engagement with Hanoi's attempts at socialist reform. Even after reforms were officially announced, his argument ran, the central leadership continued to manifest its weak hold on reality, locked inflexibly into the conception of socialism as a necessary and beautiful thing. Southerners, on the other hand, continued to exploit deviously the vocabulary of socialism while pragmatically pursuing their own ends.

## PARTY IN THE SOUTH! HAVING IT BOTH WAYS

Professor Dong's explanation of Vietnam's 1993 economic orientation placed emphasis on southern leaders' subversion of socialist policies, which were identified as northern in origin. The notion of southern leaders as 'pragmatic' could probably find no better illustration than his then senior in Ho Chi Minh City's Institute of Social Sciences, Professor Mac Duong: an ethnologist, party member, aspiring National Assembly representative and Institute Director. When I spoke to Professor Duong in 1993, his attribution of the *doi moi* reforms to the South was made in a most uncompromising manner:

> 1977 to 1980 was the period when opposition to socialist reform (*cai tao xa hoi chu nghia*) burst forth (*bung ra*). This occurred in Saigon before anywhere else in the country. It occurred precisely when pressure from Hanoi was at its greatest and took the form of private enterprise springing up all over the city. This activity took place simultaneously with criticisms from southern leaders, who felt the policies were unreasonable. *Doi moi* was actively under way in the late 1970s in Saigon (from fieldnotes).

Professor Duong's explanation thus placed emphasis on a societal reaction to socialist policies rather than on their non-implementation, practical subversion or sly evasion. Indeed the potency or actualisation of central policies had added a vital factor of 'pressure' to create the outburst of 'opposition' that occurred in 'Saigon'. His explanation fell within the resistance meta-narrative, employed by Vietnamese nationalists of diverse political persuasions, as a central theme of Vietnamese history.[22] The supposedly 'pressurising' effects of socialist policies in the South was consistent with the party's own take on the historiographical significance of resistance. History happened through resistance, in a violent reaction to oppression. People were made self-aware and fashioned into agents of history by the application of oppressive force upon them.[23]

Establishing the actualisation of socialist policies in Ho Chi Minh City lent national significance to the purported reaction to them. The city's predicament had been of a nationwide order—its subjection to the socialist reform policies later renounced at the 'historic' 6th Party Congress of 1986 as 'erroneous' and 'irrational'. The system may have only just put in an appearance in the South (the systematic collectivisation of agriculture had only began in 1977, the nationalisation of urban commerce in 1978) but it *had* arrived, uniting Ho Chi Minh City with the rest of the country as victim of oppression and providing its crucial pressurising effects. After the policy backdowns of the 1980s, Ho Chi Minh City's supposed 'resistance', was something that could be looked upon as a contribution to the nation's progress. Thus Professor Duong dated the proliferation of markets in Ho Chi Minh City late enough to be seen as 'resistance' to the policies designed to abolish them, yet early enough to be regarded as setting a national precedent.[24]

Professor Duong's interpretation was also notable for the role he asserted for 'southern leaders' in this process. The 'bursting forth' of markets had occurred 'simultaneously' with 'criticisms' from southern leaders. When questioned, he insisted that leaders like himself played a key role, assuring me that, 'we were not pre-empted by popular or spontaneous reaction.' The rational and discursive nature of this resistance was evident in the 'criticisms' they voiced about 'unreasonable' policies and their use of newspapers to express these. Like Do Thai Dong, this version attributed responsibility for Vietnam's liberal reforms to urban southern Vietnamese leaders. Yet Professor Duong considered people such as himself to have been enlightened patrons (rather than pragmatic subversives) whose championship of resistance to central policies owed to their superior understanding of the southern economy. He argued that the central government's endorsement of this outcome amounted to 'the unification (*thong nhat*) of *doi moi*', a process reminiscent of, but reversing, the northern-engineered unification of 1975.[25]

In his 1991 contribution to the *Vietnam Update* conference, Ho Chi Minh City journalist, Hoang Ngoc Nguyen was equally emphatic about the role of southern leaders in the inception of the reforms:

> I can also say that behind the liberal and radical decisions of our government, there has always been the influential opinion of some leaders who had previously held important positions in the southern provinces, most notably in Ho Chi Minh City. It has been alleged, for instance, that Resolution N. 6 of the Fourth Party Congress was the outcome of Resolution N. 9 of Ho Chi Minh City, which had been contemplated and tried out there. In my opinion, southern Vietnam has been the driving force behind reformation efforts (Hoang Ngoc Nguyen 1991:35).

Like Professor Duong, Hoang Ngoc Huyen did not portray these contemplative experiments as having occurred in isolation from national policy. He saw that the local economy had been in dynamic relationship with the operation of centralised policies:

> It is clear that southern Vietnam has reacted very swiftly and vigorously to the gradually unfolding renovation policies of the government. 'Violently' may be a more accurate term than 'vigorously', as forces in the economy had been very turbulent before. I remember a top Vietnamese leader telling a foreign newsman frankly that in the South the economy would leap forward before it had been completely untethered (Hoang Ngoc Nguyen 1991:34).

Although both of these commentators maintained some kind of a minimal relevance for the role of the central government in the reform process, just as much weight was given to Saigon's pre-1975 pre-socialist legacies. Professor Duong argued that the emergence of *doi moi* in 'Saigon' in the late 1970s had been due to 'historical' reasons:

> Since 1945 Saigon has had a commodity economy and secondly has had extensive international economic connections through its port. Hanoi lacked this. In addition it must be stressed that in the 1960s and 1970s, Saigon's Tan Son Nhut Airport was the biggest in southeast Asia (from fieldnotes).[26]

There is nothing to suggest that 1945 had been a significant year in the development of international economic connections for Saigon as distinct from Hanoi.[27] However, the date 1945 did have political significance. Since independence from France, declared in that year, Saigon's extant international links and commodity economy could be considered afresh as Vietnam's assets rather than France's. Professor Duong's characterisation of Saigon's post-independence history emphasised the city's continuous and intensifying engagement with the world economy and its status as Vietnam's commercial capital (even if foreign military aircraft had to be roped in to assist his contrast with Hanoi, its deficient rival). Due also to other factors left unspoken in his comparison,[28] Saigon had been spared the socialist structures, which had remained in force in Hanoi, until the post-war years. Ho Chi Minh City's precocious reforms in the late 1970s were a reflection of the city's head start over the national capital. According to him, Vietnam's liberal policies had a discernible place and date of inception: Saigon, 1945.

Despite its historical experience of capitalism, Ho Chi Minh City could thus be seen as both a heroic resistor and a long standing modern, arguably two of the highest values in Vietnamese communist discourse. By proposing an account such as this, Professor Duong could defend his local credentials as a leader of 'resistance', and, as an economically savvy southern leader, patiently explain the advantages of Saigon's

**Cho Lon streetscape: 'patriotic scholar', party self-promotion (long live the glorious Communist Party of Vietnam) and free-wheeling market forces**

'modernity' to backward Hanoi-ites. Such a formulation stood in stark contrast with the morose visions of those dissident intellectuals and former party members, who equated the application of socialist doctrine in Vietnam with regressive traditions and regarded the party's revolutionary rejection of colonialism as the institutionalisation of an insubstantial modernism. For such critics, 'modernity' and 'resistance' had come together in the northern half of the country in a less favourable way.[29] By contrast, Professor Duong's conceptualisation expressed the advantageous position of southern-based administrators such as himself. Having been installed to eliminate southern capitalism and subsequently claiming to have defended it, the purpose of his southern posting remained consistently in the nation's interest. His purported enlightened sponsorship of southern links to the non-socialist world rated within the nation's resistance traditions and yet also reflected his sophisticated accommodation with non-state market relations. This profitable view reflected the unique position in which many well-connected state agents in southern sinecures found themselves since unification: able to tap northern concentrations of power and southern economic resources in a wealth-creating equation unrivalled by any others within or beyond the region.

# 3

# Indigenising modernity in *Nam Bo*

*Doi moi* era commentators who offered favourable reassessments of the 1955–75 RVN period cited the growth of markets, the expansion of international trade and the emergence of new cultural and technological aptitudes as evidence of 'the South's' relative modernity vis-à-vis the North. However, these analysts did not always draw their illustrations uniformly from the area south of the 17th parallel (the territory nominally under RVN administrative control). Former Saigon and the provinces surrounding it provided the best material for those given to such north-south contrasts. The country's central coastal plain and the mountainous areas to the north of Saigon were seldom referred to and few of the examples of RVN-era 'modernisation' were drawn from there. In the late 1980s a growing number of publications explicitly singled out the more geographically restricted region of *Nam Bo*, in Vietnam's extreme south, as a place where these qualities were best exemplified.[1] Appearing on the shelves of bookstores and in journals, such as the new *Journal of Social Sciences*, these works attributed a coherent regional identity to socio-economic trends which were just beginning to become evident.

Locals recall 1989–90 as the years when Ho Chi Minh City and the provinces of the Mekong delta began to register a significant upswing in economic activity. Land prices in Ho Chi Minh City started to rise rapidly and construction activity went into high gear. Business was improving, market places expanded and shop shelves filled with a growing variety of consumer items. The city was host to an increasing number of foreign business visitors. Replacing Soviet bloc advisers in the ageing hotels constructed by their French and US predecessors, a new wave of mainly regional traders and investors began to weave the

Mekong delta and Ho Chi Minh City into a booming regional economy. The Mekong delta was largely responsible for the nation's record rice exports and was home to emerging seafood and freshwater fish industries. Provincial capitals in the Mekong delta were experiencing house building booms fuelled by overseas Vietnamese remittances. The province of Dong Nai was being consolidated as a key industrial and export processing zone. Vung Tau was thriving as a cargo port, fishing centre, domestic tourist destination and hub of the nation's oil industry. The southern region was becoming Vietnam's new frontier and immigrants from the northern delta and the provinces of the centre were flowing southwards to make their fortunes. In an era in which goals such as 'openness', the 'market economy', and 'renewal' were put forward as the ideals to which the society should aspire, this region seemed to exemplify these values in abundance.

Back in the late 1970s this area had also been distinguished, although in negative terms, by its non-compliance with the policies of agricultural collectivisation, co-operativism and the nationalisation of industry and trade. However, as attitudes and policies began to shift in the early 1980s, a number of publications appeared about the Mekong delta (*Dong bang song Cuu Long*) and the southern plain (*Dong bang Nam Bo*), which spoke about markets, trading links and cultural change, as favourable, regionally distinctive attributes. By the end of the decade writers had become more eloquent on the social and cultural distinctiveness of the southern region and were to find in its past an acceptable pedigree for events of the reform era. As economic activity and transnational cultural exchanges began to intensify, a view emerged of *Nam Bo* as a place inherently open to external influences, subject to ceaseless dynamism and constituted by processes of cultural hybridisation. These images accounted for perceived regional differences, as well as appearing to regard the region as a model for the liberal reforms and more open national approach to global integration. Such views also indicate the regime's partial accommodation with, and naturalisation of, this region's colonial and capitalist legacies, and were advanced by those who were well-positioned to benefit from the policy seachange.

## *NAM BO* AND VIETNAMESE NATIONALISM

Vietnam's southern region, or *Nam Bo*, had not always been the focus of such attention. Over the years of anti-colonial resistance and during the nation's post-colonial war, regionalism was not a popular topic among Vietnamese nationalists. Both the DRV and the RVN regimes had characterised as invalid the tripartite division of the former kingdom effected under French colonial rule. Under the RVN, the primary concern had been to emphasise uniform territorial integrity in what was an already divided nation.[2] The RVN's first president, Ngo Dinh Diem, had vigorously attacked Cochinchinese regionalism and had dispelled the power of the territorially-based political-religious groups in the Mekong delta. Ironically, it had been one of the opponents of that regime who had most forcefully advanced the issue of southern Vietnamese difference. In *The Southern Personality* (*Ca Tinh Mien Nam*), the historian and novelist Son Nam sketched out a picture of the typical inhabitant of the southernmost part of the country as a pioneer: battling unfamiliar terrain, struggling against wild animals, isolation and foreign invasion. Son Nam's southerners were rustic and uncomplicated, they were generous to a fault, spontaneous and prone to superstition, but they were fiercely nationalistic and had exhibited heroism in their resistance to the French. In a Saigon awash with foreign troops, generals who grew wealthy on corruption money and trafficking, and urban areas which swelled with refugees from the countryside, his work counterposed images of southern rural simplicity, courage, honour and struggle, implicitly suggesting the communist-led rural-based insurgency to be more consistent with the region's traditions than the RVN's supposedly nationalist leaders.[3]

The DRV and later SRVN's approach to this region was essentially the same as that of the RVN. References to *Nam Bo*, emerging after 1976, stressed the region's conformity to, or exemplification of the supposedly national traits of heroism, patriotism, love of national unity, collectivist orientation and embrace of socialism. The topic of region was only ever broached to demolish the notion of regional differences, or attack what were considered harmful, alien accretions of recent origin. For example, in 1977 the party's principal foreign spokesman, Nguyen Khac Vien, wrote about a recent journey made to the Mekong delta, his first ever to a region which he had dreamed about as a schoolboy. Entitled 'From one delta to another', it began by describing the striking differences of geology, hydrography and human ecology he had noticed between the northern and southern deltas (Nguyen Khac Vien 1977). Yet the author was quickly reminded of the unity of these deltas' human history. He reported having found residents of the Mekong delta eager to talk about the Tay Son rebels' eighteenth-century victory against the Siamese invaders, the anti-colonial struggle, and the anti-US war of resistance (Nguyen Khac Vien 1977:284). He had visited various 'bases of our resistance': Ap Bac, Ben Tre and the U Minh forest (Nguyen Khac Vien 1977:288–307). In Ben Tre he had met an indomitable heroine who reminded him of another female revolutionary he was acquainted with in the North. He listed the various patriots and heroes of 'resistance struggles against foreign aggression' produced by the Mekong delta. He discussed the region's history of economic exploitation by French colonialists and the Americans and found that only since liberation had the region begun to achieve real development by returning to the nation's 'millenary tradition' of collective work practices. He described people's joy at receiving a visitor from Hanoi. 'They peppered us with questions about the North, about Uncle Ho' (Nguyen Khac Vien 1977:303).

In a 1982 article, Tran Van Giau, influential historian and head of the *Nam Bo* chapter of the Indochinese Communist Party during the colonial era, alluded to his own return south after having spent the war years in the DRV. Giau observed that for one who had been away from the region for a period of thirty years, the rural areas of *Nam Bo* had become commercialised (*thuong mai hoa*), and, as a result, its rural inhabitants had become selfish and money-oriented. These developments were attributed to the US commodity aid program:

> Commercial trade has created a mindset of chasing after selfish interests (*cheo theo loi ich ich ky*) that smallholders and tenants had scarcely known before . . . The profit motive (*vi loi*) has advanced, while the ethic of loyalty (*vi nghia*) has declined . . . A person returning to the *Nam Bo* countryside after an absence of some thirty years cannot avoid a feeling of grief when seeing this phenomenon of psychological deterioration (*tam ly suy doi*) (Tran Van Giau 1982:206).

Nevertheless he asserted resolutely:

> At base, the southern (*Nam Bo*) peasant character retains the traditional qualities that neither France nor the American-puppets could change or annul. They remain the people whose ancestors made the adventurous journey to the extreme South to settle, armed with ploughs and hoes, who four times helped the Tay Son defeat the Nguyen feudalists, who countless times rose up against the French . . . who made the August 1945 Revolution, who fought for thirty long years under the leadership of the party and who still to this day follow the party, even despite the failings of individual party members (Tran Van Giau 1982:206).

This, until the early 1980s, was the communist tradition of writing about *Nam Bo*. The matter of regional differences was only ever raised to be invalidated, denied, or, like Son Nam, to show that by its surfeit of nationalism, the regional 'personality' distinguished itself from the so-called 'nationalist' government which had formerly held power in Saigon.

## INTIMATIONS OF INDIGENOUS DIFFERENCE

Tran Van Giau's paper was delivered at a pivotal conference on the Mekong delta held in Ho Chi Minh City in 1981. Among the contributors fellow historian, Huynh Lua, used the opportunity to discuss the pioneering exploitation of *Nam Bo* in the seventeenth and eighteenth centuries. He addressed the relevance of 'traditional' Vietnamese values in the new southern environment:

In this region, the traditional ethics of the Vietnamese farmer such as industriousness, patience, the endurance of difficulties, and the creative application of the experience of traditional wet rice agriculture, were comprehensively brought into play and yielded substantial results. In areas of recent arrival, Vietnamese migrants lived together in groups, voluntarily settling in hamlets, because village organization was the habitual infrastructural base of Vietnamese farmers—their traditions of unity, mutual assistance and mutual love were ancient legacies. Moreover, in a new land, with dense jungles full of wild beasts, deep rivers full of crocodiles, and an unfamiliar climate, they had to co-operate with each other, gather together and form hamlets, to create the conditions to help each other open the land, fight disease and resist natural disasters and wild animals (Huynh Lua 1982:87).

However, Huynh Lua also made reference to the existence of extensive market relations in the Dong Nai–Gia Dinh region (used interchangeably with *Nam Bo* in the article) during this era:

> Based on a developing agriculture, the Dong Nai–Gia Dinh region early on enjoyed thriving commerce (*mot nen thuong nghiep phon vinh*) and a developed commodity economy (*nen kinh te hang hoa*) linked by extensive market relations (Huynh Lua 1982:93).

He described such markets as 'springing up' (*moc len*) with 'many centres of international commerce', the development of handicraft industries and the emergence of a division of labour. He observed that the development of a commodity economy had stimulated the production of rice. Providing a counterpoint to Tran Van Giau's commentary on the deleterious effects of US aid on the *Nam Bo* peasant personality, this author saw the existence of a commodity economy as consistent with the maintenance of 'traditional' values, a point he emphasised at the conclusion of his piece:

> Here, it must be emphasized, one of the factors of decisive importance vis-à-vis the success [of the *Nam Bo* settlers] was their spirit of close mutual affection and assistance, the realization of communal strength, the exchange of lessons between the members of the Vietnamese community living and working here (Huynh Lua 1982:94).

The divergent interpretations of these two historians came at a time when the central government's post-war socialist reform policies were under serious challenge in Ho Chi Minh City and the Mekong delta. Exhortations to sacrifice immediate individual benefits for future collective prosperity and to maintain the spirit of resistance struggle that had purportedly animated the Vietnamese people in their military exploits had failed to mobilise the population. There had been widespread non-compliance in the collectivisation of the Mekong delta and a marked inability to secure state control of commerce in Ho Chi Minh City. The party had voiced 'self criticisms' of the drastic administrative

measures it had initially applied to nationalise bourgeois commerce in
Ho Chi Minh City and, at its 6th Plennum in 1979, there had been
calls for liberalisation in economic policy (Duiker 1989:96). Although
'socialist reform' remained on the central government's agenda, the
means to achieving this were being reconsidered. Private commerce
was being allowed in certain commodities and expectations with regard
to collectivisation had been readjusted. In many ways, the presocialist
forms in what was the country's most economically dynamic region
were subtly emerging as an alternative, if *de facto*, national approach.

Huynh Lua reassessed commodity trade, no longer viewing it as a
recent foreign imposition but as a deep-seated local institution. A
further expression of this came in 1983 with Nguyen Khac Vien's
'Socio-historical study of the Mekong delta', which summarised the
results of the 1981 Mekong delta conference for foreign consumption.
Nguyen Khac Vien argued that key indigenous, not foreign-imposed,
characteristics set the Mekong delta apart from Vietnam's 'Centre' and
'North'. In a piece which also offered qualified recognition that the US
had promoted modernisation in the Mekong delta (see Chapter 2), he
alluded to the region's even older legacy of difference. Vien wrote that
on the eve of French colonisation of Vietnam:

> While remaining essentially Vietnamese, the Mekong delta peasant had
> preserved a spirit of pioneering, even of adventure. He was always
> ready to seek new horizons, to fight and if need be, to sacrifice his
> life to defend his rights. Living on a fertile land, he was less thrifty,
> less mindful of the future than his relatives in the North and the
> Centre and generously extended hospitality to all (Nguyen Khac Vien
> 1983:345).

This represented one of the first official references to indigenous (as
opposed to foreign-imposed) regional differences within Vietnam.
Given that previous commentary, including many writings by this same
author, had considered regional differences invalid, his reference to
pre-colonial regional personality differences, firmly grounded in environmental factors, was noteworthy.

Like many others who were to write about the Mekong delta, Vien
smuggled in the city of Saigon as part of the region. Saigon for instance
featured explicitly in his portrait of the delta through its integrative
role as a market hub for Mekong delta peasants:

> The peasants were able to exploit the natural resources found in that
> virgin land: fish, shrimp, rushes, water palms, and sell the products in
> less-favoured regions, or merchants could buy and resell them in Gia
> Dinh, which later became Saigon city. From Ben Nghe port in the
> same locality, the products were sent to provinces in the centre and the
> north or exported (Nguyen Khac Vien 1983:344).

His account of Saigon as a commercial hub recast a feature that had previously been regarded as an alien implantation (the urban commodity economy) as a pre-colonial tradition. Nguyen Khac Vien's Mekong delta on the threshold of colonisation had already developed distinctive characteristics—a significant step away from the view of such differences as the product of invidious foreign intervention. This approach was even clearer in Vien's treatment of the subsequent colonial era. The 'socio-historical' impact of French colonisation was reduced to two consequences: the exacerbation of rural class divisions and the colonial cultivation of a Chinese compradore class (Nguyen Khac Vien 1983:349). Even so, as he observed, these developments were negated by the Communist Party's land reforms, the class transformations which he conceded had occurred in the late RVN period and the anti-compradore campaigns of the post-war socialist regime (Nguyen Khac Vien 1983:352). Therefore, the French colonial impact in southern Vietnam, in his view, was both limited and reversible. The regional characteristics that had endured were of pre-colonial origin.

This view, emerging as it did in the early 1980s may be linked to the policy adjustments of that time, but it remained more or less undeveloped until the end of the decade. The essays of Huynh Lua and Nguyen Khac Vien had broached the issue of southern regional difference as an indigenous phenomenon; by 1989 the concept had become a widespread staple in published discussion.

## PRE-COLONIAL MODERNITY

In 1990 Nguyen Cong Binh, then director of the Ho Chi Minh City Institute of Social Sciences, contributed a 'historical perspective' on a number of socio-economic characteristics of *Nam Bo*. The main point he sought to establish was that:

> A commodity economy (*nen kinh te hang hoa*) developed early in *Nam Bo*. It pushed forward the exploitation of a diverse and often-changing nature, to develop production and expand international commerce (Nguyen Cong Binh 1990:22).

On the face of it, this observation merely confirmed a view shared by Western social scientists of diverse theoretical orientations that the area established as the French colony of Cochinchina experienced an earlier and more extensive capitalist transformation than the rest of the country (Gran 1975, Scott 1976, Popkin 1979, Murray 1980). And yet, by 'early', Binh meant at least 1822 during the reign of the Minh Mang Emperor (more than forty years prior to French conquest of the region). The report *Gia Dinh Thanh Thong Chi*, compiled in 1822 by Sino–Vietnamese mandarin, Trinh Hoai Duc, was mined by Binh for evidence

**River port in Ho Chi Minh City's District Five**

of the importance of the pre-colonial commodity economy in the southern region:

> The greatest achievement, serving as the motor of economic, social and cultural development in South Vietnam was the development of a commodity economy. The rice market stretched from Gia Dinh to Thuan Hoa. Quite a large stratum of merchants was formed. Along with this were many famous entrepots: Cu Lao Pho (Bien Hoa), Bai Xau (My Xuyen, Soc Trang), Ha Tien, My Tho town market and Saigon—a commercial hub 'unparalleled throughout the entire country' (*Gia Dinh Thanh Thong Chi*) (Nguyen Cong Binh 1990:23).[4]

Trinh Hoai Duc's report had been submitted to the monarch of the Nguyen Dynasty, who had been instrumental in the establishment of centralised control over southern Vietnam. Binh included this dynasty 'among those former regimes' which had:

> paid attention to exploiting the unique natural features of this new region, with policies towards it of benefit to the regime, while at the same time *further accentuating the particular socio-economic features of the region*, above all its characteristics of *an agricultural commodity economy* [emphases in the original] (Nguyen Cong Binh 1990:23).

Clearly Binh placed the existence of a commodity economy prior to the founding of the Nguyen Dynasty, whose economic contribution was therefore 'further accentuating' what he deemed to be a pre-existing trait of the region.

This entailed quite significant departures from prevailing notions on pre-colonial Vietnam. The first of these might be glossed as the accusation that the French conquest of Vietnam had been abetted by the impotence of the Nguyen Dynasty. That regime's 'feudal' ideology, formalism, adherence to 'outmoded traditions' and rejection of new ideas and practices had allegedly prevented a clear assessment of, and effective response to, the emergent threat of European expansion. The country had become feeble and vulnerable to conquest (Tran Van Giau 1993a). Arguably, the enervating effects of this court ideology implied strong and unified control over the country. Accusing the Nguyen Dynasty of sinking the country into stagnation entailed a possibly unintended compliment: that it possessed the capacity to do so.

Yet Binh substantially revised this view. Socio-economic traits such as the commodity economy had pre-dated, continued in tandem with, and outlasted the Nguyen regime. The commodity economy had been an independent 'motor of economic, social and cultural development' (Nguyen Cong Binh 1990:23). He dissented from views of it as a 'modern' imposition of French colonialism, much less an 'anti-modern' or 'enslaving' effect of US neo-colonialism. Placing the commodity economy's evolution in pre-colonial times, he was rather less complimentary about the Nguyen Court's relevance to pre-colonial Vietnam than some of its critics, for this important alternative locus of social development had continued to act dynamically throughout its reign.

Having argued for the differentiation of pre-colonial Vietnam's political and 'socio-economic' domains, Binh's second departure from historiographical orthodoxy was to question the pre-colonial unity of the country. The colonial entity Cochinchina had been superimposed over a pre-existing pre-colonial entity, which Binh referred to variously as '*Nam Bo*', 'the Six Provinces' (*Luc Tinh*) and '*Gia Dinh*'. This region's natural features were 'unique', it was newly settled and, in addition to its commodity economy, he noted it possessed a substantial stratum of merchants, several significant trading ports and linkages with international trade routes. These features distinguished the region from the rest of pre-colonial Vietnam.

Such a point was emphasised the following year in a collectively authored contribution to the *Social Sciences Review*, 'On social structure and social policy in *Nam Bo*':

> *Nam Bo*'s distinct social characteristics spring above all from its most important economic characteristic, that which drives its development: *in Nam Bo, a commodity economy emerged and developed early on* [emphasis in original]. Commodified agriculture, ocean ports, trade with foreign nations, such is the portrait of *Nam Bo* from its beginning (seventeenth to eighteenth century). Favourable natural conditions, a developed commodity economy and extensive international communications, attracted to the new region of *Nam Bo* many

communities of settlers, ethnic groups, religious shadings, cultural and civilizational currents. However, differences of settlement, ethnicity, religion, language and cultural activity did not increase but rather identities dissolved (*giai toa*), linked (*lien ket*) and merged (*tu hop lai*), to form the *Nam Bo* character (*cot cach*) (Nguyen Cong Binh et al. 1991:28).

Herein lay a distinct departure from the argument developed by Huynh Lua a decade earlier. Huynh Lua, using the same pre-colonial source, *Gia Dinh Thanh Thong Chi*, emphasised that no modifications to traditional Vietnamese values had occurred when Vietnamese settled in this new land, despite their living amidst the hustle and bustle of an international trading centre. The joint authors of the later work, by contrast, described this same settlement process as one of marked cultural flux. Settlers to the new land had come from diverse origins. Traditional values had changed and divisions had been effaced in the process, leading to the creation of a new and regionally distinctive character. Another departure from Huynh Lua and other Vietnamese historians of the pre-colonial Vietnamese southward migration, was these authors' emphasis on the pull factors motivating settlement: attraction to the favourable conditions of this commercial centre versus flight or expulsion from famine, poverty and warfare.

Nguyen Cong Binh's other major challenge to received wisdom on pre-colonial Vietnam was his assessment of the flexibility of the Nguyen Dynasty in recognising and exploiting socio-economic trends and regional specificity. This had not only been of benefit to the regime but had been conducive to 'further accentuating the particular socio-economic features of this region' (Nguyen Cong Binh 1990:23). He argued that the court had acted responsively to the societal differentiation and regional diversity of pre-colonial times in a way that had profited the entire country:

> The Nguyen Dynasty, while capitulating in the face of the country's economic decline, did endeavour to find a way out by opening up new land. At the same time as preserving the system of state-owned land and village communal lands, it allowed *private rice fields* to develop in the six southern provinces. While pursuing a 'closed-door policy', it still allowed the six provinces *extensive overseas trade*: 'Gia Dinh is the regular commercial hub for several countries' (*Gia Dinh Thanh Thong Chi*). The system of private ownership of rice fields, a division of labour in a variety of ecological regions and overseas trade allowed the Mekong delta to develop rapidly a commodity economy and soon become a rice granary for the whole country [emphases in original] (Nguyen Cong Binh 1990:24).

This was positive commentary indeed for a regime whose 'backwardness' and 'conservatism' had long been blamed (not only by communist critics) for the humiliating ease with which the French had been able to take possession of Vietnam. Moreover, albeit implicitly, a case was being made that the current regime had something to learn from the 'feudalists'.

The Nguyen Court had not been alone in tailoring policies of specific relevance to *Nam Bo*, a point made in an article written the following year. The authors claimed that flexibility towards the region of *Nam Bo* had been the hallmark of all previous regimes. Such policies had served both government and the region: the potential of the region was realised for the benefit of each regime and each regime's flexibility enhanced the region's distinctive character:

> *Nam Bo* is a piece of territory that cannot be detached from unified Vietnam, yet the region has distinctive economic, social and cultural features formed over history. All former regimes had policies for *Nam Bo* to rapidly exploit the potential of this new region, each of which, as a result, augmented *Nam Bo*'s distinctiveness (Nguyen Cong Binh et al. 1991:28).

The implication was that the present regime could only benefit by continuing this tradition of recognising and promoting the region's distinctiveness. Rather than see *Nam Bo*'s distinctive identity as an invidious colonial-era innovation to be eliminated, Binh et al. claimed it as an enduring quality that would best be maintained.

Nguyen Cong Binh and his fellow contributors were not merely contributing new knowledge about the pre-colonial period—filling in gaps or oversights in the historical record. Rather, they were attacking a very persuasive scheme through which history is made meaningful: that is the distinction between a 'modern' colonising power and a pre-colonial 'traditional' society. Innovations previously dated to the colonial era—regional divisions, commodity relations and a central state responsive to, and furthering, such complexity—emerged in an earlier era. Colonial 'modernity' was anticipated by indigenous 'tradition'. The role accorded to the French in this view was to preside over or actively perpetuate processes already in full swing before their arrival.

## SOUTHERN VIETNAMESE INDIVIDUALISM

In a similar way, Hoang Thieu Khang's contribution to the volume *South Vietnam in the Renovation Task*, suggested that the individual was not a 'modern' phenomenon introduced to Vietnam from the West. His contention was that the region of *Nam Bo* was home to a kind of individual personhood which had emerged in the distinctive historical conditions of the region (Hoang Thieu Khang 1990).[5]

According to Khang, the origins of southern Vietnamese individualism lay in the era of Vietnamese settlement of the 'uninhabited wastelands' of the *Nam Bo* plain.[6] The earliest settlers had formed small communities of mutual assistance to face the challenges of an untamed nature, full of wild animals and marauding bandits (Hoang Thieu Khang 1990:313). Many of the settlers had fled an oppressive feudal regime, among them Chinese refugees likewise fleeing the Qing takeover. Thus these early communities were marked by a relative freedom from political constraint found in other regions. Khang described a process of 'spontaneous group formation' (*ket hop tu phat*) that is, groups formed in response to pressing need and bound by a 'natural moral consciousness' rather than imposed 'feudal values'. Each member had participated in such groups as a 'free member' (*thanh vien tu do*). Later political consolidation began but even well into the administrative rationalisation of the Nguyen Dynasty, the spontaneous nature of group membership was still evident. Khang argued that these legacies of early settlement continued to be evident in contemporary social relations:

> The natural moral consciousness and degree of freedom characterising this personality structure [*co che nhan cach*] offers us insights into the content of today's Southern Vietnamese personhood, and the principles of group and individual formation (Hoang Thieu Khang 1990:313).

Another significant factor shaping a distinctively southern Vietnamese personality was the existence of commodity relations. Khang concurred with Nguyen Cong Binh's account of the region's pre-colonial economy:

> Rice and cereal cultivation in Southern Vietnam developed rapidly, especially in the eighteenth century, to the extent that rice went from being adequate for subsistence to a surplus and transformed into a commodity (Hoang Thieu Khang 1990:314).

Also important was the emergence of large and internationally significant export ports in the region:

> It was thus that a commodity economy powerfully burst forth in the eighteenth century. This ensured that the economic relations pertaining at that time in Southern Vietnam bore the universal mark of global history (Hoang Thieu Khang 1990:314).

According to Khang, these were factors profoundly shaping the emergence of southern Vietnamese individualism. The region's participation in economic developments of a global nature:

> was sufficient to provide a basis for a new kind of consciousness—the consciousness of 'I' (*toi*) in its initial stages—to be closely followed by a consciousness of 'I' based on the [colonial] capitalist relations which came later (Hoang Thieu Khang 1990:314).[7]

He argued that the land clearing policies of the Nguyen Dynasty after 1802 led to the emergence of sharp class divisions and a class of landlords for whom commodity values increased in importance. In the hands of large landlords, rice had become increasingly valued as a commodity along with all sorts of handicrafts. From this a significant class of merchants emerged who became an important social force—able to shape not only economic relations but the consciousness and lifestyle of the whole of society in the region (Hoang Thieu Khang 1990:315).

Finally and briefly, Hoang Thieu Khang registered the influence of Western capitalist notions of the individual on the shaping of southern Vietnamese personhood. Yet he was at pains to stress the unique trajectory of the formation of the southern Vietnamese 'I' through this latter period, recalling its origins in the 'free membership' of the spontaneous groupings of the early pioneers:

> From an innocent and essential quality, the Southern Vietnamese person entered into a commodity ideology and subsequently into a capitalist ideology . . . The Southern Vietnamese person first stepped into individualist consciousness in an innocent manner. And because of this step, such individuality retains its innocence and natural quality—certainly not the devious individualism of a retrograde kind of capitalism (Hoang Thieu Khang 1990:317).

In his portrait of southern Vietnamese individualism, Khang down-played the impact of the colonial and 'neo-colonial' periods. The commodity economy had contributed to the development of a form of possessive individualism—but this process had already commenced in pre-colonial times. The significance of a colonialist and capitalist individualist ideology was noted and yet its influence was mediated by an 'innocent' and 'natural' individualism surviving from the earliest days of Vietnamese settlement. For Khang, southern Vietnamese individuality was an indigenous category of personhood, yet one considerably removed from typical renditions of traditional Vietnamese personhood.

## *NAM BO* CULTURE

Ho Chi Minh City-based folklorist, Huynh Ngoc Trang, promoted the notion of southern Vietnam (*Nam Bo*) as a distinct entity as cogently as any other writer in the post-war era. His writings and films ranged over a remarkable variety of genres including folk tales, ritual theatre and music, *cai luong* opera and other quasi-secular performing arts, religious iconography, sculpture, pottery and folk Buddhism, not only of the main Vietnamese ethnic group, but of other minority groups found in the region. Many of these works bore out his conviction that the *Nam Bo* region of Vietnam comprised a distinctive cultural entity;

a view to be found in its most condensed and elegant form in his essay, 'An overview of *Nam Bo* culture' (Huynh Ngoc Trang 1992).

Huynh Ngoc Trang described the cultural distinctiveness of *Nam Bo* as an enduring property—his was not a snapshot of contemporary cultural developments but an abstraction, synthesising more than 300 years of Vietnamese settlement of the region. Yet it would be inappropriate to describe this durable quality as a 'cultural tradition', for one of the properties he claimed for this regional culture was its constant propensity to change. For Trang, the paradox of *Nam Bo* was that, there, nothing could be found in its original form; both autochthonous culture and diverse alien imports were subject to constant ferment, hybridisation and transmutation. It was in this absence of originality that the region's originality could be found. His account of these properties recalls the modernist imagery of fluidity and ceaseless dynamism in Marx's Communist Manifesto (Berman 1983). However, Trang was to find these qualities present in a supposedly pre-modern society.

According to Trang, the culture of the central Vietnamese provinces of Thuan-Quang had formed the basis of *Nam Bo* culture, since most early immigrants to *Nam Bo* were from this area (Huynh Ngoc Trang 1992:59). The southern region's link to the Vietnamese cultural heartland of the Red River delta was thus blurred from the start, influenced by an area which, until relatively recently, had been on the Vietnamese periphery—heavily marked by the Indianised culture of the Chams. What is more, due to the non-elite nature of the migrants, the cultural baggage they had brought with them was the folk culture of the central coast (Huynh Ngoc Trang 1992:59). Over time this heterodox cultural base had been overlaid by court attempts to disseminate orthodox Confucian culture in the *Nam Bo* region. Yet such efforts had been unsuccessful in eliminating the folk cultural basis which itself underwent changes due to local ecological and cultural factors (Huynh Ngoc Trang 1992:60).

The settlers adopted a strikingly different resident pattern from the classic nucleated settlements of the Red River delta, settling along the streams and canals of the southern plain in a scattered, strung-out fashion. Due to the sparseness of population, settlers were extremely hospitable towards all newcomers, regardless of ethnic background or social respectability, as they helped swell scarce labour resources. These factors combined to create a cultural climate of openness and diffidence towards tradition (Huynh Ngoc Trang 1992:62). The region also saw the early emergence of the major urban centre of Gia Dinh (now found within Ho Chi Minh City precincts) which was 'renowned for its beauty and orderly arrangements of streets' and as a major international commercial centre, where 'people from the four seas' brushed shoulders. In its time, Gia Dinh was a 'fascinating beacon' for a way of life unfamiliar to most Vietnamese: 'The customs of this urban area were seen as truly fashionable and they represented an entirely different order of luxury to the ancient refinements and the rural lifestyle' (Huynh Ngoc Trang 1992:63)

According to Huynh Ngoc Trang, a century prior to French colonisation the *Nam Bo* region already had a multi-racial character. *Nam Bo* was the confluence of many cultural currents and their hybridisation proceeded apace. Chief among these was the fusion of the Indianised central Vietnamese folk culture and cultural influences from southern China—a region whose emigrants had early established a substantial presence in *Nam Bo*. This new 'Sino–Vietnamese cultural complex' exercised a powerful hold over all inhabitants of the region—strongest in the urban upper class, but still evident in the remotest rural hamlet (Huynh Ngoc Trang 1992:65).

Trang noted that this pre-colonial mix had included many elements of French cultural influence dating from the eighteenth century. He conceded that colonisation of the region had sparked a range of anti-colonial cultural resistance movements—from the revolt of the scholars to the emergence of messianic religious movements in the lower classes (Huynh Ngoc Trang 1992:66). Yet his discussion focused on the tendency of the many 'modern folk religions' (*ton giao dan gian hien dai*) to be eclectic in their borrowing of symbolism, driven by a 'miscellaneous' (*da tap*) or '*baroque*' aesthetic. The regional tendency towards bricolage, according to Trang, was typified in the Cao Dai religion's 'complex of unprincipled mixture' (*phuc the lai tap vo nguyen tac*) (Huynh Ngoc Trang 1992:67). The field of secular culture was marked by a voracious appetite for French and Chinese novels and theatre, but again he found the eclecticist spirit of *Nam Bo* more evident in popular cultural forms such as the southern reformed opera: *cai luong* (Huynh Ngoc Trang 1992:69).

For Trang, *cai luong* typified *Nam Bo* culture in its absorption of diverse musical and theatrical genres, costume styles, plots drawn from all eras and all quarters of the globe, as well as its central characteristic of constant transformation. The significance of this genre for understanding the spirit of *Nam Bo* was underlined in (appropriately) mixed metaphors:

> *Cai luong*'s quality of acceptance on no fixed principles could possibly be viewed as mere mixture, yet from a different, more open and positive perspective, this characteristic signifies what is typical about *Nam Bo*—a crossroads with doors always open to waves from all the four corners of the earth from the time of its first settlement to today (Huynh Ngoc Trang 1992:69).

His most colourful examples of the eclecticism of *Nam Bo* culture— urban cosmopolitanism, southern Chinese cultural influence, Cao Daism and *cai luong*—were not viewed as legacies of colonial times.

**Ho Chi Minh City residents visit the Holy See of
the Cao Dai faith, in Tay Ninh**

Rather, he cited these as evidence of the region's essential qualities of dynamism and cultural ferment, in play since the beginning of Vietnamese settlement.

Accordingly, French colonialism was mere grist for the voracious mill of *Nam Bo* culture. The transformations wrought in those times merely perpetuated its propensity to change. The innovations brought to bear merely catered to its appetite for the new. Huynh Ngoc Trang concluded his essay by abstracting three of the essential qualities characterising this regional culture:

1. The *baroque* cultural character of this region [means that] nothing about it is unique. Rather it should be understood as an incorporation (*thau hoa*) of all kinds of things from all different regions gathered together here.
2. As this is a busy crossroads always encountering the new, there is

not one cultural pattern, artistic form, or cultural need or taste surviving in its original form over a specified time. Everything is in constant and rapid renewal (*doi moi*) creating new forms responding to the needs and tastes of each era . . .
3. The faddishness and exoticism in cultural tastes of the people of *Nam Bo* (Huynh Ngoc Trang 1992:69, 70).

Whereas works such as this elided the significance of many colonial-era developments by finding them anticipated in pre-colonial times, others did so by omitting reference to the colonial power as the engineer of transformations during the colonial period. For example, the collectively written work, *The Culture and Population of The Mekong Delta*, referred to the enormous project of canal digging in the late nineteenth and early twentieth century which had expanded the cultivable area of the Mekong delta fourfold (Nguyen Cong Binh et al. 1990:27). The authors argued that this had led to an unprecedented level of rice exports in the early 1920s: a level which had not been attained since. Conventionally these achievements have been attributed to the French colonial project of expanding export agriculture. Yet the above-cited work made no mention of them as such. Rather by omission, these initiatives were Vietnamised, or, more precisely, indigenised as part of the distinctively dynamic history of the Mekong delta.

This approach radically disputed the tradition–modernity schema, according to which the French colonisation of Vietnam was held to have constituted a break with the past. For these authors, southern Vietnam's pre-colonial society anticipated many of the features typifying 'modernity'. Such attributes obtained in this particular part of the world up to 200 years prior to French colonisation.

These perspectives bring to mind reassessments of the states of Southeast Asia in the period preceding European colonialism as not stagnant and reactive but marked by diverse experiments with 'modernity' (Reid 1997). However, one also detects in these works, which are ostensibly about the past, the naturalisation of contemporary social relations. By downplaying the colonial legacy in Vietnam, the modernising programs of the contemporary regime could find their justification uniquely in terms of indigenous tradition (Hobsbawm and Ranger 1983). Yet as a term more commonly associated with stasis, timelessness, moral certitude and 'the way things have always been', 'tradition' is perhaps not the best concept to capture this ideological process. After all, the past being inventively alluded to was one commonly associated with 'modernity': of dynamism, commodity relations, individuation, urbanisation, restless hybridisation and the transformation of cultural forms. As such, Marshall Sahlins' evocative phrase the 'indigenisation of modernity' might be preferred as a more accurate description of this process (Sahlins 1993:21).

Sahlins' own approach promises a welcome movement away from the assumption that 'Western modernity' is relentlessly superseding 'indigenous' traditions. However, he appears to view indigeneity as a permanent condition, capable not only of robustly surviving 'modernisation', but of channelling modernity's most disruptive incursions into the reproduction of indigenous forms. By celebrating indigenous durability, in a globalising world, he thus maintains an essentialist notion of cultural differences. His defence of the concept of culture against post-structuralists and post-modernists of all hues is perhaps insufficiently mindful that tradition and indeed modernity are contested, discursive concepts. Sahlins' spirited defence of the flagging academic discipline of anthropology lacks sensitivity to the dilemmas of identity as framed by those who remain within its lens of objectification as 'modernity's' others, and it shores up the discipline's monopolisation of the authority to name what is traditional or modern. Another approach would be to recognise that people everywhere invest these terms with significations appropriate to their contemporary concerns. This, I believe, is exactly what was being done in the writings of Vietnamese social scientists of the early *doi moi* era. They were engaged in the discursive project of indigenising modernity: filling the concept of indigenous identity with a content previously only ever attributed to the 'modern' colonial or post-colonial eras.

According to these authors, the diverse markers of modernity mentioned in their works had been around in Vietnam as long as they had in the 'West'. Some authors such as Hoang Thieu Khang (1990), who stated that the commodification of social relations in *Nam Bo* in the eighteenth century 'bore the universal mark of global history', appeared to link this to the global emergence and expansion of capitalism. Yet although the date of Vietnamese settlement in *Nam Bo* (and hence, the commencement of Vietnamese modernity) did roughly coincide with an upsurge in the intensification of global capitalist relations, Hoang Thieu Khang did not propound this as the impetus for societal transformation. There was something inherent to the region that made it, and not other regions of Vietnam, able to respond. The region's propensity to dynamism was held to be a pre-existing condition.[8] Indeed, by some accounts, the 'modernity' of the region manifested itself long before the dates that a Habermas (1987) or a Giddens (1990) might give for its emergence in Europe, let alone its expansion to other parts of the globe.

## THE ARCHAEOLOGY OF *NAM BO* MODERNITY

Le Xuan Diem, an archaeologist based in Ho Chi Minh City, argued that the cultural legacies of the ancient peoples who preceded Vietnamese settlers in southern Vietnam had a bearing on contemporary social relations in the region. In his contribution to the volume *South Vietnam and the Enterprise of Renovation*, Diem wrote that 3000 to 4000 years ago, two ancient peoples emerged more or less simultaneously: the Sa Huynh people (*nguoi Sa Huynh*), in central Vietnam's coastal plain and the Dong Nai people (*nguoi Dong Nai*) 'in the *Nam Bo* plain' (Le Xuan Diem 1990:298). The geographical extension Diem attributed to the Dong Nai people was identical to the *Nam Bo* of the 'modern historians'. However, many of the distinctive traits of *Nam Bo*, identified by Diem's colleagues as qualities dating back to the seventeenth and eighteenth centuries, were, according to him, anticipated by about two millennia with the emergence of the country of Phu Nam (Fu-nan) in the southern plain.

According to Diem, the Indonesian (*Anhdonedieng*) people who settled the *Nam Bo* plain 3000 to 4000 years ago led a fairly humble existence for almost two millennia, their agricultural and trade activities eclipsed by the East–West struggle between the civilisations of China and India for cultural predominance in the region (Le Xuan Diem 1990:298). Yet their ocean-going traditions saw the Dong Nai people become active participants in significant pre-Christian-era global exchanges:

> In the *Nam Bo* plain, the people of Dong Nai conquered the Mekong delta, built a life on the swamplands and opened up economic activity—trading with the rapidly-developing trans-oceanic business routes of their day. The Mekong plain rapidly became a central commercial destination with many important international ports: Nam Chua, Canh Den, Can Gio, Oc Eo (Le Xuan Diem 1990:300).

In other words, this region's ancient integration into the global economy anticipated the supposedly radical rupture posed by French colonisation by more than two millennia.

The culmination of the Dong Nai people's development of their economy and opening up of trade links was to come with the emergence of the Mekong delta 'civilisation' of Oc Eo and country of Phu Nam, about whose global significance, Diem waxed hyperbolic:

> The world-famous Oc Eo civilization (*van minh Oc Eo*) was born and expanded in those lively historical events. At the same time, they were the clear proof that the ancient people of Dong Nai were familiar with 'renovation' (*doi moi*) in accordance with their times. They simultaneously continued to exploit the agricultural potential of the highlands, began flooded agricultural activities, quickly exerted themselves to create new potentials, oriented themselves to the sea and were active in trade, building the fortunes of the country of Phu Nam with its economic, political and cultural influence throughout the Southeast oceans in the early Christian era (Le Xuan Diem 1990:300).

The diversification and innovation evident here recalls Nguyen Cong Binh's (1990) account of the complexity and dynamism of *Nam Bo* in the concluding centuries of the pre-colonial era. Dong Nai people's 'renovation in accordance with their times', also recalls Huynh Ngoc Trang's notion of *Nam Bo* as a crossroads, where 'everything is in constant and rapid renewal, creating new forms responding to the needs and taste of each era' (Huynh Ngoc Trang 1992:69). These regional characteristics were backdated by Le Xuan Diem almost two millennia: 'Here, in the past, existed a region of the most lively assemblage of historical cultures and peoples' (Le Xuan Diem 1990:298).

Referring to Oc Eo as the most ancient of the cultures of *Nam Bo*, Hoang Thieu Khang, in his contribution to *South Vietnam and the Enterprise of Renovation*, reiterated this point (Hoang Thieu Khang 1990:310). He argued that the archaeological vestiges of Oc Eo culture (*van hoa Oc Eo*) show it to have been a melting pot of many currents of religious thought: both 'Aryan' and 'Dravidian' streams of 'Hinduism', lesser vehicle Buddhism with strong Brahmanic influence, 'Sanskrit Buddhism' as well as 'orthodox Buddhism'. Their complex hybridisation in Oc Eo times was characteristic of:

> the ancient *Nam Bo* people's logic of biochemical (*noi sinh hoa*) combination of thoughts of foreign origin, *a logic of assemblage (hoa hop) and integration (hoa nhap)*, enabling their coexistence [emphases in original] (Hoang Thieu Khang 1990:310).

This quality, according to Hoang Thieu Khang, was of more than historic significance for 'the imprint of such thought and such a style is clearly evident today' (Hoang Thieu Khang 1990:310). He argued that the influence of the ancient culture of Oc Eo still manifests itself: 'in the thought, the outlook on life and the style of thinking . . . (in short), in the modern spiritual life of the people of *Nam Bo*' (Hoang Thieu Khang 1990:311).

In a similar vein, Le Xuan Diem argued that the socio-economic characteristics of the ancient cultures of South Vietnam 'made them important foundations for the socio-economic and cultural developments of the succeeding [Vietnamese] era' (Le Xuan Diem 1990:299). Or in other words, 'their progeny are still in full evidence' (Le Xuan Diem 1990:304). Vietnamese settlers' debt to the ancient peoples of *Nam Bo* could be seen in two ways. First:

> . . . the Vietnamese of *Nam Bo*, terminal point of Vietnam, assimilated the experience of millennia of generations of Vietnamese in opening up the land in the south *with that of the local communities here since long ago* [emphasis in original] (Le Xuan Diem 1990:303).

Second, the complex and dynamic society created by the Vietnamese reverberated with the experience of Phu Nam:

Here, [the Vietnamese] quickly transformed the Mekong plain into a multi-formed agricultural area, linked with trade activity beyond the region. This agriculture was marked by the synchronous development of wet rice, orchards, forestry, fisheries in conditions of a rich, multi-formed natural environment. *Here we can see it is as if the experience of Phu Nam was re-established* . . . [emphasis in original] (Le Xuan Diem 1990:303).

Le Xuan Diem did not elaborate on the factors of continuity linking the achievements of previous peoples settling the *Nam Bo* region ('Dong Nai', Cham, Cambodian) to those of their successors, the Vietnamese. Indeed, his few allusive references to this continuity were already quite surprising, the prevailing line on Mekong delta settlement history being that the first Vietnamese settlers had arrived in a region (including contemporary Ho Chi Minh City) described as deserted (*hoang phe*) and wild (*hoang vu*).[9] Such a history-writing convention minimised the presence of Khmers (and others) in the *Nam Bo* region and fell silent on the Nguyen Lords' political and military actions that had neutralised the Khmer state's control over the lower Mekong delta.[10] In contemporary party histories references to the 'southward advance' (*nam tien*) conventionally depicted the Vietnamese arriving as pioneers in a deserted land, turning their millennial tradition of struggle to profit against nature—a happy framing of an encounter that both lent moral legitimacy to their presence and reinvested with relevance the tradition that made settlement of the region possible. Beyond denying Cambodian claims to the region, the view of Vietnamese as heroic instigators of settlement in a deserted land also served the cause of national unity. To be any more explicit than Le Xuan Diem or Hoang Thieu Khang already were about continuities with an ancient pre-Vietnamese entity of *Nam Bo* would be an unwanted invitation for other interested parties to advance arguments for regional autonomy or annexation.[11]

While toeing the official line that the land was deserted, Le Xuan Diem turned an archaeologist's perspective to it in a manner that greatly extended and enlivened the notion of *Nam Bo*'s indigenous dynamism. The rupture between an ancient *Nam Bo* civilisation and Vietnamese settlement, proposed in the trope of reversion to deserted land, allowed those with an eye to the *longue durée* to suggest that the sequential rise and fall of civilisations in the region was evidence of its inexorable and profound dynamism. Diem saw such a quality to be a property of the Dong Nai people's Oc Eo civilisation, as well as of the much later Vietnamese settlement. Yet in contrast with these 'micro'-dynamisms, by incorporating both civilisations into a *longue durée* perspective he advanced the case for a 'macro'-historical dynamism. This was a view investing dynamic agency in the region itself:

South Vietnam with its numerous stages of historical cultures described
here is a region with a truly lively social life, seen in few other areas,
a region of 'open' space (*khong gian 'mo'*), a major human-cultural
meeting point, with a continuously 'renovating' (*'doi moi'*) and
creative history [quotation marks in original] (Le Xuan Diem
1990:304).[12]

Not only was such ferment found in each of *Nam Bo*'s historical
cultures, but it was evident in the sequential progression of civilisations
through this region as well. This was a creative use of the reversion-
to-wilderness thesis, for asserting a hiatus between civilisations allowed
presentation of a more dramatic *longue durée* account of rising and
falling civilisations than if a thesis of cultural continuity were maintained.

The collectively authored work of the Institute of Social Sciences,
*Culture and Population of the Mekong Delta* (Nguyen Cong Binh
et al. 1990), ran a very similar, book-length argument to Diem's
article.[13] While more than half of the book was devoted to contemporary
Mekong delta society, this was situated within a *longue durée* perspective. Indeed the work represented something of a vehicle for
archaeologists. In it, the accomplishments of Diem's 'Dong Nai people'
were treated as the more coherent 'Dong Nai culture' (*van hoa Dong
Nai*) and its inception was pushed back at least another millennium, to
5000 BP. Furthermore, the Oc Eo period was treated more respectably
as a discrete culture (*van hoa Oc Eo*) rather than as the mere crescendo
of the Dong Nai people's activities. Hence, when the patterns of the
*longue durée* were evoked, it could be done with greater scope and
through greater detail than could Diem alone, who was always struggling to evoke the historically sublime with only two case studies.

The central theme of the book was a familiar one: to describe the
distinctive dynamism of the *Nam Bo*[14] way of life:

That is a life, neither closed nor secretive, neither autarchic nor
self-sufficient; a way of life always integrating the new, always
assimilating with different communities, both far and near (Nguyen
Cong Binh et al. 1990:426).

The region was inherently dynamic in that it was constantly assimilating the new and undergoing transformation. This property was evoked
in three major senses. First, it had been evident since ancient times:

The Mekong delta clearly is an ancient, diverse and vital (*song dong*)
cultural area. In this place many Eastern and Western values have
co-existed, and many human communities and peoples have lived
alongside each other. Also this place is home to many different ancient
traditions, which have continued to be cultivated and 'renovated' (*cach
tan*) in today's modern life; with many purebred (*thuan chung*) peoples

mingled (*hon chung*) into one place and integrated into each other (*hoa nhap vao nhau*) (Nguyen Cong Binh et al. 1990:423).

The second approach was developmentalist. The distinctive character of the region had been emerging in a relentless manner over several millennia:

> The diverse and unique socio-cultural space in the Mekong delta has gradually formed in the course of many thousands of years of history. This is linked to major environmental changes in the delta, changes in the ethnic population and activities which have widened economic and cultural communicative relations over many distinct historical eras (Nguyen Cong Binh et al. 1990:423).

Third was the sense of dynamism, evoked by Le Xuan Diem, of a vital progression of cultures through the region. Such a view drew strength from its analytical separation of Dong Nai and Oc Eo cultures as well as retaining the view of 'an interval of time and of cultural and historical rupture' between 'Oc Eo Culture' and the 'Gia Dinh Culture of the *Nam Bo* Vietnamese':

> Closely following the course of history, we can easily see this plain is one of the most vital (*soi dong*) regions. Wave after wave of people have come to settle and earn a living. Layer upon layer of cultures overlap and mix (*hoa tron*) with each other. Amongst these, the three most important cultures are: 1. *Dong Nai* culture of the Indonesians, 2. Oc Eo culture of the *Phu Nam* Indonesians and Thien Truc people of ancient India, 3. Vietnamese culture in Gia Dinh of the *Nam Bo* Vietnamese and Khmer, Hoa, Cham, Ma ethnic groups in *Nam Bo* (Nguyen Cong Binh et al. 1990:425).

*The Mekong Delta: Its Location and Potential* (Tran Hoang Kim et al. 1991) also lent a millennial cast to the distinctive character of this region. It was published as a bilingual edition aimed at inducting foreign investors into appreciation of the region's unique properties. While the poorly-translated English version thus represented an influential document in its own right, I have retranslated the Vietnamese original to recapture its more coherent and nuanced voice.

The bulk of this book was devoted to detailed description and copious statistical data on the agricultural, aquacultural and industrial potential of the various Mekong delta provinces, clearly laid out for the benefit of potential foreign investors and traders. This was introduced with an essay detailing the region's outstanding performance in responding to the liberalisation of the late 1980s. It concluded in a manner seemingly pitched at reassuring foreign investors that they would be understood and well received if they chose to do business here. It noted that:

**Passenger boat terminus in the Mekong delta river port of Long Xuyen**

> [t]he Mekong delta early developed as a region of commodity trade and international relations. Once, traders from India, China and European countries frequently stopped here to purchase agricultural products, rice, sugar, handicraft items such as silk and art products made from gold, silver and tortoise shell (Tran Hoang Kim et al. 1991:26).

Contemporary investors have found that:

> . . . the inhabitants of the Mekong delta have received them in the broad-minded manner of *Anh Hai Nam Bo* (*Nam Bo* eldest brother) following the Vietnamese tradition 'four oceans are the same house' (Tran Hoang Kim et al. 1991:29).

In this manner of life, the people of the delta were implicitly contrasted with those of other regions of Vietnam:

> Although living in an agricultural area, with small production still widespread, life is not bound to the mould, closed-in, secretive nor self-sufficient. An open-hearted way of life is a clear characteristic of the inhabitants of the Mekong delta (Tran Hoang Kim et al. 1991:35).

The authors presented this quality as an inherent characteristic of the people of this region. Fortunately for the inhabitants of the delta, at the outset of the 1990s, history was finally moving in a direction that would allow them full self-expression:

In this epoch, when economic, cultural and social activities are breaking down the barriers between people, when borders between nations are now only geographical divisions, the soul (*tam hon*) and manner (*phong cach*) of the inhabitants of the Mekong delta will easily allow them to assimilate (*hoa nhap*) to the rhythm of the age (*nhip song thoi dai*) (Tran Hoang Kim et al. 1991:36).

The era of globalisation was evoked to show history moving in a way that would allow the full realisation of the region's identity. If the people of the Mekong delta were able to fall easily into stride with contemporary global developments, it was because their own local history was of such a dynamic character. By way of demonstration, the authors focused on the era of Vietnamese settlement of the delta, agreeing with authors such as Huynh Ngoc Trang (1992) and Nguyen Cong Binh et al. (1991) that here, cultural legacies from elsewhere had undergone dynamic transformation:

> Since long ago, the people coming to exploit this waste region have brought with them cultural characteristics from every region of the country. Through many generations, the inhabitants of the Mekong delta have maintained the national essence, simultaneously renewing (*doi moi*) and developing it to construct a separate, original cultural history of their own (Tran Hoang Kim et al. 1991:35).

The authors found strongest proof of the region's ability to adapt to a new 'epoch' such as the present one in its millennial history of successive cultures:

> If we follow the course of history, we find this place has seen three consecutive cultures: *Dong Nai* culture, *Oc Eo* culture and *Gia Dinh* culture. The transition of these cultures proves that the inhabitants of the Mekong delta by birth carry in their blood a sensitivity to the times and they can always find the quickest way to adapt their way of life to new situations (Tran Hoang Kim et al. 1991:35).

The sensitivity to the new or 'exoticism' which Huynh Ngoc Trang (1992) described as a cultural constant of seventeenth- to twentieth-century *Nam Bo* culture was here given an ancient cast. The present authors found in the region's history the relevance of distinctive biological factors. Innate or transcendental attributes of 'birth' and 'blood' supposedly enabled the inhabitants of the Mekong delta to invariably adapt to new situations.

## MODERN BY NATURE

Arguments which proposed that the alleged dynamism of the *Nam Bo* region was ancient essentialised the region's character in a manner that emerged explicitly in Tran Hoang Kim et al.'s account. If in this work recourse was made to the qualities of regional 'soul' and 'blood', others were to see geographical or environmental factors as more significant in promoting such continuity. This was as true of those authors who dealt with the Vietnamese colonisation of *Nam Bo* as those who dealt with earlier periods.

In his treatment of the regional history of the Mekong delta, Nguyen Khac Vien placed much emphasis on its unique ecology in shaping local forms. In his account, society in the delta bore the imprints of nature more deeply than in other parts of the country. In the southern delta, social solidarity sprang from nature rather than tradition. He sketched an image of the region's typical settlement pattern:

> The houses, instead of pressing close to one another inside a bamboo hedge, [a classic reference to the Red River delta in northern Vietnam] were now scattered along waterways and facing them. A number of houses were built on stilts. Each family had a boat for transportation and fishing. The roads and lanes, practicable only in the dry season were at many places connected by shaky 'monkey bridges', made of a single coconut palm or bamboo trunk (Nguyen Khac Vien 1983:342).

In this environment, the pressing constraint upon its inhabitants was not society, but nature. As a result, social similarities with the northern delta could be deceptive:

> The villages were bound by very strong solidarity which sprang not from strongly established institutions as in the north but rather from the pioneers' joint efforts in the face of common dangers (Nguyen Khac Vien 1983:343).

Nature left its marks too in the cosmology of Mekong delta peasants, accounting for the proliferation of apocalyptic sects, animism, 'fetishistic practices' and less attention to orthodox creeds such as Confucianism, Buddhism and the cult of the ancestors. The reason for this was that:

> the hold of the (feudal) system here was not as strong as in the north and the centre, the inhabitants having always the possibility of leaving the village to reclaim land elsewhere (Nguyen Khac Vien 1983:345).

As a result of these ecological factors:

> liberation from Confucian shackles opened the door to many a creed and superstition . . . Facing a redoubtable nature, deprived of the support of strongly-structured village communities, the pioneer with all his courage needed the comfort offered by various religions and creeds (Nguyen Khac Vien 1983:346).

The unique basis of the formation of social solidarity in the Mekong delta—the challenge posed by a perilous, untamed natural environment—was cited by many authors. This approach rested on a conception of the region of *Nam Bo* as a wilderness prior to Vietnamese settlement. The social solidarity that had emerged from this, as authors from Son Nam (1992) to Hoang Thieu Khang (1990) argued, was characterised by the emergence of a distinctly individualist mentality. Thus, as Khang noted, the early pioneers' mutual reliance in the face of an overwhelming nature resulted in 'spontaneous' communities predicated on free membership. Contemporary southern Vietnamese individualism derived from this pioneer-era valuation of individual autonomy.

Nguyen Khac Vien also noted that the ready availability of land in the context of a still redoubtable nature resulted in the spread of religious heterodoxy. Others carried this ecological argument further, whereby southern religious innovation was attributed to the imprint on settlement of *Nam Bo*'s unique hydrography. Ho Chi Minh City historian, Tran Van Giau, also commented on the way houses in the northern delta were 'tightly clustered in villages surrounded by bamboo hedges, while dwellings in the south[ern delta] were scattered along the Mekong river's tributaries' (Hiebert 1994:18). In an interview with *Far Eastern Economic Review* journalist, Murray Hiebert, he argued that this had been influential in shaping the different dispositions of peasants in the two regions: 'In the north, the bamboo hedge determines the village . . . It keeps villagers in and outsiders out. If you have no fence you have no limitations' (Hiebert 1994:18).

Tran Van Giau argued that this explained the different receptivity to the message of the early Catholic missionaries arriving in Vietnam in pre-colonial times. According to Hiebert:

> Giau says southern peasants are more susceptible to outside influences because they do not have fences. For example, early French missionaries were more successful in finding Roman Catholic converts in the south than in the north. In the north, their first converts were traders and fishermen who lived outside traditional, fenced-in Confucian villages (Hiebert 1994:18).[15]

Likewise, Huynh Ngoc Trang found *Nam Bo* culture's fascination with the new, and restless hybridisation of forms, to be best exemplified in the furious eclecticism of the Cao Dai religion. The aesthetic of 'unprincipled mixture' which he claimed Cao Daism embodied, derived from *Nam Bo*'s geographical remoteness from the orthodoxy of the centre as well as the open structure of southern villages. Such geographical and ecological factors accounted for the catholicity and mutability of Cao Daism and other syncretic folk creeds as well as quasi-secular artistic forms such as *cai luong*. Indeed, for Trang, the hydrography of *Nam Bo* provided an inexhaustible fund of metaphor for his account of its general cultural traits. *Nam Bo* represented a 'cultural confluence' into which 'streams' of influences 'from the four seas flow', 'mingle' and 'mix'. His *Nam Bo* culture had properties of 'absorption' yet nothing about it was 'stable' or 'fixed'.

The oft-mentioned abundance of cultural inputs into the southern scene was accompanied by common reference to the relative material abundance of the southern plain. The region was conventionally described as well-endowed with fertile soil, abundant rainfall, plentiful watercourses (needing fewer flood control measures than in the rest of Vietnam) and moderate seasonal temperature variations. These natural endowments meant the inhabitants of *Nam Bo* were less often pushed to the limits of survival as was deemed to be frequently the case in the central and northern parts of the country. While a 'dangerous' or 'redoubtable' nature was seen to have posed a challenge to the survival of the early pioneers (Nguyen Khac Vien 1983, Son Nam 1992, Hoang Thieu Khang 1990), the natural abundance of the delta also created a disposition towards openness, immediate gratification of desires, lack of concern for the morrow and the abandonment of traditional practices geared towards survival still evident in Vietnam's ecologically harsher central and northern regions.

Natural and geographical factors operating in this region over the *longue durée* were also invoked to explain the openness and innovativeness of its inhabitants. The historian Tran Quoc Vuong argued that the Cham and Khmer civilisations that pre-dated the Vietnamese in this region were oriented to the sea. This made them open to external influences such as Indian culture. In contrast, 'Hanoi had no seaport; it was the capital of the peasantry'. He argued that in the course of their long southward migration, Vietnamese migrants left behind much of their Confucian inheritance, dating from China's earlier colonisation of Vietnam. Arriving in the southern region, the Vietnamese became influenced by the Cham and Khmer world view. 'The Cham and Khmer were open to the sea, so the new arrivals became more open-minded' (Hiebert 1994:9). While this explained the relatively liberal outlook of southern Vietnamese, those remaining in the North remained bound by tradition. According to Tran Quoc Vuong, 'in the north, people always have one eye looking back [to the historical legacy of China]' (Hiebert 1994:9).

On the operation of ecological factors over the *longue durée*, it might be appropriate to conclude with Nguyen Cong Binh's (1990) account of pre-colonial Vietnamese society in the region of *Nam Bo*. According to him, the region's propensity to dynamism was a long-standing property in effect since the Oc Eo era. Indeed he viewed the rise and fall of 'Oc Eo culture' as illustrative of a vitality which ultimately inhered in the ecology of the region:

> This is a region both ancient and modern, a region of very diverse ecological forms in constant change. Rapid change over time, diversity

in space governs production and human life. In ancient times, Oc Eo culture once developed to great splendor, then withered right away, returning to a natural wilderness. The first Vietnamese settlers coming to Dong Nai-Gia Dinh also experienced dizziness at the prospect of this new and strange place (Nguyen Cong Binh 1990:22).

Undergirding the presence of humans in this region, whose transitory civilisations had risen and vanished, lay a nature whose constant property was dynamism—a nature perpetually at war with itself. The natural conditions of *Nam Bo*:

> demanded that human society recognize and master the extremely great hardships brought on by nature: disputes between the river and the sea, conflicts between the rainy season and the dry season, downpours and droughts, the contradiction between plenty and paucity, differences between fresh-water silt, saline earth and acidic soil (Nguyen Cong Binh 1990:22).

As the indigenous dynamic propensities of *Nam Bo* assumed millennial proportions and obtained permanent, ontological grounding in 'nature', the belittlement of the relevance of colonial modernity was complete. In the process of indigenising the conventional markers of 'modernity'—global commodity relations, individualism and ceaseless revolutionising—European colonial pretensions to have introduced modernity were dismissed and the societal transformations wrought by the French in Cochinchina discursively appropriated. Yet however complete this assault on the prestige of the colonial project may seem, the quarrel was never with the former colonial power nor its historian apologists.

The distinctiveness of *Nam Bo*, echoing throughout these works was explicitly contrasted with the rest of the country. The southern region's permanent ontological modernity was set against the equally inherent orientation of other parts of the country to closure, autarchy and stasis. Rejecting the view of southern dynamism as a recent occurrence or a colonial innovation indeed downplayed differences between indigenous 'tradition' and contemporary 'modernity'. Yet the full force of that temporal distinction re-emerged in a geographical distinction seen to hold supra historical relevance between a timelessly modern *Nam Bo* and the timelessly 'traditional' remainder of the country.[16] If colonial or post-colonial contributions to 'modernising' Cochinchina were obscured in assertions of the indigenous or 'natural' modernity of *Nam Bo*, it was arguably due to the high value placed on such contributions. On the other hand, the assumptions of post-war reformists, whose attempt to abolish the southern region's distinct legacies had been unsuccessful, could be considered little more than prejudices brought from less dynamic parts of the country.

These ideas about Vietnam's southern plain flourished in the late 1980s and very early 1990s, at a time when the powerhouse of Ho Chi Minh City was breaking out of the fetters that had bound it, leaving the rest of the country far behind. It occurred in a brief interval of time, when it looked as if the liberal reforms might both pay dividends and allow the party to preserve its monopoly of power, that is, before the contradictions between political monopoly and economic opening became clearly manifest. The early success of reforms in southern Vietnam shone a harsh light on the inadequacy of depictions of the South as either land of degraded tradition or pawn of foreign powers. Casting *Nam Bo* as a place of essential modernity represented a happy stroke: an explanation of the region's breakaway success and a defence of its integrity in so doing. It may appear ironic that this regionalist discourse was substantially penned by members of a party usually associated with the defence of national unity. Included among contributors were the self-same cadres who had been originally posted to the South to administer its capitalist legacies out of existence. However, as substantial beneficiaries of the reforms—as power holders located in the country's most promising economic frontier—their celebration of the region's openness, commerce and qualities of transformation was perhaps not hard to understand. Herein lay a clue as to why these particular images of *Nam Bo* tailed off as the decade progressed, indeed just as parts of southern Vietnam were becoming truer than ever to the *Nam Bo* stereotype: subject to increasing commodity relations, urbanisation, individualism, external commerce and cultural hybridisation. The invigorating images of a region, open to the world, effortlessly able to change and to absorb repeated shocks of the new, proved inconsistent with the authoritarian goals of the regime and indeed were unpalatable to many southerners less favourably placed to benefit from the reforms. Different images of southern Vietnam soon emerged, casting it as a threatened, or alternatively, threatening place.

# 4

## Reinventing modernity as threat

Despite significant transformations in the regime's orientation in the mid-1980s, the central government's ambivalence about Ho Chi Minh City, the city which had formerly served as the enemy's capital, persisted into the reform period. Indeed, as contradictions between economic and political objectives emerged in the early 1990s, praise for the city's outstanding level of engagement with the wider world began to be displaced by warnings and expressions of anxiety about the possibilities for subversion that this brought. While southern Vietnam and southern cadres had been credited with the nation's liberal reforms, they were also to attract continuing criticism as points of national vulnerability. As the 1990s unfurled, the regime's increasingly chilly outlook on the city's international connections reminded any who fostered hopes for political liberalisation that the integrity of the party's monopoly on power remained the regime's foremost goal. Over the first half of the 1990s, many Ho Chi Minh City intellectuals were also to question the impact of the economic reforms on what they construed as Vietnam's 'traditional' culture. While the urban context in which they worked was clearly informed by the logic of the market, their disposition towards liberalisation differed from those enthusiasts who, in the late 1980s and early 1990s, had normalised commercial relations as inherent to the southern region. The converging neo-conservatism of the Hanoi-based leadership and of southern urbanites was one indicator of progress made towards national integration in the post-war years. This response was also an example of ideologies of essentialist identity which were to become widespread in a decade which saw a concerted push towards global free trade, an uptake in transnational exchanges and the expansion of new communications technologies such as faxes, satellite broadcasting and the Internet. However, there were also important differences between the views of these city residents and the increasingly besieged view of the regime. The former group's reconstitution of their home city as a repository of threatened tradition included a critical assessment of the effects of the regime's own policies in this region. Southern urbanites' espousal of their identity as 'traditional', and threatened, was a reaction to those who were to unleash changes on southern Vietnam in the name of 'modernity'.

## AN ENEMY WITHIN

When the *doi moi* reforms were announced in 1986, attention was so riveted on what were described as historic shifts away from the regime's commandist mindset[1] that the continuation of the imposition of socialist structures in South Vietnam was momentarily overshadowed. This was a project in the throes of a crisis, which only deepened as the better-known 'reforms' kicked in. Well into the 1980s the South remained an intractable subject of socialist reform and continued to attract criticism for lifestyles, 'alien' cultural products and ideas considered detrimental to the consolidation of central power. Perhaps the most unexpected problem was the adverse effect this was having on the representatives of the new regime. Nowhere was this problem more evident than in the former economic hub of French Indochina and former capital of the Republican enemy, Ho Chi Minh City.

For several years after unification, official media outlets carried reports of lingering 'vestiges of neo-colonialism' (*tan du cua thuc dan moi*) in the city. One irate columnist, writing more than a year after liberation, complained of young people who continued to gather together and play music of the pre-liberation era, often employing ruses to hide the nature of the music:

> Whoever has business or returns from work late can see youths gathered together in many places, especially in narrow lanes. At first these groups sing a few songs with the new content in order to camouflage things. When there is a moment of quiet, the faint sounds of 'heart' songs—sick, sentimental, bourgeois songs of the old period sound forth (*Saigon Giai Phong* 5 August 1976a:4).

The author concluded by asking, 'Shouldn't disguised "artists", who act foolishly and disturb people, be pacified immediately?' The survival of such 'vestiges' was considered to present a serious risk: that the 'old way of life' might infect the cadres of the new administration. The ideological confusion or, worse, corruption of this sector of society posed the most serious threat to the project of unifying socialism. Indulgence by cadres in the goods, lifestyles and cultural items left behind by the old regime (circulating illegally in Ho Chi Minh City markets) undermined the distinction the regime sought to maintain between the 'old' and 'new' style of administration and to claim the latter's higher level of morality and responsibility. Cadres' corruption, which reduced their resolve to stamp out illicit distribution networks, would expose the whole of society to ongoing harm. Their 'contamination' by 'neo-colonialism' threatened the efficacy and the legitimacy of the national unifying project:

> Neo-colonial 'culture' died almost three years ago but its stench (*mui hoi thoi*) and baneful germs (*vi trung doc hai*) still spreads disease (*gay benh*) among quite a few compatriots and has caused a number of party and state cadres to be poisoned (*bi nhiem doc*) (Ha Xuan Truong 1978:66).

In a letter to the editor of the national newspaper *Dai Doan Ket*, in April 1977, a reader, identifying himself as 'a cadre living on Vo Van Tan Street', complained about his neighbours in downtown Ho Chi Minh City:

> A cadre husband and wife living near my home have a 'fashion' of living which is worthy of censure. Nearly all night and day, from their home, sounds the despicable music left behind by the enemy. From tape deck to cassette, Khanh Ly to Thai Thanh, oh honey, oh sweetheart, love, purple colour, bewitched, etc., in unbroken and lulling voices, this addiction and sickness is intolerable to many and makes me throw up (*Dai Doan Ket* 1977:6).

A columnist for *Saigon Giai Phong* also wrote of high-ranking cadres in Ho Chi Minh City passing off their passion for forbidden pre-1975 'yellow' music as 'research'. He reports a conversation with a cadre whom he was surprised to find listening to such music:

> 'From whom did you borrow these tapes?'
> 'I did not borrow them, I have been collecting them to listen to them.'
> 'Collecting them?'
> 'Yes, I am collecting them to listen to what they are singing about. With anyone else you would have a right to be concerned but how can we cadres be influenced by them?'
> Another cadre was more secretive, 'I borrowed them from a cousin in order to "research" them and find out what the tastes of youth are like. I must listen to them so I can learn how they are wrong and "teach" this to youths!'
> Several months after I first met them, the two cadres mentioned above were still 'researching' these songs in such great detail that it seemed they had not concluded how to teach the young generation (*Saigon Giai Phong* 23 September 1976d:4).

In these comments the threat posed by the musical legacy of the former regime in South Vietnam was seen to have ominous new significance. The reported 'infection' of northern troops stationed in the South, as well as the appearance north of the 17th parallel of 'neo-colonial poisons' suggested their ability to 'invade' and wreak damage independent of the assistance of an occupying power. In 1977 a report in *Quan Doi Nhan Dan* (the *People's Army Daily*) warned of: 'neocolonial cultural works which are causing damage in one way or another in our units', describing confiscated books, magazines and music records as:

'Silent Bullets'

The above refers to the neocolonial cultural works which are causing damage in one way or another in our units. When we attacked to liberate areas occupied by the US-Puppets, all of us were told that we must be on our guard against those silent weapons.

Many units did a good job of obeying orders from above: Regiment 2 was stationed in the middle of Saigon for a year but there was not a single violation of discipline regarding the use of reactionary publications. The regiment's reconnaissance company often had to be dispersed in the neighbourhoods, where there were still many old publications, but not a single comrade concealed or read such cultural works.

Meanwhile, unit X (military region Y) carried out an equipment inspection in two companies and confiscated 119 reactionary, decadent books. One soldier had 84 yellow music records. A number of comrades were infatuated with reading adventuristic books or romance novels, or looked at the drawings and photographs in decadent pictorial magazines.

In Battalion N, there was a soldier who borrowed a wig and women's clothing and went to have his picture taken!

Although the cultural bullets make no noise, they are very dangerous and often bring about unforeseen consequences (*Quan Doi Nhan Dan* 14 August 1977a).

Another article in the same issue addressed the need to be vigilant against 'surreptitious infiltration of the troops by the cultural and artistic poisons of neocolonialism' (*Quan Doi Nhan Dan* 14 August 1977a). The author noted that in some units, 'various types of evil poisonous cultural works were eliminated [and] unwholesome ways of life which appeared were criticized':

However there are also units which waited until there were serious infections before treating them, or which prevented them solely by purely administrative measures, which resulted in the continued presence of hidden cankers in units which superficially seemed to be pure.

Furthermore, even in a number of units stationed in the North there have been scattered instances of reading bad books, listening to provocative music, or imitating the backward way of life of some people in society at large (*Quan Doi Nhan Dan* 14 August 1977a).

The problem of northern vulnerability to southern cultural forms was acknowledged in an article appearing in the journal *Arts Research*, entitled, 'The struggle against bourgeois culture and art'. The author argued that despite twenty years of socialist reform and construction, the continued existence of small-scale production and 'vestiges of the old society', meant that the North remained fertile ground for the penetration of 'reactionary thought and culture' from the South. Therefore:

> We are not surprised that after the South was liberated, a number of bad social and cultural factors which had long ago been eliminated in the North reappeared, including such backward tastes as liking of hedonistic, flashy, weak, provocative and decadent 'arts', which the people of the newly liberated areas are struggling to eliminate (Ha Xuan Truong 1977:15).

He then went on to state the problem of cultural and artistic reunification as a continuation of war on a new 'front' (*mat tran*):

> The effect of the bad will expand if we do not promptly promote the enterprise of building the new culture . . . and resolutely struggle against all manifestations of the slave, reactionary, bourgeois society. Although the conditions and circumstances of the various regions are not yet identical, the requirements of the struggle to determine 'who defeats whom' on the culture and art front are the requirements of the whole nation (Ha Xuan Truong 1977:15).

The author identified lack of vigilance, corrupt elements in the domestic administrative structure and lingering 'backwardness' in the North for these developments. Yet the perceived problem also refocused attention on the alien quality of the South—no longer a disease under localised control but having a potent irrepressibility and, more seriously, contagious qualities.

An additional danger of 'neo-colonial vestiges' was that they purportedly kept open a channel for continued external interference and might possibly serve as bridgeheads, facilitating the reoccupation of Vietnam, as a report on lingering problems in Ho Chi Minh City by Nguyen Khac Vien warned:

> On the economic level, the principal obstacle is the consumer mentality inherited from twenty years of US domination. In the West, the consumer society grew out of scientific and technological development; here it was created *ex nihilo* by US Aid. This aid was interrupted five years ago, but the habit remains of consuming imported goods and of maintaining at all costs a standard of living far above the country's possibilities.
>
> On the social plane, this consumer mentality has given rise to the proliferation of a strata of merchants and traffickers who have caused prices to rocket and who have been getting scandalously rich, even tending towards recreating a bourgeoisie ready to call in foreign

imperialists to help them establish their influence (Nguyen Khac Vien 1981:186).

Meanwhile, foreign imperialist powers were accused of continuing to focus on the recently liberated South, targeting the sphere of culture and cultivating domestic reactionaries to further their hostile aims. A 1981 article in the party's theoretical journal, *Tap Chi Cong San*, detailed ongoing interference of such kind:

> One of the enemy's current activities aimed at sabotaging our ideology, culture and arts and letters is to aid the remnants of the neo-colonialist culture and arts and letters and encourage reactionary bourgeois artistic and literary tendencies. The struggle to wipe out reactionary and decadent cultural products was and is being vigorously conducted in Ho Chi Minh City and a number of other localities. According to still incomplete statistics, a fairly large number of these products has been confiscated during inspection and suppression drives in a number of provinces and cities (Tran Tho 1981:65).

The article included comparative data on material confiscated during such 'inspection and suppression drives', in the six months to June 1981, which illustrated the enormous gulf between Hanoi and Ho Chi Minh City:

**Cultural material confiscated in 1981 compared by city**

|  | Books | Music tapes | Songs/paintings |
|---|---|---|---|
| **Hanoi** | 167 (copies) | 1216 | — |
| **HCMC** | 60 (tonnes) | 41 723 | 53 751 |

*Source:*    'Tu lieu ve dot truy quet van hoa pham phan dong doi truy rua qua (some data on the recent phase of wiping out reactionary and decadent cultural products), *Tap Chi Cong San* (10), pp. 62–3.

The author warned of a collusion between hostile internal and external forces who were actively engaged in reproducing the vestiges of neo-colonial culture and continuously infiltrating new material:

> Obviously, the cultural products we have confiscated are not only the remnants of the old neo-colonialist culture in the South, which is trying to rear its head again. They also include material smuggled into our country since the South was completely liberated, in an effort to promote and restore neo-colonialist cultural activities and to co-ordinate acts of sabotage against our country (Tran Tho 1981:65–6).

The rapidly growing diaspora constituted a further threat; the packages they sent home were believed to contain subversive material:

> Through the international postal service, many reactionaries living in exile overseas have sent home letters, goods, cultural products and so

forth to propagandise Western bourgeois lifestyles and incite people to flee the country (Tran Tho 1981:66).

Such a threat was concentrated in the South and in Ho Chi Minh City in particular, from which most of the diaspora had come:

Many papers and magazines published by Vietnamese 'refugees' in foreign countries, such as *Que Me, Van Nghe Tien Phong, Vuot Tuyen, Hon Viet, Trang Den, Chuong Saigon, Saigon-My*, and so forth, have appeared in Ho Chi Minh City and a number of other localities. Most of the authors of the articles carried by these publications are hired pens who served as lackeys of US imperialism in the past (Tran Tho 1981:66).

Long after it was liberated, Ho Chi Minh City remained vulnerable to infiltration by new enemies and forms of external manipulation. In the late 1970s the People's Republic of China (PRC) joined the sphere of hostile imperialistic powers who were seen to be engaging in internal subversion. The article noted that:

As of late 1981 the Beijing reactionaries had smuggled 40 different kinds of leaflets into our country, of which 24 contain material designed to slander our party, sow division among various nationalities, incite rebellions, lure people into fleeing the country and so forth (Tran Tho 1981:66).

With the PRC in the role of imperialist power, the city's perceived vulnerability to foreign cultural subversion was reinvented. As ethnic Chinese were concentrated there, the threat it posed was believed to be particularly severe. This was contradicted by the fact that PRC influence had been far stronger in the nation's northern capital. The PRC had bankrolled, advised, trained and provided a model for Vietnam's Communist Party for over thirty years of waging war and constructing a socialist state in the North. Much of the official culture of the DRV was modelled on the PRC. Quite ironically, the PRC's imperialist interference in the South was denounced as 'hegemonist plotting' (*am mu cua chu nghia ba quyen*), a term borrowed by Vietnam's leaders from the PRC's own foreign affairs lexicon (Chanda 1986:240). An editorial in an early 1983 edition of the party journal noted that the South had only recently emerged from the clutches of neo-colonialism and had only made a few tentative steps towards socialist reform. It noted that there, the struggle between the 'two paths' was still strong, even within the ranks of party cadres. Moreover, party cadres had become strategic targets for the Chinese in their war of sabotage against Vietnam (*Tap Chi Cong San* 1983:2).[2] The unholy alliance between the PRC and USA completed this hydra-headed assault on the Vietnamese regime's cadres:

Moreover we are now facing a multifaceted war of sabotage (*chien tranh pha hoai nhieu mat*) by Chinese hegemonist expansionism (*chu nghia banh truong ba quyen*) allied with US imperialism. One of the evil schemes of the enemies is to sabotage our party. They use many psychological warfare activities, distorting and criticising our party's path, arousing and spreading alarm within the party apparatus (*Tap Chi Cong San* 1983:2).

This was written at a time when the party's central committee was attempting to rein in the Ho Chi Minh City party leadership, accused of non-implementation of policy and straying from the party central committee's socialist blueprint. The editorial urged errant party members to augment their spirit of discipline in the face of organisational fissuring caused by external enemies (*Tap Chi Cong San* 1983:1).

Despite the novelty of the problem—the emergence of new external enemies (the overseas Vietnamese, the PRC, the US–PRC alliance) purportedly acting on a new target (the party's power structure in the post-war South)—the image of the capital of the former South as a place endangering national integrity persisted long after its liberation. This perception was still strong as late as 1985, when Phan Van Khai, then Chairman of the People's Committee of Ho Chi Minh City, in summing up 'ten years of socialist transformation and building in Ho Chi Minh City', wrote:

> Politically, after their defeat in the war of aggression, the US imperialists, working hand in glove with the Chinese expansionists and hegemonists are frenziedly carrying out a multi-faceted war of sabotage against Vietnam. In this war of sabotage, they regard Ho Chi Minh City as a target of prime importance. Taking advantage of conditions in a newly-liberated city, they are trying to destroy it politically, militarily, culturally and ideologically, in the hope of fomenting a rebellion leading to the overthrow of the revolutionary administration (Phan Van Khai 1985:14).

This view of this southern city's cultural identity as being compromised or determined by hostile and alien forces lingered up to the *doi moi* era, despite the enormous resources mobilised to achieve cultural unity. Even though fundamental realignments of political geography were unfolding, the significance of southern difference went through several modulations over the first post-war decade. The nation's administration became 'infected' on regional lines, unification turned the North into a new cultural 'front', the harmful influence of new enemies was most evident in the South, and the administration's vulnerability to their subversion was strongest there.

## THE CULTURAL CONSEQUENCES OF REFORM

The 'reinvention' of national identity (Turley and Seldon 1993) that occurred in the 1980s was to unleash a new set of challenges to the nation. Among these was a challenge to the nation's cultural integrity perhaps greater than that posed by the incorporation of the former South Vietnam into the Socialist Republic of Vietnam in 1976. From the perspective of the northern half of the country, the liberal reforms represented a 'seismic shift' in national orientation (Kerkvliet 1995a:1). In the early 1980s Vietnam had been host to hundreds of advisers and experts from the socialist bloc. At the beginning of the 1990s its burgeoning hotel sector could not keep up with the influx of investors, traders, and official delegations flooding in from the capitalist world. The lifting of the International Monetary Fund (IMF) lending restrictions and of the US trade embargo in 1994, promised to accelerate this process, although well in advance of this investors from neighbouring countries in the region as well as others such as France and Australia had rushed to the new economic frontier in the early 1990s. Exhortative billboards urging emulation of resistance war heroes and socialist models were outshone by advertisements for foreign companies and consumer products. The major cities appeared to have been colonised by Ancient Rome with office signs and billboards displaying a proliferation of acronyms such as 'VIETRONIMEX',[3] 'SEAPRODIX' and 'LEGIMEX'. Soon these were dwarfed by massive billboards bearing the new buzzwords of consumer culture: JRC, SONY, Heinekin, Daewoo and Cheng Fong. Legalised private markets were awash with new consumer items. Classrooms were crammed with students taking private language classes in English, Japanese, French and Mandarin. Drab, official reportage on TV was supplemented by foreign-made advertisements for foreign products. Foreign money poured in and a sizeable consumer class emerged with an enormous appetite for the labour-saving, sense-provoking, status-marking objects of mass production and above all, for all things foreign.

The instigation of reforms did not receive unanimous support at the political centre. Analysts somewhat opaquely referred to differences between Politburo 'reformists' and 'conservatives' over the desirability of various steps towards liberalisation. The consequences and changes unleashed by the reforms were subject to mixed appraisal. While some leaders welcomed these transformations and talked up the need for continuing reform, there was an equally audible voicing of concerns about the perceived ill effects of the 'open door' (*mo cua*) policy and economic liberalisation.

In the late 1980s articles appeared in the official press and the party's theoretical journal, which linked the new policies to a serious rise in social problems and a looming moral and cultural crisis. A number of articles decried a flood of 'bad cultural products' (*van pham xau*)[4] entering the country after the promulgation of the open door policy. Some authors noted a sharp increase in the incidence of gambling (*co bac*), prostitution (*mai dam*), drugs (*ma tuy*) and theft (*trom*

**Gambling, a 'social evil' in Ho Chi Minh City**

*cap*), sometimes labelled 'the four collapsing walls' (*tu do tuong*), as well as an increase in 'superstitious' (*me tin di doan*) practices (Mai Chi Tho 1988). Concerns about an upsurge of criminal activity ranged from reports of increased juvenile delinquency (*Dai Doan Ket* 1989) to an explosion of economic crimes such as fraud (*lua gat*), smuggling (*buon lau*) and corruption (*tham nhung*) (Tran Dao 1993). The latter was seen to have reached epidemic proportions and was subject to a particularly urgent debate. Paralleling an increasing number of reports on corruption came a shift in its designation from the euphemistic 'negative phenomenon'[5] to the shrill 'national catastrophe' (*tai bien ca nuoc*).[6] Added to these were concerns at the degradation of Vietnam's educational and cultural infrastructure. Numerous newspaper articles reported that economic liberalisation was accompanied by a decline in the quality of education, a rise in illiteracy (*mu chu*), a decline in the range of cultural services for ethnic minorities and disinterest in the preservation of cultural relics.[7] The emergence of 'individualism' (*chu nghia ca nhan*) (Nguyen Van Huyen 1996), the 'cult of exotic taste', dizzying pace of borrowing, resurgence of a cultural inferiority complex (*mac cam van hoa*), (Nguyen Sinh Huy 1996:86) and emergence of consumerism (Dang Canh Khanh 1996:71), were further negative cultural consequences of the open door policy which state-employed intellectuals worried about in official publications.

The explanations offered for the social turbulence of post-reform Vietnam were characteristically complex, officials often identifying multiple causes, unintended consequences and vicious circles of causality. Some leaders viewed the upsurge in crime and decline in ethical behaviour as an inevitable consequence of switching to a market economy in which money was the sole measure of value. This was the view of Colonel Tran Dao, deputy head of the economic police department, Ministry of Interior, writing in the party theoretical journal in 1993:

> The motive force of the market mechanism is profits and superior profits . . . The way to make superior profits easily is to engage in smuggling, trade contraband goods, evade paying taxes, produce and sell bogus goods and commit fraud (Tran Dao 1993:51).

Another serious consequence of societal commercialisation, identified by the Minister of Culture, Tran Van Phac, was a flood of 'depraved' or 'culturally inappropriate' items pushed by 'unscrupulous' profiteers. According to Hiebert, the Minister told the National Assembly in mid-1989 that: 'The spread of videotapes and music of an unhealthy decadent nature has reached an alarming rate and seriously affected the young' (Hiebert 1989:23; see also Dang Canh Khanh 1996:71). The problem was partly due to private entrepreneurs. Yet crackdowns on commercial venues selling pornographic videos in 1989 also led to the discovery that many policy and army units as well as party mass organisations were using such illicit commerce to raise funds (Hiebert 1989:23).[8]

Increasingly complex chains of causation were held to prevail in the deterioration of cultural and aesthetic traditions. A report in *Nhan Dan* identified the increased incidence of smuggling with a net decline in the nation's cultural integrity:

> Smuggling brings into our country cultural products with reactionary, decadent, ideologically provocative and anti-socialist themes, encouraging violence and sex, corrupting many young people and leading to crime. At the same time, it is also the route for illegally exporting many cultural antiques and historical relics from temples and imperial tombs (*Nhan Dan* 6 July 1990:3).

**A Cu Chi billboard cluster which identifies a range of 'social evils' such as superstition, alcoholism, gambling and 'negative phenomena' such as corruption and smuggling, also urging family planning and national defence**

The article offered a complex and nuanced explanation for the potentially sensitive issue of cultural degradation across national borders. On a familiar note, it included schemes of sabotage by enemies and reactionaries among the factors causing this problem. However, the article presented a far more complex portrait of the problem than would have been the case perhaps only five years previous. Apart from naked profiteering by private individuals, the problem stemmed partly from lax management by border protection units. These were accused of often aiding and abetting smuggling in return for bribes. Many such cadres were degenerate and corrupt and were themselves protected by corrupt local party and state hierarchies. Some localities systematically profited from their location on borders to maintain illegal private crossing points. Cadres and soldiers coming to investigate them had even been beaten up (*Nhan Dan* 6 July 1990).

Some authors noted that decentralisation and commercialisation of state functions had reduced the ability of state agents to exercise responsible leadership in the cultural sphere. On the other hand, many authors and high ranking leaders blamed the persistence of 'subjectivist' (*chu quan*) approaches to cultural reform from the pre-*doi moi* era. The Minister of the Interior, interviewed in 1989, argued that Vietnam's socio-economic crisis was due in some measure to:

> the devaluation and neglect of spiritual and moral values by some localities and sectors within the state apparatus, whose emphasis on

material results had allowed pragmatism to grow and had led to the chase after money at any cost' (*Dai Doan Ket* 1989:1).

He argued that dismissal of the importance of culture and the arts had led some state agencies to neglect to police these sectors, leading to a flood of inappropriate and harmful imports, influencing the thinking of the young (*Dai Doan Ket* 1989:1). Writing in the party's theoretical organ, one author argued that 'pragmatism' (*chu nghia thuc dung*) and the 'cult of money' (*dao tho tien*) was exacerbated by a long-standing failure on the part of the state to pay attention to the 'national essence' (Ho Phuong 1991:10). Another argued similarly, that the cause lay with not valuing the 'original cultural and spiritual abilities of the people' (Phong Le 1991:17). Minister of the Interior, Mai Chi Tho, agreed, arguing that due to 'subjective voluntarism' in the 'ideological and cultural revolution' (excessive zeal in building the 'new socialist person' and 'new socialist morality'), the nation's 'fine cultural and moral traditions' had been neglected (*Dai Doan Ket* 1989:1). According to one contributor to the party's theoretical journal, cultural decline had already set in prior to the *doi moi* reforms, in an environment of 'monotony and authoritarianism' (Do Huy 1989:17).

Awareness of the complexity of factors involved differentiated official commentary in the early 1990s on the contemporary crisis of Vietnamese culture from similar commentary in the 1970s. Greater attention was given to internal dynamics in contrast to the previous weight placed on foreign factors. The simplicity of conspiracy theories gave way to awareness of more diffuse factors and the language of unintended consequences. The suprematism of a revolutionary meritocracy ceded to highlighting the ambiguous position of state agents. Self-confident assertions of uniqueness and militant voluntarism gave way to an awareness that Vietnam was not unique in its plight nor able to engineer its own cultural purity. Such an awareness was evident in an article by Dinh Gia Khanh, entitled 'Tradition and modernity in culture', in which he put the problems facing Vietnam into a broader comparative framework. He argued that the dizzying shifts being experienced in Vietnam were formidable challenges facing the entire world:

> The unconscious and rapid urbanization, the process of disintegration of traditional social units (village, clan), the emergence of so-called consumer society, with the daily changes in fashion and taste, with the fast, dizzying rhythm of life, the contempt for spiritual values, the crisis of the family and the so-called generation gap . . . all [these are] real facts of life in the world. This is not only real in the capitalist world. In socialist countries, similar problems of culture are being dealt with (Dinh Gia Khanh 1990:32).

He argued that the culture of capitalist countries was constantly making its influence felt in socialist countries due to modern transport and mass media. Yet these influences also included models for articulating and handling the relationships between tradition and change. In specifying these, he seemed to suggest that the way such problems were being approached in Vietnam were themselves borrowed from the West:

> There are two extreme tendencies in handling this relationship in the Western world. One is . . . people want to negate all traditions which they consider to be appropriate to the old rhythm of life only. The other extreme is, being fed up with the fast living style of modern society, people want to 'go back to the origin' by idealising the ancient patriarchal society of the East (Dinh Gia Khanh 1990:32).

Khanh asserted that 'we do not subscribe to either of these extremes', although he stopped short of specifying where he did stand. However, in the 1990s a great deal of reflection on the problem of Vietnam's integration with the wider world did indeed sit between these two poles. Awareness of the complexity of the factors contributing to the nation's contemporary cultural crisis led to rumination on solutions between the poles of isolationism and surrender.

During my residence in Vietnam in the early 1990s I encountered much discussion among state-employed intellectuals and cadres about other nations' policies with respect to preserving tradition and promoting cultural diversity. France's stand in the GATT convention of 1993, reserving the right to protect its film industry from Hollywood incursions was widely applauded. The attention paid to cultural preservation in France was contrasted with the cases of the Philippines and Thailand which many deemed to have 'lost their national identity' (*mat ban sac dan toc*) in a catastrophic confrontation with the West. The Philippines was often viewed stereotypically as having 'lost' its culture while Thailand, rife with AIDS and environmental degradation, had succumbed to a worse crisis. Lee Kuan Yew's doctrine of Asian value relativity and the virtues of the Singapore model were prominent topics of discussion. I was also frequently asked about Australia's policy of multi-culturalism by those thinking about it as a model for handling ethnic diversity in Vietnam.

## THE THREATENING OPEN DOOR

Despite the increasing complexity of official explanations of, and solutions to, the perceived cultural crisis facing Vietnam, continuities with earlier approaches were evident. The uncompromising terms 'cultural poisons', 'alien influences' and 'spiritual pollution' (*o niem tinh than*) remained common currency in official discussion of the question of cultural influence from abroad (for example, Draft political report of the Central Committee of the Communist Party (7th Congress) 1996:112; Schwartz 1996:15). From time to time throughout the 1990s the bunker mentality of the late 1970s rose to the fore. In early 1994, just after the US embargo against Vietnam was lifted, research staff at Ho Chi Minh City's Institute of Social Sciences were assembled by their director and told to step up their vigilance against an impending 'US cultural invasion'. The audience was told that, in 1975, the US had been 'defeated militarily'. In 1994, with the lifting of the embargo, it had been 'defeated economically'. Now all its resources, including spy satellites and fax technology would be massed on the new front of culture and the coming fight would be more intense than ever (from fieldnotes).

A campaign to maintain vigilance against 'peaceful evolutionism' (*dien bien hoa binh*), which was announced in the early 1990s, was representative of this attitude of cultural crisis and echoed the stark antinomies of the early post-war years.[9] According to the official commentators who identified 'peaceful evolution' as a threat, the intentions of some people who were currently visiting, or engaging with, Vietnam in the early 1990s were anything but peaceful. Writing in the People's Army newspaper, one author warned against attempts by 'hostile forces and reactionaries' (*luc luong thu dich va phan dong*) to employ this means to topple the regime by stealth. He argued that 'enemy' schemes included 'spreading many psychological warfare documents and many degenerate cultural materials in our country' (Duong Thong 1991:42). Since the crisis among socialist countries had begun:

> The American imperialists and the enemy forces have regarded Vietnam as one of the focal points of attack. They have quickly implemented their plot of 'peaceful change' using many insidious stratagems. In this they have given particular attention to destroying us ideologically (Duong Thong 1991:41).

The author wrote that party cadres represented a prime target of such schemes and cited the case of dissident author Duong Thu Huong, arrested on 14 April 1991 on charges of 'compiling and smuggling out materials harmful to national security', as an example of enemy forces' successful, 'peaceful' subversion of the party apparatus (Duong Thong 1991:41).

Another senior military figure warned that 'our country is in the direct "viewfinder" of the "peaceful development" plot of the imperialists'. He noted that Vietnam's international exchanges and co-operation had strengthened recently:

> On the other hand, along with the widening of multi-faceted and multidirectional exchange and co-operation, ideological and cultural views and ways of living of all kinds also gain access to our people's political and spiritual life. The wishes for goodwill in relations are also mixed with unwholesome, even wicked and dark schemes (Major-General Le Hong Quang 1993:28).

In February 1996, ten years after the official announcement of the *doi moi* reforms, the government mounted a high profile campaign against 'social evils' (*te nan xa hoi*).[10] According to a *Far Eastern Economic Review* report, the main targets were 'prostitution, drugs, gambling' and other 'toxic cultural imports':

> Tens of thousands of pornographic or overly violent videotapes have been confiscated, while hundreds of massage parlours and *karaoke* bars have been closed or severely restricted. Both Hanoi and Ho Chi Minh City have promoted the campaign with public bonfires of unsuitable videos, calendars, books, posters and playing cards (Schwartz 1996:15).

Included in the litany of 'social evils' were advertisements for foreign products and companies whose presence in Vietnam the regime had been assiduously courting for the last decade (Chalmers 1996). According to the *FEER* report, advertising billboards were stripped of foreign-language slogans and company logos and some company offices were forced to pull down their signs. As evidence of a 'xenophobic tinge which has crept into official commentary' (Schwartz 1996:14), the article cited former Prime Minister Pham Van Dong's expression of 'distaste for the vice and corruption which he said had been introduced into Vietnam by the switch to a market economy':

> There has been a deterioration in lifestyle, in social and cultural matters, and [increase] in the bad influence of Western culture, particularly on young people in cities (in Schwartz 1996:15).

The campaigns against 'peaceful evolutionism' and 'social evils' (there was a renewed campaign in 1997) witnessed a hardening of the terms of the debate over the impact of reforms on Vietnamese society. Both these campaigns articulated the threat posed to contemporary Vietnamese society and culture as foreign in origins. The campaign against 'peaceful evolution' articulated the issue most starkly—the circulation of 'depraved' culture and the corruption of cadres represented a wilful conspiracy by foreign enemies to destroy the regime. The bunker mentality, militaristic language and methods adopted to 'combat' this and other threats[11] were reminiscent of the 1970s, when the dominant approach was to reduce the issue of non-socialist bloc cultural influences to national security considerations.

## INESCAPABLE AMBIVALENCE

Given this continuity, it was perhaps not surprising that the South, and Ho Chi Minh City in particular, was the place where such enemy subversion was seen at its most threatening. Comments made in the post-reform era showed that Ho Chi Minh City was unable to shake off the accusation that its cultural identity was compromised or determined by hostile or alien forces. In the aftermath of war, the city's cultural identity had been seen as wholly compromised by US 'neo-colonialism'. In the 1990s the evil of the 'peaceful evolution' campaign was also seen as concentrated there in a way which threatened the entire nation's cultural integrity.

This predicament dogged the city since reforms were first initiated. In his 1981 speech to cadres responsible for artistic and cultural management, Vo Van Kiet criticised cafe owners and other entrepreneurs' interpretation of preliminary steps towards economic liberalisation (Duiker 1989:95) as a licence to return to playing the 'degenerate' music of the old regime. Liberalisation in a place like Ho Chi Minh City was fraught with the ever present danger of revival of the 'old' way of life:

> Under these conditions, it suffices only a minute of relaxation for the old [person], the old way of life to reappear . . . In this spontaneous, noisy development [can be seen] the egocentric tendencies of the old society, tendencies which try to make a comeback, inciting people to shirk their duty, to run away from reality, to turn their back on the life of labour and the struggle of our people . . . Cadres, dazzled by the new phenomenon [of pop music], have unconsciously created the conditions enabling this exciting music to get the upper hand (Vo Van Kiet 1981:32–4).

Two years later the regime's foreign spokesperson, Nguyen Khac Vien, warned that market reforms opened up a 'dangerous' route back to the consumerist ills of the old regime. He described Ho Chi Minh City as poised at a fork in the road between socialist and non-socialist futures:

> The city will become a production centre, a socialist city where education, the social health service, the arts continuously develop, where everyone is paid according to the work done, where there is no excessive income differentiation—or a consumer city where a few social strata grasp vast amounts of riches, where social services are neglected, where social evils reappear and last, but not least, where luxury goods imported from highly industrialized countries dominate the market (Nguyen Khac Vien 1983:393).

In 1990 a strongly worded report appeared in *Nhan Dan*, the organ of the central government, which identified 'unfavourable trends' and 'openly antagonistic and destructive activities by the enemy' unfolding in Ho Chi Minh City. On the 'cultural front', the article reported:

> While we respectfully support every good work of art, fine film and performance bearing the knowledge and aesthetics of socialism, in every nook and corner of the city are sex videotapes of every kind, spreading violence, sexual desire, superstition and heresy, and unwholesome pre-liberation publications, directing mankind toward a

life of urgency, pragmatism and existentialism are now being displayed and sold in abundance (Nguyen Kien Phuoc 1990:21).

It noted that inspections had been held 'with the confiscation of scores of sex videotapes, thousands of foreign music tapes with reactionary themes, many bad publications sent from foreign countries, etc. (Nguyen Kien Phuoc 1990:21). A conspiracy of domestic reactionaries and imperialists was held to be behind this phenomenon. The former had not been willing 'to abandon its scheme to destroy the revolutionary undertaking of our people'. On the other hand, the US imperialists were still trying to 'achieve the American postwar plan'.

The dangers posed by such dark schemes were compounded by serious problems in Ho Chi Minh City's state and party apparatus. The article warned that 'a number of cadres and party members, including some in authority, must pay a high price for their degeneracy and deviance'. It noted that many in such positions 'possess an indifferent combat will, a lack of personal self-cultivation, disregard for the law and a tendency towards selfishness and individualism' (Nguyen Kien Phuoc 1990:21).

In the same year, *Quan Doi Nhan Dan*, the People's Army newspaper, published a stinging exposé of Ho Chi Minh City state and party cadres. The piece described their enthusiastic patronage of bars offering 'beer in cans with sex' and their free spending and fraudulent ways. Cadres were described as 'parasites on society', 'abscesses on the body of the party and state machinery', 'bad monks', and were 'so depraved that even thugs crooks and dishonest business persons . . . have to respect and consider them their teachers' (Bui Dinh Nguyen 1990:22). Later that year *Nhan Dan* newspaper again reported that a clean-up in the city's party structure was urgently required as 'weak fighting will', 'decadence' and 'deviance' had even led some of the city's party members to work as 'lackeys for the enemy'. The article reported that:

> a part of the party membership . . . has shown a degrading way of living, become corrupt, taken bribes, wasted public funds, gone after pleasure and debauchery and shown disrespect for organization and discipline (Le Huyen Thong 1990:8).

Two full decades after the country was formally unified, Ho Chi Minh City was still being viewed as unusually vulnerable to the intervention of hostile forces. In an interview with *Cong An Thanh Pho Ho Chi Minh*, Ho Chi Minh City's police newspaper, the party's Secretary-General, Do Muoi, said:

> The city is . . . the place hostile forces consider prime ground for 'peaceful evolution', causing political disorder, sabotaging the economy, causing social and cultural pollution, aiming to overthrow the regime established by great personal sacrifices (Reuters 1996).

While such comments implicated local authorities in disorder and 'cultural pollution', Ho Chi Minh City authorities themselves were at the forefront of campaigns to eliminate harmful influences. In late 1997 city authorities hosted a cultural purification ritual of late 1970s proportions. Given the city's notoriety, what appears particularly striking in the following news report was the role of the city as the purifying centre for the whole of the Mekong delta region:

> Hanoi: Police in Ho Chi Minh City burned 15 tons of banned compact discs, videos, magazines and other items in a show of resolve to purge Vietnam of what the government calls culturally impure items, a local official said Friday.
>
> The contraband material, much of it pornographic, violent or anti-communist, was set ablaze Thursday in a massive bonfire, said the official from the culture department of Ho Chi Minh City's People's Committee, who declined to be named.
>
> More than 16,000 videos, 6,300 music cassettes, 600 laser discs and 13,000 CDs were set alight, the official said.
>
> The material had been confiscated by customs officials and culture ministry inspectors from shops in Ho Chi Minh City and areas in the Mekong delta region of southern Vietnam (AP-Dow Jones News Service 1997).

A paradox was evident in these representations of the former capital of South Vietnam. The city was viewed simultaneously as degenerate and vulnerable, attracting constant fretful attention to its endemic impurity and impending defilement for more than two decades. This quality gave it a special place in debates about the effects of reform on Vietnamese culture. Due to its more intense involvement in contemporary global exchanges, the preservation of its cultural purity was considered of the highest urgency. Yet it was simultaneously depicted as the country's most degenerate site. The city was confined in this enduring ambivalence, setting it apart from the rest of the country.

Ho Chi Minh City's unique predicament recalled those depictions of Vietnam's extreme south, or *Nam Bo*, sketched by Huynh Ngoc Trang (1992) and others, as having a distinct identity, assertions in which the city had featured prominently. Some had construed *Nam Bo* as a melting pot, a place of cultural exchanges and constant change. The region of *Nam Bo*, allegedly having no stable, fragile tradition at stake, might therefore have been considered exempt from the cultural crisis purportedly facing the entire country. Considering the region's millennial involvement in commerce, 'liberalisation' might have posed more of a challenge for the rest of the country. Similarly, pragmatism and individualism were allegedly familiar *Nam Bo* traits and thus hardly a recent problem. On this reasoning, concerns about a cultural crisis were more relevant to the rest of the country, but from which *Nam Bo* would be immune. Such a view was anathema to the notions of purity or pollution. While both notions did see the city as distinctive, in terms of its legacy of external influences and potential for ongoing engagements, the former view was celebratory, while the latter paranoid. The former spoke of assimilation and renewal, the latter of subversion and degeneracy. Those who lamented the cultural consequences of the reform policies differed too from those who asserted that the 1955–75 RVN era had entailed the 'modernisation' of the southern half of the country. According to one Ho Chi Minh City journalist in 1993 southerners would take the challenge posed by liberalisation in their stride:

> Southerners know how to tell a genuine foreign investor from a fake, and good ideas from garbage due to twenty years of experience with the Americans. Northerners risk losing their traditions or committing the worst kind of aesthetic gaffes due to inexperience, as they have been closed for so long (from fieldnotes).

From this perspective, while the North was opening to the world for the first time, and thus risked being devastated by exposure to the worst global culture had to offer, the South was returning to a process interrupted by unification. Experience had taught southerners to be more discerning and therefore they could sail more smoothly through the storms of the reform era, identity unscathed. However, this was disputed by those who construed the city's identity to be at risk in the *doi moi* era. Furthermore, it was a view not all southerners shared.

## CONSTITUTING *DOI MOI* AS CULTURAL CRISIS

As a place of constant subversion (or assimilation), having been severed from its roots (or having confidently discarded them) long ago (or only recently), Ho Chi Minh City has been constructed variously as a site where it is no longer relevant to speak in terms of 'tradition' or original culture. Yet the conduct in Ho Chi Minh City in the early 1990s, of an animated debate on the adverse impact of the liberal reforms on tradition and national cultural identity called these views into question. This supposedly uncharacteristic occurrence forced reconsideration of constructions of the South as a place which threatened, or was antithetical to, such an identity.

The period was a tumultuous time for those working in the city's cultural field: teachers, journalists, actors, musicians and academics. Rapid decentralisation and commercialisation of formerly state controlled activity such as teaching and publishing, and a surge of foreign investors, gave a shot in the arm to all intellectual and cultural activities linked to the domestic reception of foreign capital. The demand for all those with foreign language teaching experience was at a premium. Even a smattering of foreign language was to become a valuable asset.

Economics and business courses multiplied, followed quickly by computer literacy classes. Print media went through a similar explosion in demand for translated textbooks, novels and self-help manuals. Journalism hit boom times with an insatiable demand for translated articles and reports on new commodities and investments, in a mushrooming series of newspapers and magazines. Local and foreign corporations began to pour unprecedented amounts of money into advertising. By the beginning of the 1990s the key sectors employing intellectuals: schools, universities, publishing houses, the media and administration, illustrated the largely accomplished commercialisation of the Vietnamese economy (Fforde 1991). An enormous demand for knowledge prompted a virtual information explosion, boosting the economic fortunes of many who had languished in a low-paid state-dominated sector which offered few practical opportunities for advancement. Yet while the economic boom benefited southern intellectuals, many came to doubt the capacity for market forces to promote the sustainable development of their country's intellectual capital.

These doubts were first raised for me in 1993 by a professional astrologer and geomancer (*Thay tu vi, dia ly*). Having gained university qualifications and teaching experience as a historian and geologist under the former regime, he had made fortune-telling his core profession since reunification. His career had flourished (despite the fact that it was, and still is, outlawed as 'superstitious' by the current regime) mostly thanks to a long and mutually profitable accommodation with local authorities.

Summarising the history of his practice, located behind the mausoleum of former Gia Dinh viceroy Le Van Duyet, a site renowned for its magical potency, he divided the last twenty years into three periods. From 1975 to 1981, most of those who sought his advice had wished to determine the outcome of a planned escape from the country. From 1982 to 1989 the bulk of his clients had been those seeking sponsorship to go abroad or awaiting emigration with the Orderly Departure Program. From 1990 half of his clients were business people (mostly female marketeers), the other half cadres, seeking advice on promotions and business but also to know the outcome of pending corruption charges.

Although a successful fortune-teller, my interlocutor told me that his profession was under siege in the new market conditions by a host of rivals who satisfied increased demand for occult practices with the merest patina of esoteric knowledge. He said that from time to time he received clients whose intentions were patently to pick up a handful of tricks for immediate exploitation on the market. Under today's conditions of high demand for his knowledge, an hour's consultation with him might suffice to launch the career of such an individual, even though he himself had served a seven-year apprenticeship in his art

**A cut-price fortune-teller in Ho Chi Minh City**

(which in turn was only a third of the time expended by his own teacher in acquiring the requisite skills). Not only was he critical of the way his profession was reproduced and degraded in such a perfunctory way, his own reputation was being eroded by market forces. While only ten *Thay tu vi* had operated in the Saigon area from 1975 to 1989, more than a thousand had now sprung into business. In his lane alone could be found five fortune-tellers who worked under the same name as his, crudely capitalising on his fame to net customers who had been referred to him. Of the many fortune-tellers in practice, he estimated that '99 per cent of them were charlatans' operating with rudimentary knowledge, hustling relentlessly for work, practising palm and physiognomy readings (*coi tay, coi tuong*) and card readings (*boi bai*) from photocopied pre-1975 popular manuals. He stressed that his profession was bound by two key ethical precepts: to do no ill and to do no advertising. Yet he alleged the new class of fortune-tellers broke both requirements. He went on to outline this as a malaise gripping the entire field of contemporary intellectual endeavour. He argued that nowadays one found journalists who did not know how to write a good story and English teachers who did not know English, let alone how to teach. Unprofessionalism and raw greed were sweeping the professions, a consequence of the commercialisation of knowledge and the poor quality of education students received at school.

These views were confirmed by a number of acquaintances, speaking of a range of institutions in which they had worked over the past three to four years. An English teacher who had worked in Ho Chi Minh City since the 1980s, lamented that foreign language courses had wildly multiplied in recent times, yet after working with several schools, she had only once worked under an English program head with even rudimentary English. Many of the teaching staff, on the other hand, were highly trained individuals—engineers, physicists, philosophers and former regime officials—who had dredged up the scraps of English acquired in the pursuit of their prior careers, to recycle themselves as successful language teachers. The Vietnamese language programs at various Ho Chi Minh City universities were among these institutions' prime money spinners and, in the early 1990s, they were expanding dramatically, adding rooms and purchasing computers and fax machines at a furious rate. Yet teachers at one university, with whom I spoke, noted that little investment was being made in teacher training. While teachers received less than one USD an hour, irrespective of class size, the program itself could earn more than ten times that if enough students were crammed in. The program's teachers, mostly pursuing degrees themselves, were increasingly overworked, with little share in the lucrative fees from their efforts, no time to improve their teaching skills, nor time to pursue their studies. In another university in the city, a staff member from the Department of History made a similar complaint:

> This university is just chasing after money. For example, the Department of History used to teach about Vietnam's revolutionary traditions and do local history research in the countryside. Now it has opened a Journalism department to earn money from fee-paying students. They have hundreds of students in that course and there's no time or space left for teaching History. At the same time, the Philology department also opened a Department of Law for full fee-paying students. And then the entire university turns into a massive private English-teaching business in the evenings, classrooms crammed with fee-paying students. There is just one qualification for entry in these courses: money (from fieldnotes).

Parallels could be found at other institutions in the city. The Institute of Social Sciences rented out many of its offices as accommodation to visiting foreign academics and its seminar rooms and conference hall were rented to private classes run by other institutions for far more money than its researchers could attract in research funding. Researchers saw little of these earnings. Some of those who were working on a national poverty alleviation program commented ironically that they were as poor as any of those whom they encountered in their research. All over the city and provincial towns of the Mekong delta, primary and secondary schools led double or treble existences, mutating into private schools in the afternoon and evening. Humble, fading school signs were outshone or obscured by noisy banners announcing language, business and computer courses. Every available classroom was filled to bursting. In pursuit of profits to be made from private classes, time and space available for state-funded courses and research tended to shrink. Private courses slowly invaded the schools. Even the playgrounds were filled by those operating private bicycle- and motorcycle-minding services. As financial reward increasingly determined educational priorities, degrees became increasingly reflective of financial status. The quality of students in private education was reported to be as poor as that of the staff employed to educate them. One teacher who worked in a government-funded school by day, and taught the same subject in its privatised incarnation by night, reported a plummeting in the quality and commitment of students and staff that nightfall brought.

These concerns were repeated by others working in other domains of the arts and culture. One writer who had worked as a journalist for the last forty years lamented that the recent explosion in print journalism in Ho Chi Minh City had been accompanied by a decline in the quality of writing and intellectual content:

> Most papers merely carry translations of foreign articles and reports on personalities, societal trends and fashions of little relevance to contemporary Vietnamese life. Journalists endlessly recycle their work reselling an already thin story to numerous outlets with minimal alterations (from fieldnotes).

He argued that, gripped by money fever, newspapers had abandoned their role of watchdog: of political and societal critics. They merely conformed to, and fed, the consumerist fever gripping Vietnamese society. A high school teacher lamented the targeting of the youth market by certain pulp magazine publishers. Full of sex, violence and lives of the glamorous rich, she said she understood why they had attained such popularity among her secondary school students, as there was so little else of relevance for them to read. Lack of state investment in youth cultural issues had led to the colonisation of her students' imaginations by unscrupulous profiteers.

Theatre, film, music, and fine arts were other cultural domains where similar criticisms were being voiced. Stripped of subsidies and forced to operate as commercial ventures, these fields' artistic values and capacity to provide social commentary were seen to have greatly diminished. The influx of cheap videos and cassettes was blamed for further undermining the value of the local arts scene. Given the label 'instant noodles' (*mi an lien*), to describe the rapid production time, domestically-produced films were widely scorned for their poor sound and image quality, predictable stories and melodramatic nature. Musicians too lamented little development in the local music scene, indeed all innovations were seen as coming from abroad. Actors told me that

**A state-owned cinema displaying a banner greeting the Seventh Party Congress in 1991**

theatre was suffering in competition with foreign videos—the price of a theatre ticket averaging at ten to twenty times the rental cost of a video. One acquaintance's theatre company was forced to rush through rehearsals to cut costs and play for increasingly short seasons to fill the theatre. Meanwhile artists were selling paintings like never before, however the quality was considered by many to be low, due to the chase for profits. One artist pointed out the fetishistic representation of breasts dominating her male colleagues' work as representative of contemporary art's maximisation of sales by exploiting cheap titillation.

Most of those who worked in the cultural field in Ho Chi Minh City led hectic, fragmented lives.[11] It was not rare for writers, teachers or musicians to do three or more jobs a day and divide their efforts between many fields of activity. I would often hear them criticise the lack of intellectual substance, morality or aesthetic value of the chaotic field of production they were involved in. They expressed powerlessness to change their predicament, saying it was an evil of life in a commercialised world. Their comments offered further food for thought on the identity of the southern Vietnamese cultural scene. As residents of Ho Chi Minh City, their critique of cultural degradation sat uneasily with official constructions which described the city as having 'lost its roots' or as representing a site of endemic depravity and cultural impurity. The logic of such critiques denied southerners the discriminating capability to criticise commercialisation or be articulate about their inundation by foreign ideas and forms. Southern urban intellectuals' critique of the decline of tradition in the face of *doi moi*-era commercialisation also called into question the idea that southerners had familiarised themselves with the market in the 'modernisation' of the RVN era or had embraced commercialisation in resistance to socialist reforms in the South in the late 1970s. Finally, the disaffected intellectuals I met in the 1990s were not acting as typical representatives of *Nam Bo* culture. They lamented a loss of tradition, the degradation of culture and an 'invasion' of things foreign, displaying little of the 'exoticism' or *laissez-faire* attitude supposedly distinctive of the region of *Nam Bo*.

## THE 'DIGESTIVE' DILEMMA OF *CAI LUONG* OPERA

A particularly graphic counter-example to the presumption of an all-accommodating southern cultural scene could be found in a prevalent critique of the fate of the *cai luong* operatic form under the impact of the market economy. That such a critique might exist at all was at odds with the view of southerners as open to all changes and unconcerned with the preservation of tradition. That it was directed at perceived degradation in this particular art form was more surprising, for the nature of this form was supposed to exemplify the principles of mutability and openness to new influences. For Huynh Ngoc Trang it represented an archetype of southern cultural 'baroqueness' (Huynh Ngoc Trang 1992:69). Others, however, in criticising its deterioration, recognised that even this distinct southern cultural form had limits to its adaptability.

Phan Thanh Van, who had performed *cai luong* in the past and had written about the ups and downs of the genre for many years as a journalist for a Ho Chi Minh City newspaper, told me in 1993 that, 'in recent years, *cai luong* has met its nemesis with the flood of foreign films, videos and music coming through the open door'. Attempting to compete for the audience's attention, '*cai luong* productions have increasingly resorted to cheap stunts, weird, inappropriate borrowings and spectacular fighting scenes'. He argued that audience numbers were dwindling due to the high price of tickets and the genre's slide into the 'crude and melodramatic'. He said '*cai luong* is famous for its capacity to digest the new, however in the contemporary situation it looks as if it is about to choke to death'. Several other performers, scriptwriters, choreographers and avid *cai luong* followers with whom I spoke confirmed this view. The contemporary genre was labelled 'repetitive and boring', 'catering to the lowest denominator' and 'bereft of artistic value' (*thieu gia tri my thuat*). As was also the case for theatre, rehearsal times had dwindled, and *cai luong* troops had lost their *esprit de corps*, with a handful of stars flitting from troupe to troupe. According to one disaffected *cai luong* buff:

> the only thing keeping the industry alive is the cult of a few *cai luong* superstars. Now their personal lives are the only magnet attracting audiences. People talk more about their affairs and holidays than their skill at performing (from fieldnotes).

The number of troupes was said to have shrunk from around fifty in the late 1970s to five or ten in the whole South in the 1990s.

Phan Thanh Van illustrated the predicament of contemporary *cai luong* by citing its analogous predicament of near-extermination in the late Republican era. He told me:

> In the late 1960s it looked as if *cai luong* was going to be crushed to death under the boots of an occupying army and its accompanying baggage of foreign films, music and fashions (from fieldnotes).

This had been the official view of the predicament of Vietnamese culture in the Republican South. Yet Van's evocation of that period as having constituted a crisis analogous to the contemporary era turned the new regime's critique of the RVN against its own policies. The RVN and the current regime's contemporary policies were equated as common enemies of this southern Vietnamese cultural tradition.

For some of those who viewed the late 1960s and early 1990s as analogous periods of cultural crisis, the intervening period of relative isolation and social reform represented not only a respite but a regenerative opportunity for the region's much compromised cultural integrity. This indeed was the self-image promoted by leaders and spokespersons of the unifying regime. For example, in the early 1980s Ho Chi Minh City's party secretary, Vo Van Kiet, had spoken of revolutionary artists' redemptive role 'to light up dark and confused souls' (Vo Van Kiet 1981). Socialist construction of the South had been aimed at sweeping away the taint of corruption and poison contracted by Vietnamese under the RVN and reminding the erstwhile 'puppet' population of their heroic identity. This project had been equally beneficial to the *cai luong* form, according to Phan Thanh Van, who argued *contra* Huynh Ngoc Trang that, despite its 'good digestion', the form had reached its limits to assimilate the new in the late Republican era.

According to Van, the 1975–86 period represented a return to the 'golden age' of *cai luong* of the 1940s and 1950s. The clampdown on foreign music, banning of many Western films and plays, and the diminution of the influence of the urban Chinese had allowed this indigenous folk form to thrive for the first time in two decades. The return to Ho Chi Minh City of several *cai luong* troupes which had been located in the North during partition had injected new energy into the southern *cai luong* scene. He argued that Soviet-trained directors had introduced fresh and imaginative innovations into the staging of performances, responding to the form's appetite for the new. The crackdown on urban cultural forms such as popular music had indeed led to disaffection and the flight of intellectuals and artists overseas but this had not affected *cai luong* artists to the same extent as those in other genres, given *cai luong*'s predominantly rural-based following. Van argued that peace had enabled the repopulation of rural areas and more favourable opportunities for touring, giving an enormous stimulant to the reinvigoration of the form. *Cai luong* troupes mushroomed and its audience greatly expanded. The new regime's policies of social reform were aided by this form's popularity as, he argued, *cai luong* had traditionally carried a message of social reform (*cai cach xa hoi*) and moral restructuring (*cai tao dao duc*). In turn, the form's integrity as a vehicle of social criticism rather than mere entertainment (*giai tri*) was restored through its mobilisation to the regime's reformist ends.

## CONSTITUTING SOCIALISM AS CULTURAL THREAT

Those who agreed with Phan Thanh Van's view of the 1960s and 1990s as analogous moments of cultural crisis did not necessarily share his depiction of the intervening period. Truong, a journalist on a state-run newspaper, and critic of cultural upheavals during the late Republican and contemporary *doi moi* periods, reserved even harsher criticism for the intervening period. To illustrate his concerns he sketched out a timeline depicting the main factors impacting on 'cultural values' (*gia tri van hoa*) in the recent past. There were the threats posed to tradition by 'social factors' such as the presence of foreign troops or foreign investors. He thought that the impact of the latter in the early 1990s was approaching the seriousness of the impact of the former in the early 1970s. One would also have to consider the impact of 'politics' on culture, in particular what he called the party's 'period of error' (*giai doan sai lam*), which he dated from 1975 to 1982, followed by a four-year transitional period until the official policy reverse in 1986. His attribution of blame to the party for its destruction of traditions during its era of 'error' was particularly uncompromising:

> From 1975 to 1982, politics (*chinh tri*) exerted a negative impact on cultural values. The party's policies of this time damaged traditional social roles. For example, it downgraded the status of teachers. They became poor and they couldn't upgrade their knowledge. As a result, their position in society slipped and people no longer respected them. Another category affected was friends. During the period of error, friends were encouraged to turn on each other. People no longer trusted each other. It became impossible to celebrate happiness with each other (from fieldnotes).

Referring to the predicament of South Vietnam after unification, Truong rejected the notion that the post-war era had amounted to the purifying and revitalising of Vietnamese culture. Framing that era as one of damage to tradition, Truong refuted the assumption that, on liberation, the South had been devoid of tradition or a place of alien invention. Indeed, his comments inverted official views, in reframing the unifying regime as destructive alien and the former South as repository of culture.

This was confirmed in a subsequent conversation during which he unleashed a more vociferous attack along the same lines:

> From 1945 to 1975 in the North, the traditional culture of Vietnam was lost, attacked by the communists who were blinded by the Stalinist dreams of building socialism. They attacked the role of pagodas and religion, weddings became rubber stamp affairs at the People's Committee offices. People could marry without even the need to ask their parents. Socialist equity was placed above traditional values so that children were asked to denounce their parents as compradore bourgeoisie.
>
> By contrast, Vietnamese traditional culture was preserved in the South up until 1975. This is a feature which southerners hold much more strongly than northerners. Families preserved an altar to Buddha and traditional family relations were preserved (from fieldnotes).

Truong's critique employed the same terms exploited by the regime in the late 1970s to characterise the effects of 'neo-colonial cultural poisons', which had allegedly 'stupefied' and impeded the senses of the South Vietnamese population. He said the reason these depredations had occurred in the North was because of the 'stupidity of the disciples of Ho Chi Minh'. He described them as 'uneducated' (*vo hoc*). 'Due to this they "blindly" followed the lead of Russia (*Nga*), yet Russia is not Asia.' He argued that, in contrast, RVN president Ngo Dinh Diem had been a great patriot: 'a man who had loved and contributed to his country.' True, from the late 1960s Vietnamese culture had really begun to disintegrate under the distortions of the US presence. Yet he considered that development to have been the fault of those who came after Diem, presidents Nguyen Van Thieu and Nguyen Cao Ky, whom he also described as 'uneducated'.

This view of Vietnamese tradition in the South as constantly under attack paralleled that vein in official commentary which, since unification, construed Ho Chi Minh City as a place of unremitting cultural subversion. Truong's perception of tradition assailed was equally contradictory. That a quality such as tradition could be open to such repeated assaults was by definition impossible, for the effect would have been the undercutting or changing of 'tradition'. Unlike Van, he proposed no theory of how tradition might have regenerated after each turn in the destructive cycle. Yet Truong's argument also differed in emphasis from official perspectives in that he saw a degree of merit in the RVN era, while placing the post-war regime among the ranks of alien entities destructive of tradition in the South. The cultural nationalism of this state-employed urban intellectual may not have been logically consistent, however, it meshed with what many fellow southerners had to say about the negative cultural impact of the post-war government's policies.

A frequently encountered criticism of the new regime in the South was that, under the influence of Maoism, the respected role of intellectuals in Vietnamese traditional society had been undermined. This was noted by Bui Tin who argued that, after Maoist class policies had been adopted, ignorance had become permanently entrenched as a qualification for leadership for no-one at the top had the intellectual capacity to reform the status quo (Bui Tin 1995:24, 146). This critique was expressed to me by a foreign language teacher in the city of My Tho, who had taught under the former regime, and who said he had been out of work for ten years from 1975 due to the new leaders' 'inferiority complex' towards intellectuals. In both rural and urban contexts I met many professionals who denounced the new regime's valuation of 'redness over expertise' (*hong hon chuyen*) for promotion to responsible societal positions. Studiousness or intellectual brilliance had been less guarantee of a student passing a course or securing employment than the political background of his or her parents. Those from non-revolutionary backgrounds had only been able to redeem themselves in the new society by political militancy, by doing non-intellectual labour (volunteering to join the army, engaging in public works or working in a new economic zone) or by bribing the school authorities.

Post-war attacks on the status of intellectuals were sometimes described as part of a larger assault on the traditional occupational hierarchy which Vietnam had inherited from China. A common criticism was that the prestige of scholars, expressed in the formulation:

1st    scholars (*Si*)
2nd    farmers (*Nong*)
3rd    workers (*Cong*)
4th    traders (*Thuong*)

had been rejected and they had been pushed to the lowest social rank, alongside traders, who remained a despised category under the new regime. According to some, the new regime's own hierarchy was expressed in the two-tiered formula:

1st    *Cong–Nong–Binh* (workers–farmers–soldiers)
2nd    *Si–Thuong* (scholars–traders).

An equally pervasive critique of the new regime was its reversal of traditional valuation of seniority. Youth had been considered the most valuable weapons in the fashioning of a new society. Young people had been mobilised through the Youth Federation, through schools, 'young pioneers' or 'advance guard youth' as well as through military conscription. Youth had been used as instruments in various 'movements' (*phong trao*) and 'campaigns' (*chien dich*) to 'strike the bourgeoisie compradors' (*danh tu san mai ban*), abolish reactionary culture (*bai tru van hoa phan dong*), banish ignorance (*thoat dot*), fight illiteracy (*phong trao chong mu tru*), and 'go to the new economic zones' (*di vung kinh te moi*). This had not only placed young people in a position of societal leadership, but it very often had pitted children against their own parents and senior relatives. Articles appearing in *Tuoi Tre* in 1977 urged children to see the school as an alternative family with fellow pupils as siblings, teachers as parents and the portrait of their benevolently smiling 'senior uncle', Ho Chi Minh, displayed prominently, in place of familial ancestors. A generation of school children had grown up calling themselves 'the nephews and nieces of Uncle Ho' (*con chau bac Ho*). Children had been encouraged to report wrongful activity wherever they saw it, even if at home. Praise and rewards were given if they did so. Emphasis on the school and, by extension, the state as the child's real family had served to police the newly subject population as much as to fashion new national citizens.

This policy was criticised as having caused severe problems of trust across generations. The new regime's undermining of the family and the traditional valuation of seniority was traced back to the early 1950s. I often heard the story of how former party secretary Truong Chinh had denounced his own father in the land reform campaign in the North in the early 1950s. Even in the early 1990s, some parents told me that they still had to exercise caution in disciplining their children. They were worried that if their children became too resentful they might make comments to their teacher that could result in a visit from the police.

The traditional family structure was also seen to have been devastated in the first decade after the war as a consequence of failed economic policies. A number of social scientists from Ho Chi Minh City told me that to their surprise they found the tradition of 'three generations under one roof' to be more commonly practised in urban areas of Ho Chi Minh City than in the relatively 'traditional' rural areas of the Mekong delta. The factor they considered as decisive was the failed collectivisation policy of the late 1970s to late 1980s, which they said had 'unleashed disorder' (*gay lon xon*) upon the countryside. Due to inhibition of production, rural families were impoverished and a whole generation of children had had to leave their family home to look for work. As a consequence, families in the Mekong countryside were torn apart. The oldest children had been usually the first to leave and this led to an overturning of the convention whereby the eldest child tended the household's ancestral altar.[12]

Criticisms of the new regime's approach to intellectuals, seniority, gender relations and religion were directed at the violence done in the building of a 'new life' (*cuoc song moi*) at the expense of cultural traditions. Criticisms of the restructuring of temples, from places of worship, to museums of 'resistance traditions against foreign aggression', focused on the neglect of rich spiritual traditions in pursuit of an overly narrow conception of tradition as anti-foreign resistance. Criticisms of the new regime's traditionalist credentials were ultimately directed at its pretensions as a cultural purifier. Many saw the new regime's campaign to sweep away the 'alien', 'noxious' and 'mongrel' 'vestiges of neo-colonial culture' as quite the opposite: that is, a campaign aimed at eliminating Vietnamese culture and replacing it with foreign contents and forms.

## MUSIC AND IDENTITY: SHADES OF OPINION

This view was particularly evident in discussions I had with Ho Chi Minh City residents about the music policies of the post-war government. The banning of the diverse genres of popular music played under the former regime led to the 1975–85 period being described by some local musicians as the 'era of non-Vietnamese music'. According to these critics of government policy, with the exception of *cai luong*, the only music that people could legally listen to was so-called '*nhac cach mang*' or 'revolutionary music': comprising songs from the resistance wars and the period of building socialism or music from other socialist countries. Occasionally groups from the Soviet bloc would tour the country. During this period, the playing of Western classical music or easy-listening instrumental music was allowed, but not given much airplay. However, instrumental arrangements of pre-1975 music from the South were not permitted. In the early 1980s some Western pop music with lyrics began to be broadcast on the radio, but never on television.

As for the 'revolutionary music', it was derisively referred to as 'red' music (*nhac do*) in reference to the 'yellow' music it was supposed to replace. Many with whom I spoke saw it as directly borrowed from Soviet bloc and Chinese repertoires. Added to this were the melodies borrowed from Eastern Europe, China or Cuba. One southern music critic described red music's repertoire as restricted to three themes, 'productive labour (*lao dong san xuat*), struggle (*chien dau*) and love of the country/party/Uncle Ho (*yeu nuoc/Dang/Bac Ho*)'. He argued that the expression of love in this music was also restricted:

> Red music spoke of love for compatriots, the country, the building of socialism, the fight against the Americans, never of love between two people or for one's family. Neither did it refer to disappointments in love, nor to feelings of sorrow or loneliness (from fieldnotes).

A socialist-realist aesthetic of optimism prevailed. Compositions had to be 'positive' (*tich cuc*) and take a 'definite' (*quyet dinh*) emotional stance. Emotions such as sadness, bitterness and nostalgia were not addressed, nor did the music contain nuances of emotion that signified 'indeterminacy'. Lyrics which could be interpreted ambiguously were forbidden:

> For example there was a song which contained the line, 'On the 30th, I was unable to express my emotions'. The line was referring to feeling mixed emotions on the eve of the new year. However the authorities thought it might be referring to the 30th of April 1975, the date Saigon fell. Therefore they banned it just in case people drew that inference. That instantly made the song extremely popular in Saigon because the lyrics had been given a 'definite' meaning by the government's action! (from fieldnotes).

Many who construed the post-war proscription of 'yellow' music to have been an era of 'non-Vietnamese' music, likewise disputed the notion that this period constituted a 'golden age' for the *cai luong* opera. With most of the music played in the South before 1975 banned, *cai luong* became the only popular music form bridging the old and new eras. Yet the 'health' of this form in the new era depended very much on one's view of the changes made to it and uses it was put to by the new regime. Phan Thanh Van argued, for example, that purging the form of many Chinese costumes, stories, melodies and choreographic items that had taken place in the late 1970s was 'a good thing, for they were not *cai luong*—they were very Chinese-looking'. Also purged were Western melodies, musical genres from the tango to love songs, eclectic foreign costumes, use of Western stories and motifs drawn from sources as varied as Ancient Rome, Egypt, India and the US Wild West. According to some former *cai luong* fans, these excisions had represented a severe breach with the genre's tradition of eclecticism and sensual stimulation. It had greatly impoverished the form, making performances monotonous and predictable. The moral message of post-war *cai luong* had been directed against the 'old way of life', urging youth to give up 'decadent', 'harmful' and 'foreign' culture and embrace the 'new' life of 'purity' and 'sacrifice'. To many, as both victim and vehicle of post-unification cultural reform, *cai luong* had become didactic and unappealing.

One of the worst depredations, according to one critic of the new regime's music policies, had been misuse of the sorrowful and nostalgic melody called *vong co*, which is widely regarded as *cai luong*'s central element. Representing an emotional register proscribed by socialist realism:

> there was initially suggestion that this component of *cai luong* be dropped as the melody was 'weak', destroyed one's will and drove one into solitude. However, it was concluded the *vong co* melody was too popular and central to the *cai luong* tradition to be dropped. Next an attempt was made to set lyrics expressing positive feelings of struggle to the melody, yet the result was so jarring that it was quickly dropped. Ultimately it was used for certain characters to express sorrow or desperation at some predicament, providing the opportunity for the hero of the play to counter such emotions with a martial melody full of optimism and resolution to overcome the problem. For example, on seeing her son sent to prison, a mother would express sorrow in a melancholy *vong co* refrain, but her son, a communist militant, would reply expressing his optimism for eventual victory and even encouraging his mother to feel joyful! (from fieldnotes).

This critic contrasted the socialist-realist heroes of post-1975 *cai luong* with those in the former period. Formerly, heroes would express a range of emotions: doubt before going into battle, sorrow at separation from loved ones, fear for their survival, joy at being reunited with their family and tenderness at rejoining their wives. By contrast, post-unification heroes' emotional register was improbably limited to fearlessness and optimism:

> In one play, a cadre even rejoiced when his own daughter—a beautiful girl leading a debauched life—was sent to prison. She sang using *vong co*—'you are not my father you are so cruel.' Her mother agreed. But the cadre father would not bend. He was so full of revolutionary morality that even the most sad and beautiful *vong co* melody couldn't shake him. He replied, 'I would rather lose a daughter than society lose its purity.' She was sent to gaol. Then, her formerly criminal lover would come to his senses and visit her in gaol encouraging her to appreciate re-education and admire her father's actions (from fieldnotes).

Not only were these characters impossible to relate to but the enemies against whom they fought were caricatured in crude ways:

> Americans were depicted by big actors who used white make-up, hairy beards, spoke Vietnamese badly, walked awkwardly, but mysteriously sang *vong co* beautifully! They were portrayed as lecherous, aggressive, sinister and unfeeling (from fieldnotes).

The heavy hand of the government was all too evident in the new productions according to several long-time followers of the genre:

> Some pre-1975 personnel such as actors and costume and make-up specialists continued on in the new troupes but each troupe had a political cadre—either a northerner or a former southern regroupee. In

this era, *cai luong* went from being a private or commercial art form to a tool of the regime (from fieldnotes).

One remembered *cai luong* in the 1980s as a tool of military and political mobilisation: '*Cai luong* was mainly used to mobilise people to fight the Pol Pot and the Chinese or to attack the old way of life' (from fieldnotes). Another former *cai luong* follower dismissed all *cai luong* since 1975 as 'just government lies and propaganda' (from fieldnotes). Such observers disputed Phan Thanh Van's notion of the 1975–86 period as a 'golden age' of *cai luong*, seeing it as a time when the genre became impoverished and lost its relevance to people's lives. In doing so they inverted the official position that it had engineered the restoration of a more 'wholesome' and 'vital' culture in the South. Rather, the unifying regime was constituted negatively as central to the erosion of traditional culture.

As for pop or non-folk music, the early 1980s saw the music of some Western groups such as Abba, Smoky and Boney M. given qualified official approval. Provincial radio stations reportedly added these to their play lists, although the accompanying video clips were never shown on television. In conjunction, 'revolutionary music' itself was softening its military strains and broadening the themes it addressed. One musician with whom I spoke believed this to have been prompted by the authorities' realisation that pre-1975 Vietnamese music, available widely on the black market, remained far more popular than the official variety:

> The composer Pham Duy was probably the most popular musician in the South before liberation. But the communists really hated him as they said he had betrayed the resistance and fled to the South after 1954. After 1975 a book appeared entitled *How did Pham Duy Die?* which made the claim that popular opinion had rejected Pham Duy. Yet I've heard that a few years after that, composers in the state conservatorium in Hanoi were studying Pham Duy's music, trying to discover the secret of how it was able to reach into people's souls (from fieldnotes).

By several accounts, the attempted fusion between revolutionary themes and sentimental melodies, or the reverse, that had occurred during this era of experimentation was an unmitigated failure. One wit dubbed the end product *nhac cam* or 'orange' music:

> After 1980 there was an attempt to render revolutionary themes in the melodic register of some pre-1975 or 'yellow' love songs. Later, with some relaxation of control, there was an attempt to write about romantic love using 'red' melodies. Both efforts produced something I call 'orange' music that was awful to listen to and had the same effects on the soul of the listener as did the US Army herbicidal agent of the same colour on South Vietnamese jungles (from fieldnotes).

Many musicians saw the decentralising and liberalising policies of the government as having allowed 'the return of Vietnamese music'. This coincided in the mid-1980s with a policy of rehabilitation of some artists and musicians who had long been out of favour, entitled 'Restoration of human values' *(Phuc hoi nhan pham)*. Yet some attributed the rehabilitation of 'yellow' music more to the pressure of popular opinion than to the leadership of the party.

According to one observer, a Ho Chi Minh City-based musician, only in 1985 had 'Vietnamese' music again been played legally in Vietnam, at a concert commemorating the composer Van Cao, at which a number of his pre-war songs had been played. During the concert, popular southern musician Trinh Cong Son sneaked in a rendition of his own 1960s hit *Diem Xua*, which had not been played in an authorised context for ten years. His audacity reportedly earned him a prolonged, emotional ovation from the audience. The musician told me that, in response to an increasing number of such occurrences, in 1986 the government issued a list of 36 acceptable songs from pre-liberation times. This had opened the way for a wholesale, but largely informal, return of most pre-1975 music to popular venues as well as that composed or rearranged by the overseas Vietnamese community *(nhac hai ngoai)*. By the 1990s lists of acceptable music were reportedly no longer issued, although a list of forbidden music which included 'ARVN music' *(nhac linh cong hoa)* was still in circulation. In the early 1990s the Ministry of Culture was reportedly promoting new musical compositions which it dubbed 'green music' *(nhac xanh)*. It was hoped these compositions would reflect the aspirations of the new, *doi moi* era and capture the affection of Vietnamese youth, for whom the conflicts of the past had limited relevance. Yet the prospects for locally-produced 'green' music to ever gain the widespread airplay that both 'red' and 'yellow' music once commanded, in the contemporary era of a globalised musical market, appeared to some critics (who might as well be labelled 'jaundiced') an unlikely prospect.

None of those who lamented the impoverishment of *cai luong* during the era of socialist restructuring believed the genre had made a comeback in the *doi moi* era. Indeed, most saw that the genre had reached its worst ever moment of crisis. Competition with foreign videos, taped music and *karaoke* cafes saw *cai luong* struggling to survive. In pursuit of profits, performances were dominated by cheap stage effects, showy fighting scenes and costumes, and a turn towards superficial and melodramatic stories. Many doubted its survival. In the early 1990s audiences at *cai luong* performances were nearly exclusively female. Most audience members with whom I talked worked as marketeers, hairdressers and in other service industries. I was routinely told that contemporary audience composition differed greatly from 'before 1975', when the genre was still popular among urban and rural intellectuals and attracted many male followers.

Such critics' diagnoses of the contemporary crisis of *cai luong* shared common ground with analysis appearing in state-controlled media outlets on the contemporary crisis of Vietnamese culture. Yet they diverged from the idea that the origins of this crisis lay with hostile, foreign forces. Rather, the crisis of *cai luong* was seen to flow directly from the damage done to it in the supposedly restorative era between 1975 and 1985: '*Cai luong* made itself irrelevant, therefore people lost interest. Now they prefer to follow foreign music and fashions.' This was a perspective encountered in several discussions.

A music critic who was particularly scathing about the impact of 'Stalinism' on the genre of *cai luong*, surprised me in late 1993 by saying that he sincerely hoped that the US embargo would not be lifted for some time. This was because of the poor preparation of youth for the 'foreign cultural invasion' (*xam luoc van hoa nuoc ngoai*) that would undoubtedly be unleashed by the normalisation of relations between the two countries. He feared that young people would not be able to distinguish good cultural imports from bad, as for many years they had been subject to a cultural invasion from the Soviet bloc. This had swamped Vietnamese musical traditions such as *cai luong* and had passed itself off as 'national tradition'. As a consequence, youth had entirely lost interest in their nation's culture. He hoped that the lifting of the embargo would be delayed in order to give teachers, musicians and critics such as himself the chance to reawaken young people's interest in Vietnamese traditions and music and to give youth some kind of education in aesthetics that could help them be more discriminating when the floodgates were eventually opened.

This recalled a comment that the fortune-teller made around the same time, although by then he felt that the capitalist flood had already truly surged through Vietnam's open door. He grieved that immorality, pragmatism and a kind of 'law of the jungle' (*luat rung*) were sweeping the country. He attributed this largely to the deficits of the education system in the pre-*doi moi* era. History, geography, literature, even maths had been primarily concerned with inculcating in students a sense of their innate heroism as Vietnamese:

> Even arithmetic was taught along the line of 'If you shoot X number of enemy troops, how many are left?' After two decades of saturation in deeds of military heroes and emulation of the Soviet Union, youth have emerged from classrooms with no philosophical or moral framework to guide them in their daily lives. Knowledge is now only meaningfully assessed on pragmatic criteria: that which enables the fastest and greatest accumulation of wealth (from fieldnotes).

## CULTURE IN AN ERA OF COMMODIFIED POWER

In the 1990s *cai luong* performers, choreographers and teachers told me that another legacy of the immediate post-war era, casting the contemporary survival of *cai luong* in doubt, was ongoing tight state control of the genre. Political commissars were still attached to each troupe, enabling tight control of the content. Increasingly, pre-1975 southern directors and writers were participating in productions. However flamboyant and public such figures might be, the real artistic control remained with a party cadre filling a more innocuous position in the troupe.

This ongoing control was seen by some as fatal to the effectiveness of the genre, for it limited autonomous exercise of cultural criticism or the exploration of ideas and models not authorised by the party. Most significantly it prevented critical discussion of the legitimacy or competence of the party itself. One critic of contemporary *cai luong* believed this guaranteed to sound the death-knell for the genre. Traditionally it had been followed as a vehicle for critically assessing the socio-cultural trends of the day. Intellectuals had enthusiastically patronised the genre, attracted to it as a popular and vibrant medium of social commentary, he told me. One of the major questions brimming among contemporary Vietnamese was whether the current authorities had the moral qualities (*duc*), and the competence (*tai*), to secure national prosperity, equity, and retention of identity. If such questions could be discussed through the vehicle of *cai luong*, its popularity would return overnight.

Such observations were repeated in other cultural sectors I investigated. State control was duplicated in all sectors of the arts, the press, in schools, universities and research institutes. Commercialisation had allowed an explosion of cultural activity and full-time employment of those with the merest scrap of knowledge to capitalise on. Intellectuals were expressing themselves as never before but, with the question of the party's authority to govern off-limits, perceptions were rife among southern Vietnamese intellectuals that they were but canaries singing in a gilded cage. As a long-time journalist noted, 'liberty under *doi moi* means that now we are free but to make money only'.

The combination of a commercialised system and a party claiming the sole authority to govern provided fairly obvious conditions for systematic corruption. This was the final reason given for the perceived decline in the value of indigenous cultural traditions in the face of foreign competition. Party cultural commissars and arts, media, research and educational administrators were seen by many as chiefly interested in using their positions of power to enrich themselves at any cost. These people did not often exhibit artistic gifts, an understanding of their genre or an ability to steer the institution for which they were responsible through crisis. Their thirst for profits triggered wholesale importation of cheap cultural products on the basis of their profitability in the Vietnamese cultural market rather than any other criteria. The southern music critic who craved a stay in the lifting of the US embargo cited eradication of this 'red aristocracy' (*qui toc do*) as the other major house-cleaning exercise that was required to ensure that, by the time Vietnam's external relations were normalised, traditional musical culture might have some chance to survive. He argued that the field of culture was dominated by mere political appointees with no qualifications to preside in such offices, less spark a cultural revival. In addition, years of absolute power had made them irresponsible and attuned to augmenting their own privileges. He argued that the 'red elite' had turned into 'red capitalists' (*tu ban do*) presiding over a decline into rule by the law of the jungle.

Referring to the collusion of cadres with foreign companies in the building of golf courses, hotels and bars, one widely published Ho Chi Minh City novelist and short story writer described such cadres as 'no longer Vietnamese'. Such investments, she considered, were developed for the combined profit and pleasure of both foreigners and the 'red class' (*giai cap do*). She claimed that these investments did not benefit ordinary people. They could not use them, nor would any of the financial benefits reach them. They would only suffer from a depleted environment. However, to protest was futile, she argued. The publication of critique was forbidden. She admitted that even in her bestselling stories she was unable to speak the truth. Such was reserved for her diary alone. This sentiment of a cultural defection by the city's political leadership was shared by many of the city's working class, unemployed and trade sector. Lien, who worked as a waitress, saw a growing gap between cadres and foreigners on the one hand, and the poor and uneducated on the other. She cited the case of a Ho Chi Minh City factory closed down to build a hotel with Singaporean money. Asked did she not think this would create jobs for everyone, she replied, 'only for the good-looking and fluent in English. And being able to speak English is a product of wealth anyway, so the development aids only those who are already wealthy and already powerful.'[13]

One explanation for the party's instigation of reforms, widespread among southern urbanites, was the self-interest of state and party cadres. Having consolidated their hold on southern society, they were now in a position to extract maximum benefits from its re-commercialisation. The way the reforms unfurled confirmed this cynical observation. Since the promulgation of the foreign investment law in the late 1980s, foreign investment capital had been monopolised domestically by state and party localities. Reform of the land law had reportedly only occurred because party members, as Vietnam's major private landowners, needed secure title over their properties. The banner of socialism was reportedly still waved as a means of ensuring that southern party members could maintain centrally authorised control over this trend. Reverses and checks in liberalisation, rather than being the work of party 'conservatives', were seen by some observers as motivated by envy internal to the party apparatus and by others as attempts to prevent the capacity to make profits from slipping out of the tentacles of the revolutionary elite. This explained the central government's campaign to restore 'spiritual values' (*gia tri tinh than*), eliminate 'social evils' and step up vigilance against 'peaceful evolutionism'. Such cultural purification campaigns impacted most upon those private publishers, teachers, artists, booksellers and film and video distributors, whose activities eroded the party's monopoly to extract profit from the commercialisation of cultural and intellectual property. Even the widespread publication of books and articles on Vietnamese cultural traditions was seen by a teacher in Ho Chi Minh City as an example of the government's monopolisation of lucrative commercial enterprises. Sold to rich overseas Vietnamese and foreign academics concerned with the threat of commercialisation on the preservation of Vietnamese cultural traditions, these works, issuing from select, party-approved publishing houses, were themselves seen to exemplify commercial rather than cultural traditions. Variations on this critique of the regime's venality, which were prevalent among southern urban intellectuals, belied the image of southerners as rational economic actors and disputed ideas of Ho Chi Minh City's divorce from, indifference to, or loss of, Vietnamese cultural traditions.

# 5

# Civilisation in the orchard: The unpublished history of a Mekong delta village

In the early 1990s, while urban areas were unquestionably responding to the *doi moi* reforms, rural Vietnam was facing a serious crisis. The countryside (*nong thon*), home to the nation's poorest, and formerly a place of widespread hunger, had indeed benefited from economic liberalisation. However, very little investment was taking place there, socio-economic differentiation was on the rise and the gap between city and country was growing (Kerkvliet and Porter 1995). The countryside represented one of the biggest anomalies in socialist Vietnam. Championed by the party as Vietnam's most exploited group under colonialism, the peasantry had been described as the nation's historical avant-garde. At war their revolutionary consciousness had been supposedly heightened under enemy bombardment, while in peace, mobilised agricultural labour was to be the locomotive of national development. The war claimed close to two million peasant lives and devastated rural communities, while post-war economic policies brought the countryside to crisis point. In the early years of the *doi moi* era, southern-based social scientists had depicted the Mekong delta as a site of RVN-era 'modernisation' and as a place where 'modernity' was indigenous and indeed natural. While most of the benefits of the reform policies were to come to the cities, it was the city which felt the sharpest pangs of change and it was there that criticisms of the too-rapid pace of reforms were articulated. That such shifts and rebuttals surrounding the location and periodisation of modernity in Vietnam strongly reflected urban Vietnamese concerns became apparent when I began to spend time in the countryside. During an extended residence in a Mekong delta village, I encountered staunch criticisms of the marginalisation of this area of rural Vietnam, which challenged urban perspectives. Elderly villagers contrasted the somewhat grim picture of contemporary rural conditions with a remembered image of their village's high level of 'civilisation' (*nen van minh*) in the days of their youth. Their critical comments about the failings of their local leadership engaged with, and disputed, meanings projected onto the countryside by a range of authorities, from the local to the national level, and yet they did so in a way which underlined how widespread was the notion of modernity and its cognates in Vietnamese discourses of identity.

## BOUND FOR THE BOONDOCKS

On notifying urban acquaintances that I intended spending some time doing research in a rural village of the Mekong delta, I was met with responses ranging from anxiety through bemusement to embarrassment. For all their published representations of the Mekong delta as a site of exceptional modernity, Ho Chi Minh City-based social scientists expressed a different set of concerns in personal communication with me, which emphasised their own experiences in the countryside. Some of their concerns focused on health: I might not survive the basic diet of three rice meals a day, and risked stomach upset from poorly prepared food and certain poisoning by home-brewed rice alcohol. Some feared infection from washing in water drawn from agricultural ditches. Others thought I would find 'inconvenient' the precarious toilets erected on stilts over ditches and fish ponds. Most focused on the political situation in the countryside. Rural cadres in general and those from the province of Tien Giang in particular, were politically 'conservative' (*bao thu*), I was told. Compared with the relative freedoms of association and expression in the big city in the era of 'openness', I would find the countryside five or even ten years behind the times, cadres mistrustful and the general population afraid of the consequences of speaking with outsiders. Some doubted that I would be allowed to do research or that villagers would feel comfortable talking to me. Such critical and anxious views, based on their own difficulties researching in the countryside, were contrary to the confident promotion of the region as expressive of Vietnamese modernity.

Similar contradictions were found among those urban acquaintances who had expressed worry at the deleterious impact of reforms on the nation's traditions. Despite the constitution of their home as a site of endangered tradition, few of these urbanites were in doubt about their temporally advanced (*tien bo*) status when considering the situation in the countryside. The rusticity of the Mekong delta countryside was a byword among such urban friends. This was not without its charms. The southern delta was an anachronistic but a quaint land. The speech of its inhabitants was simple, forthright and full of charmingly archaic turns of phrase. Southern peasants (*nong dan*) were idealised as frank (*that tha*), simple (*don gian*), and open (*coi mo*), and I would be safe from the crime and guile of city life. Yet as the reverse side of the coin, I could expect limited horizons, low education and life experiences limited to rice and fruit growing and the drinking of home-brewed rice wine (*ruou de*). Binge drinking, low schooling, and prevalence of superstition (*me tin*) were equally prevalent and linked with each other. Lack of schooling led to credulous minds, few work opportunities and, with opportunities foreclosed, a resort to alcoholism. In a word, the place for which I was headed was perceived as 'backward' (*lac hau*). For them, the southern Vietnamese countryside was a touchstone: a symbol of tradition, yet one in which they would not like to spend too much time.

Many of those who had themselves only recently arrived in the city from the country, were more forthright about the 'backwardness' of the countryside. Such people expressed their bewilderment at why I should want to waste my time in such irrelevant backwaters. The countryside was described as 'sad' (*buon*), with few cultural offerings, entertainment activities or consumer opportunities to distract me. I was warned there would certainly be no TV or refrigeration. Electricity might be sporadic or non-existent and all my neighbours would retire at sunset and wake at sunrise in a daily miserable grind. When I mentioned that the district I intended to reside in was nationally famous for its milk apples (*vu sua*), the uproarious verdict was that I was heading for the international capital of 'breast'-fruit. Another feature of local history was the emergence of the southern musical form *cai luong* or 'reformed' opera, there in the 1920s. Seen by male intellectuals as an entertainment for 'uneducated' (*that hoc*) and 'common' (*binh dan*) market women, the association of my proposed field site with this art form convinced my urban friends that I was heading for a backwater of rustic simpletons. Expressions of enthusiasm for the art form only provoked embarrassed laughter. To such newly established cosmopolitans, the countryside was anachronistic and unrepresentative: a kind of aberration from the urban world they embraced and celebrated. They had eagerly welcomed me as an emissary of all the excitement, strangeness and foreign sophistication the 'open door' policy had promised to bring and were not overjoyed that their new-found source of entertainment was to be lost to a rural black hole.

## FORMALITIES, TRADITIONS AND WAR

Arriving in the province of Tien Giang, I discussed field site locations with the director of the provincial party school who was also a member of the provincial People's Committee (*Hoi Dong Nhan Dan*). He was to be my patron, in charge of securing permission for me to do my fieldwork. The field site I had in mind was a village which, during the

Republican era, had been divided between government and insurgent control. A variety of religious traditions were represented there, including the Hoa Hao and Cao Dai (both indigenous to southern Vietnam), two Buddhist pagodas, one Catholic and one Protestant church and a Chinese temple. The village's economy was equally diverse, divided between rice growing, fruit trees, animal husbandry, aquaculture, and a number of food processing plants. To me it was representative of the complexity of Mekong delta society. However when I suggested it to him as a potential field site he dismissed it out of hand.

Enthusiastic about my project to study a village in his province, he felt that the candidate for such a study was beyond doubt the village of Vinh Kim, 'the most typical village of Tien Giang province'. Asked why it was typical, he replied that the village was one of the earliest Vietnamese settlements in the province. He strode over and indicated a map of Tien Giang province:

> More than 300 years ago, Vietnamese from the central coast of
> Vietnam came southwards and entered the Mekong through these
> mouths. They came upstream and settled first around Vinh Kim, due to
> the many small freshwater streams in the area, providing a year-round
> supply of fresh water (from fieldnotes).

The village was a place where traditions ran deep, none of these more so than its proud 'tradition of resistance' (*truyen thong khang chien*). Vinh Kim was what was known as a 'heroic village' (*lang xa anh hung*), famed for its very old tradition of heroism. He told me it had been the key battleground for the repulsion of a major Siamese invasion in the late eighteenth century. Also leading the way in resistance against French colonialism, the village was a 'cradle of the revolution' (*noi cua cach mang*), being the site where the first Communist Party cell in the province had been established in 1930. During the 'War against America' (*Chien tranh chong My*), he claimed, the Americans themselves had used a phrase recognising the militancy of the village: 'Enter Vinh Kim on foot, leave it on your back.' With such an exemplary history, there could be hardly any question of an alternative research site.

The party school's secretary, Brother Hiep, helped me make my preparations. On a map in his own office, he showed me the way settlement in the village followed the bends of the stream, with fruit trees clustered around the dwellings and rice paddies out behind. During the war, Hiep said, the orchards in Vinh Kim had been defoliated to deny the 'Viet Cong' cover and many people had fled for the city. Hiep said he had left Saigon to avoid conscription into the ARVN, which would have occurred when he turned eighteen. He had been stationed in the Plain of Reeds (*Dong Thap Muoi*) in the northwest of the province, where he had spent several years fighting. Hiep said that during the war, the liberation troops (*giai phong quan*) had subsisted on rice from unoccupied fields, on frogs, snails and crabs and on fish, big as his arm, and so numerous that he could scoop them up from the canals by hand. I was told that the Vietnamese people had been successful in their war against the Americans due to the strength of their traditions. He explained to me that in southern Vietnam, people had a tradition called 'splitting sorrow and combining happiness' (*chia buon va chung vui*):

> In times of misfortune, we visit and help each other out. For example, if someone has lost a family member, we will drink with each other and light incense for each other. That way, the misfortune of one is split between many. If, on the other hand, someone has cause to celebrate, then we will again drink with each other to augment that person's happiness. This custom of sharing is how we were all able to defeat the Japanese, the French and the Americans (from fieldnotes).

Brother Hiep assured me that although having been enemies during the war, our countries were now at peace and I would find myself included in village life and treated hospitably in social activities. To emphasise his point he shared his glass of home-brewed rocket fuel with me, setting the lead for everyone else at the table to 'combine happiness' with me.

On arrival in the village I was introduced to the village president, a man in his early forties. I was most welcome in the village, however, several special provisions would apply. I was to be lodged with the head of hamlet security. Visits to neighbours in my hamlet were to be accompanied by the household head or a member of the household, who were responsible for my security. Trips to the neighbouring village were to be accompanied by a village police officer. The president informed me that these restrictions were imposed for my own safety. Locals, with the memories of war still fresh in their minds, might take me for an American and take an angry pot-shot at me. For similar reasons I was told not to accept invitations to eat with anyone except my host family to avoid possible poisoning.

Introductions to the hamlet in which I was to reside were conducted by its administrative representatives. The very first social occasion I was invited to in the village was hosted by the party secretary (*bi thu dang*) responsible for the hamlet. It was his grandfather's death anniversary celebration (*dam gio*). Brother Three's house was a simple structure of thatched palm leaves on wooden poles over an earth floor. Members of his family were busy with preparations for a substantial feast in the front room where I was invited to sit and sip tea with a number of elderly guests. Delicious-looking dishes were laid out on the elegant ancestral altar which dominated the small room. Three explained that his grandfather had been forcibly drafted by the French to serve in Europe during World War I. He reached up and pulled down the frame which contained photographs of his ancestors. His grand-father was sitting erect in the largest of the photographs, with the delicate scalp, translucent eyes and wispy goatee of a Ho Chi Minh and wearing Three's pencil-thin moustache. Medals lined his breast. The picture of his grandmother was crumpled and brittle, giving her an anguished and decaying look. The only image of his father was his identity card, in which Three's moustache appeared again in faded black and white.

Outside the front door, a low table had been set up. 'An altar for fallen soldiers', he explained, arranging bowls of rice, steaming soups and roast duck and pouring out rice wine for five settings. 'It is a Vietnamese custom for all soldiers who have fallen defending Vietnam.' He came inside and, with lit incense, murmured an invitation to his grandfather and other ancestors to join the feast. He then moved outside and repeated the invitation to the fallen soldiers. Preparations complete, he rejoined us inside. He thanked his guests for coming to celebrate his grandfather's death anniversary. He said it was a particularly great honour to be receiving a foreign guest. He addressed me: 'During the war, this celebration couldn't have taken place. This whole area was a particularly ferocious battle zone.' He pointed out the front door at the profusion of fruit trees lining the road. 'If you looked out there, you would have seen nothing. The colour green did not exist.' He stood by the doorway and pointed to the land around him saying, 'during the anti-American war, this was what they called a "free-fire zone". Whoever wanted to shoot at anyone just went ahead and shot. Yet Vietnamese people still lived here during that time. Any other people would have left long ago' (from fieldnotes).

A few grunts of protest emerged from other guests. 'Come on, let your guest eat,' grumbled a grey-haired figure in a military uniform. Three quickly refocused on his responsibilities as a host to the living and proceeded to share a glass of rice whisky with each guest at the main table. He invited us to make ourselves at home. The sound of chopsticks and clinking of glasses replaced our host's welcoming formalities. Food and drink were consumed in large quantities. Endless combinations of toasts were proposed. Three disappeared outside to share liquid hospitality with guests seated at tables in the front yard. Half an hour later, when everyone at my table was finished eating, he reappeared, face flushed, staggering slightly. With one hand holding on to the edge of the table for balance, the other to a freshly charged glass, he proposed a special toast to me, his foreign guest: 'I want us to drink as friends, to the possibility of friendship between Vietnam and, and . . . your country', seeming to forget where I was from. Three clasped my hand and his voice grew suddenly intense. 'When the Americans came here, they destroyed this country of ours. They committed unfor-gettable atrocities. The Vietnamese people cannot forget the Americans.

Could an American return here, I ask you?' His voice trailed off uncertainly. His hand almost slipped out of mine. Had he just remembered that Australian troops had also fought in Vietnam? The glass hung in the air. There was complete silence in the room.

He began another tack. 'The Vietnamese people don't hate the American people, only the American government.' His voice grew more certain as he steadied himself against my grip. 'It's the American government, not the American people that we hate.' His voice broke, showing great emotion. The glass of whisky now hung by his side, spilling over slightly. The probability of it getting drunk seemed to be vanishing rapidly.

One of the senior guests broke the uncomfortable silence. 'You know, the Australian government was one of the first to start helping Vietnam,' he addressed the table of elderly men at which I was sitting. His words, or was it just the sound of his voice, catalysed Three's whisky-bearing arm into action. 'We'll drink as brothers,' he said, eyes clasped to mine. 'Elder and younger brothers. I'll drink first as I'm the elder.' Feet braced, he flung back the better part of the glass. He released my flagging hand and I drank off the remaining whisky. The cup was taken from my hand, quickly refilled and sent off across the table on a new mission of sentimental bridge-building.

## THE VILLAGE COSMOS

My landlord and officially-prescribed minder in the village turned out to be one of Three's senior guests: a 67-year-old farmer and civil head of one of the village's five hamlets (*truong ap*). The substantial orchards surrounding his house represented a small fraction of what his grandfather had once owned. All of the 250 families in the hamlet were well known to him, he said, although the rapid proliferation of hamlet children was hard to keep track of. Over the course of the next two months I made the acquaintance of many of his age group, accompanying my host on social calls to his friends and receiving invitations to a range of household festivities organised by family, friends and neighbours. As hamlet head and active socialiser, my host received many such invitations to death anniversaries (*dam gio*), birthdays (*sinh nhat*), weddings (*dam cuoi*) and funerals (*dam ma*), sometimes attending as many as ten in one week. Accompanying him, I inevitably found myself seated at a table of elderly men. The seating at such festivals sharply reflected age and gender hierarchies with elderly men seated and served first, women and younger men served later, sometimes in a second or third 'shift' at the same table. After two months of such intense socialising, fuelled by choice delicacies and potent rice alcohol, I got to know his age and gender cohort fairly well, far better than any other group in the village. Such fragmentary exposure to rural society

**Elderly male villagers celebrating together**

was repeated at the domestic level. Three meals a day were shared almost always exclusively with my host and occasionally one of his sons. Having prepared the meal and offered it ritually on the ancestral altar located in the front room, my host's wife or daughter-in-law would serve us and then retire to eat together with other female family members in the small kitchen area at the rear of the house. During our meals, my host would discourse tirelessly on various matters in his weary didactic twang, punctuating the air with his chopsticks.

In conversation with him and members of his age group, I was struck by the breadth of their interests and knowledge of the wider world. I was impressed to be informed about the rivalry between Sydney and Melbourne over location of the Australian capital that had led to the founding of Canberra, dial-it fast food, France's film importation policy, American irrigation methods, warlordism in Somalia. I was also struck by my hosts' scrupulously pedantic efforts at sourcing such information. For example, one old-timer told me, 'although I have not been to Hanoi, my older brother was there and he told me that the temperature in summer there is actually hotter than in the Mekong delta' (from fieldnotes). Another example came from a group discussion about eating habits in foreign countries: 'The younger brother of my father, whom I refer to as junior paternal uncle (*Chu*), returned here from Canada last year to visit his family. On that occasion I spoke to him and he told me that most of the food Canadians eat is packaged' (from fieldnotes). After hearing me mention a detail that interested them, my hosts would often repeat what I had said and seek confirmation they had heard correctly. I would often hear such facts, impeccably sourced back to me, repeated and offered up as gems of information at later festive occasions. In addition, I was endlessly asked to confirm the veracity of reports about the wider world and sensed my hosts yearned for engrossment in a detailed, nuanced and critical assessment. Interest in the wider world was matched by enthusiasm for history. My host once led me into his front garden and showed me an ornamental shrub which he speculated might be older than the history of white settlement in Australia. In his ever sceptical manner, he once told me, 'there are historians who claim Vietnam has existed for 4000 years. I cannot say for sure whether this is true, yet what can be said for certain is that the Vietnamese nation is a mere infant compared with Grandfather China (*Ong Trung Quoc*)' (from fieldnotes). Pride and awe at the relative depth of his country's existence was evident, yet even here, was tempered by awareness that his knowledge of this was second-hand and thus possibly erroneous. He followed this comment with a mini-lesson in history: a good example of his sceptical style, in which making the source of his knowledge transparent was as important as conveying its content:

> I am not a well-educated man, but I have had a chance to read a number of books and in them I read that the history of Vietnam is 4000 years old. The Vietnamese are the descendants of Au Co and Lac Long Quan whose union produced one hundred eggs. The first Vietnamese emerged from one of these and we are descended from this ancestor. This occurred before there was writing. The reason we know this is that the story was passed down from generation to generation until a system of writing arrived from China and the story could be written down. That is the origin of Vietnam (from fieldnotes).

He paused, then added. 'Of course I have to tell you this because that is what I was taught at school.' His face creased into an enormous grin.

Breadth of interest in the events of the wider world matched the rich life experiences of most of this cohort. Most of the group whom I got to know had been educated for at least two years in the colonial period (which they equated with six to eight years of schooling under the present system). While all came from farming families, most had travelled beyond the provincial borders during the colonial period. All said they had participated in the anti-French resistance war of 1945–54, which had brought them into contact with revolutionaries from other regions and saw them operating beyond the confines of the village. After 1954 all those with whom I had a chance to speak had left the village, either working in one of the provincial capitals or in Saigon, serving in the Republican army or regrouping (*tap ket*) to the North to serve under the Democratic Republic of Vietnam (DRV) for the twenty years prior to unification. Coming back to the hamlet from these diverse locations in 1975, most had returned to farming lifestyles, some serving in the village administration. Each had relatives abroad and each household at least one member residing in the provincial capital or Ho Chi Minh City.

Members of my host's generation and gender cohort expressed honour that I had selected their home village (*que huong*) to study and were effusive in singing its praises. Selections from encounters with three proud villagers revealed a substantial consensus on the character of their homeland. 'Uncle Four', a 72-year-old former regroupee, brought a whiff of Soviet-style diplomacy to our first encounter. Raising both hands up, palms forward, in greeting, he said:

> I want to welcome you to our village. We deeply value the assistance
> of foreign friends such as Australia, especially in the field of technical
> assistance and training. These are exciting times for Vietnam and
> thanks to our foreign friends we have witnessed many positive
> developments (from fieldnotes).

Stepping forward, he completed his genial greeting with a bear-hug, thumping my back in time with his laughter. He congratulated me on my 'choice' of residence, saying my host was both prosperous and had received many visitors due to his intelligence. He explained that my host's prestige (*uy tin*) was based on his intellectual (*tri thuc*) accomplishments. Uncle Four said that my host had entered the third year of school in the colonial era, an impressive achievement considering the high standards of those times. He said the village was full of such clever people yet they had lacked the financial means to get a degree. However, Vinh Kim had many winners of doctorates in its history, some taking their degree more than 100 years ago. Many of them had gone abroad, for example his son, who had studied in Kiev and was now residing in Uzbekistan. He showed me a photo of his son and a copy of his degree, displayed on the front table alongside a plaster bust of Ho Chi Minh, proudly enshrined with pink plastic flowers inside a small glass aquarium.

The next person I spoke to was a 63-year-old retired teacher, referred to by all as Teacher Quang. A native of Soc Trang, he had moved to Vinh Kim in 1967 to live with his locally born wife. Consequently, he said he could tell me very little about village history; however, from an outsider's perspective, the village was distinguished by three characteristics: its hospitality, the early development of a high level of culture and the arts, and a proud tradition of resistance. Asked how locals regarded their history, he replied that the people of Vinh Kim were proud (*hanh dien*) of their village's 'grand traditions' (*truyen thong lon*) of culture/education (*van hoa*) and resistance (*khang chien*).

He told me that although village educational standards were low in comparison with the city, they were still higher than other rural areas, for example, his own home village. From one who came from the saline infested rice fields of the eastern delta, he saw the extremely fertile soil and year-round fresh water in the village as central to the development of its prosperity and reputation for generous hospitality. Benevolent natural conditions had allowed people to focus on their education and cultural development. The village had received many famous visitors, he argued, drawn to its exemplification of 'civilisation' (*van minh*) in a rural context. Its environment of abundance had prevented mental rigidity. Diverse cultural, religious and intellectual influences had combined here and were widely absorbed, which proved that 'we southerners (*nguoi Nam Bo*) are not fanatical' (from fieldnotes).

The third villager, 'Uncle Two', was a 63-year-old former newspaper editor who had ceased work in Da Nang and returned to his native village in 1975. Uncle Two was the most effusive about the distinctiveness of his village, calling it '*dia linh nhan kiet*' (miraculous earth whence heroes spring). His version of village history, articulated in several conversations with me, may be paraphrased as follows. Under the late Nguyen Dynasty the village had produced one of southern Vietnam's few doctoral candidates, Phan Hien Dao. Under the French many villagers had studied in Hanoi and had taken higher degrees abroad and today its children now served as doctors, lawyers, teachers, professors, technicians and administrators throughout Vietnam and in many foreign countries. From pre-colonial times to the present, the village had been a hub of regional education. Just as the talented sons of the region had flocked to receive education from the village's doctoral candidate in the nineteenth century, so today did surrounding villagers continue to send their children to study at Vinh Kim secondary school, the only one in the immediate region offering classes up to final year. Local scholars had also fanned out to teach in schools throughout the Mekong delta. The village was foremost in the development of *cai luong*, the southern Vietnamese reformed opera, and had exported performers and impresarios throughout the country. One of the founders of this genre, a local son, Tran Van Khe, had taken his doctorate in musicology at the Sorbonne and was now professor of music in Paris. A land of plenty, the village had entertained many distinguished guests and had acquired a wide reputation as a centre of rural civility and learning: for its 'civilisation of the orchard' (*van minh miet vuon*). Resistance against the French had been a village-wide phenomenon. Landowners (*dia chu*) had led the way, showing generosity and understanding in distributing their lands in Viet Minh-inspired land reforms. Village administrators had shown solidarity in resistance against colonial oppression by resigning from their positions, so that in 1928 the village had been without an administration for three months. Throughout the war of 1960–75, locals working for the 'Republic' (*Cong Hoa*) as administrators had shown an open and enlightened attitude in executing their duties. No village son whether Republican soldier or guerilla fighter had ever lifted a hand against fellow villagers, he claimed, nor had they engaged in looting or the destruction of property.

This view of the village as an exceptional place of learning, culture and enlightened resistance was frequently encountered among men in my host's age group. On several occasions I was pointed to a publication published in 1972 on village history and personalities entitled, *A Formidable Page in the History of Vinh Kim Village (Trang Su Oai Hung cua Xa Vinh Kim)*. With prefatory acknowledgments to the local US military commander, the slim booklet was dedicated to a deceased village intellectual who belonged to the generation of most of my acquaintances, born in the 1920s and 1930s (Nhieu tac gia 1972). The theme of outstanding feats of resistance evident in the title, featured prominently, with accounts of local participation in the 1940 'Southern Uprising' (*Nam Ky Khoi Nghia*) against the French (following their surrender in Europe), the 1945 August Revolution, and the 1945–54 anti-French resistance. It also included biographical sketches and tributes to accomplished local intellectuals, including doctors, musicians and doctoral winners. Completing the presentation of the village as a haven of culture and learning, the booklet contained poems and songs singing the village's praises, some composed by school children, interspersed through the historical narrative. During my stay in the village, only one moth-eaten copy of this booklet could be located, although many recommended it as an authoritative introduction to village history. Despite its scarcity, however, most of my host's age group were familiar with its content and frequently recounted episodes featured therein such as the three-month strike of administrators, the 1940 Southern Uprising and severe French reprisals, and the local villagers' seizure of power in August 1945.

## TAKING A BOW ON THE NATIONAL STAGE

Conversation with a wider range of villagers revealed persistent attempts to inscribe the village as a site of national significance. Examples of such posturing were encountered in a wide range of topics. For instance many villagers boasted that the daughters of Vinh Kim were widely acclaimed as the most beautiful in Vietnam. The main feature of this feminine beauty was their white skin, although reasons given for this diverged. Some said that the clear complexions of local girls were due to the village's protective canopy of fruit trees, which shielded them from exposure to the sun. Others argued that it was the

**At a village wedding, the bride and groom serve cake to senior male guests**

diet of fruit that produced such results. Still others argued that in conformity with the strong respect for Confucian traditions in the village, families kept their daughters indoors, preventing them from widespread socialising, and therefore their skin remained unblemished by the sun. Proof of the incomparable beauty of village daughters came with the fact that 'Uncle' Ton Duc Thang, the first president of united Vietnam himself, had married a Vinh Kim girl. Others asserted that Le Duc Tho, former Central Committee power-broker had also married a local girl. The competitive nature of assertions of such a locality's national relevance was evident on visiting neighbouring villages. At festive occasions in three of the surrounding villages, I met locals who asserted that it was in fact *their* village from which the nation's leader had selected his wife. Despite the reported polygamy of the national party leadership, discussed critically for example by Bui Tin (1995:107), which might support the scenario of a wife drawn from each village, it seemed safer to assume that their competitive assertions were attempts to claim some national significance for their locales.

When the localisation of a national trait ('Vietnamese history is heroic', 'Vietnamese women are exceptionally beautiful') occurred, it resulted in an exemplary formulation; as 'heroic', the village typified the nation's history and as 'beautiful', its daughters exemplified Vietnamese feminine beauty. When, however, a singular event was localised, it produced an exception, the village as a nationally significant place. Rivalry in the localisation of general traits produced, in the former instance, a confirmation of the national stereotype. The more Vietnamese villagers termed themselves 'heroic', the more the exemplary heroism of the Vietnamese villager was confirmed. Rivalry over singular events, however, produced anomalies. It fractured singularity, suggesting multiple parallel occurrences. One example of this came with local interpretations of an event described as singular in contemporary histories, the decisive victory of the Tay Son general Nguyen Hue over the Siamese in 1785. Foreign, national, provincial and district histories all located this battle at Rach Gam Xoai Mut, the confluence of the Rach Gam stream and the anterior branch of the Mekong river delta, where Tay Son troops ambushed the Siamese navy (for example, Nguyen Khac Vien 1987:106). However, locals from four separate villages, even including one which had no border with the Mekong, each claimed their own village as 'Rach Gam Xoai Mut', the historical victory ground. Three of these villages were also among those producing the wife of the national president.

The contexts in which I heard such claims were similar—during visits to these villages for festive events. They tended to come early on in the process of introductions when I mentioned my interest in the history of the neighbouring village of Vinh Kim. The claims flowed immediately from this statement of my research interests: 'Oh, did you know *this* village is the "second homeland" (*que thu 2*) of Uncle Ton Duc Thang. His wife comes from here.' Or: 'this village is the site of "Rach Gam Xoai Mut", where Nguyen Hue defeated the Siamese pirates' (from fieldnotes). Stating my interest in a neighbouring village's history instantly evoked instances of their own village's brushes with history. The cumulative effect of such encounters was to kaleidoscope the singular, creating the impression of a multi-sited battle or a polygamous president.

Such multiple localisings of events of national significance, while competitive, were not necessarily subject to dispute. The reason for this owed much to the nomadic and often inebriated state of the recorder of such claims, being myself, the sole repository of this particular accumulation of claims dispersed in space and time. More importantly I was not concerned to verify and dispute competing claims, being more interested in the terms in which contemporary Vietnamese located themselves than the true location of historical personages and events. The main result of this process of travelling and listening was to find that in certain contexts people would competitively inscribe themselves into the national narrative, emphasising their home village as nationally exceptional.

Among the events subject to contemporary competitive narrative localisation was the 'Southern Uprising' (*Nam Ky Khoi Nghia*) of 1940.

Several elderly men from Vinh Kim and surrounding villages had taken part in this and it was recalled by people of all ages as an important historical event, with local participation exemplifying the nation's history of anti-colonial resistance. For many the Southern Uprising also exemplified the brutal face of French colonial rule. Accounts of the uprising, by locals from various villages, agreed on the central facts. Following a sizeable and noisy march from surrounding villages into Vinh Kim's central market hamlet, prolonged demonstrations, and the seizure of the French garrison stationed there, colonial reprisal had been swift and bloody. Forty locals had been killed in French aerial bombings of the market place and many of the uprising's local organisers and participants had been executed, or gaoled for up to five years, to be released with the Japanese surrender in 1945.

On the first night of my sojourn in Vinh Kim my host received a visit from a 75-year-old friend from the neighbouring village of Long Hung. This individual had been gaoled from 1940 to 1945 due to his role in the uprising. Hearing of my plans to research Vinh Kim's history, 'Grandfather Seven' was eager to introduce the significance of his own village. He asked me if I had ever heard the name 'Long Hung' in reading about Vietnamese history: 'Long Hung could be called the cradle (*noi*) of the Southern Uprising.' Over the next two months he repeatedly made offers to give me a guided tour of the key sites in his village where this uprising had unfolded, offers I could not take up due to restrictions that had been placed on my movement to other villages by Vinh Kim officialdom. However, in conversation with yet another of my host's friends, a native of Vinh Kim, I was informed that I would be missing very little by not visiting Long Hung. Grandfather Seven's account was patently incorrect. Those who claimed that Long Hung village had been the 'cradle' of the Southern Uprising were merely showing their ignorance. It was incontrovertible that Vinh Kim village had been the true cradle of the uprising. For it was not only in Vinh Kim village that the uprising had been executed. It was there that it had been conceived.[1]

The contest over where the Southern Uprising had originated was of a different order to disputes over the birthplace of the president's wife or the site of an eighteenth-century battle with the Siamese. In my conversations with villagers, it featured less as an introductory pleasantry or random topic of discussion than as a persistent focus of concern. For those who most often raised it—my elderly host's generation and age cohort—it was an abiding memory, and a particularly vivid one. What had been a stirring challenge to colonial authority had quickly turned catastrophic, resulting in the deaths of forty villagers and the execution and arrest of many more. The uprising was also an authorised 'event' in the nation's history. The 'Southern Uprising' featured as one of the sacred defining events of Vietnamese Communist

Party history. Much print had been expended on this, one of the largest rebellions organised by the fledgling Indochinese Communist Party. People's constant reference to their involvement in the uprising was also illustrative of the means by which contemporary political advantage was augmented, by linking personal biography to the official history of the party. To prove participation in such an officially sanctioned historical event, or to be related to someone who had, was to gain 'revolutionary merit' (*cong voi cach mang*). From the party's perspective this was considered the highest of virtues and, at the time of research, remained a most valuable commodity for those seeking office or membership of the Communist Party.

The Southern Uprising had also been the topic of a recent historical study initiated by the party chapter of Tien Giang province. Investigators from the 'Committee for the research of Tien Giang province's party history' (*Ban nghien cuu lich su dang Tien Giang*) had come to the village and quizzed locals on their involvement in the uprising. The book, published in 1985, was entitled, *Tien Giang in the Southern Uprising* (*Tien Giang trong cuoc khoi nghia Nam Ky*).[2] Two years later the party chapter of the local district had published a book entitled, *History of the Revolutionary Struggle Tradition of the People of Chau Thanh District 1930–1954* (*Lich su truyen thong dau tranh cach mang cua nhan dan huyen Chau Thanh*).[3] This work also prominently featured the uprising. Again researchers, this time employed by the district party chapter, had come and had combed Vinh Kim village for information. Such activities had jogged memories and had stimulated discussion about this event in various village fora.

Proud of their village, Vinh Kim locals awaited publication of these texts with anticipation, hoping to see the importance of their home town recognised in an official publication. However, to the consternation of several of my elderly acquaintances, both these accounts had emerged, proclaiming neighbouring Long Hung village to have been not only the district but the provincial 'seat' (*tru so*) of the uprising (1985:53; 1987:61). The district account described how, in early 1940, key meetings of the district party chapter had been held in Long Hung, at which decisions to mobilise the population into an uprising against the French had been taken (1987:51) and preparations for mobilisation had begun (1987:52). Both works described Long Hung's communal house (*dinh*) as the site of the provincial 'seat' of the post-uprising revolutionary administration and the place where the gold-starred flag was first raised (1985:52; 1987:61). Both publications displayed a photograph of the Long Hung communal house: 'seat of My Tho Province's uprising committee.'[4] The provincial party publication included a photograph of a stone 'used to sharpen weapons used in the uprising at Long Hung' and another of a wooden tocsin 'from the Long Hung communal house' which had been used to signal the start of the uprising. It also displayed two photographs of Long Hung native, and currently high-ranking party member, Nguyen Thi Thap. In one of these she was depicted introducing visitors to the 'base of the uprising' (*can cu cua khoi nghia*) in Long Hung (1985:46). The medium in which such contentions were made set them far beyond the boastful assertions of a neighbouring villager whose ideas could be jokingly indulged, irritably dismissed, or ignored. They emerged as politically authorised versions of the event, in editions of 5000 and 3000 copies respectively, set as required reading in the province's history classrooms and readily available in book stores in the provincial capital.

## QUESTIONING OFFICIAL HISTORIOGRAPHY

My elderly acquaintances in Vinh Kim village were quick to dismiss the authority of these works. According to one the district party chapter's published history of the district's 'revolutionary struggle traditions', where it referred to the 'Southern Uprising', comprised 'only 40 per cent of the truth'. He derided the provincial party chapter's publication, although solely devoted to the uprising, as 'of even lesser value'. He claimed that both erred seriously on places and dates. Both accounts also exaggerated the role of 'certain key party cadres' from Long Hung and (misleadingly, he argued) suggested that the uprising had been organised in that village before flowing on to Vinh Kim village. According to him organisation of the uprising had taken place in Vinh Kim prior to the gathering of protesters in Long Hung. That Long Hung had become enshrined in published texts as 'cradle of the Southern Uprising' suggested to him the play of contemporary power politics.

More than one villager conveyed cynicism about the way official historiography served contemporary ends. I was urged by one to seek out rival histories to those emerging under the current regime. They might not necessarily be more true, but at least could provide a different perspective. He suggested I consult histories published under the old Saigon regime or those by southern Communist Party writers currently out of favour with the party. Typically party histories were political exercises, sponsored by certain individuals in high places, as a way of self-servingly promoting their own involvement in key events of revolutionary history. I was told that, as Long Hung village had sons and daughters in very high places, it was inevitable that it would emerge as a central actor in the province's political history.[5] Had Vinh Kim only produced higher-ranking party members it might well have been accorded the credit it deserved.

Not only had these official accounts removed the village of Vinh Kim from centre stage, appropriating what many saw to have been a defining moment in their own village's history, they proposed a history that differed radically in its view of the significant actors and processes, seriously misrepresenting the *nature* of the revolt. According to my acquaintances, Vinh Kim villagers' participation in the Southern Uprising had expressed the high educational level, cultural accomplishments and cosmopolitan sophistication their village had attained by the eve of World War II. This was referred to by several individuals as a 'civilisation of the orchard' (*van minh miet vuon*). Prosperity, hospitality, Confucian cultivation, admixed with French primary education and the enlightened patronage of landlords, had led to revolt against the worst despotism of colonial rule.

Yet the provincial history publication, for example, extracted a different meaning, which may be paraphrased as follows: The first Vietnamese settlers arriving in the province had need to draw on their heroic traditions of struggle from the beginning of their encounter with the depopulated wastelands of the Mekong delta (allegedly devoid of people, such as Cambodians):

> In our Vietnamese nation's several-thousand-year history of 'building and defending' their country, the people of Tien Giang province have a history of over three hundred years to which they are deeply attached. The people of Tien Giang have expended inestimable effort and sweat into opening up and cultivating waste lands and building a populous and wealthy region and have poured immeasurable quantities of bones and blood alongside the people of the entire country in defending their fatherland (Dang Cong San Viet Nam 1985:10).

No sooner was some kind of hold purchased on the unforgiving delta than came the challenge of foreign invasion in the form of the Siamese Navy. Yet with ingenuity and heroism, typifying the most glorious episodes in Vietnamese history, the Tay Son forces defeated the Siamese 'bandit aggressors' (*giac xam luoc Xiem*) in the battle of Rach Gam Xoai Mut. The province saw the early development of class stratification and the extension of the 'degenerate' (*thoai hoa*) feudal administration of the Confucian court. Yet local people tirelessly manifested their aspirations for equality in 'continuous uprisings' (*lien tiep noi day*) against feudal despots (Dang Cong San Viet Nam 1985:11). French invasion was followed by severe rural stratification and oppressive taxation and corvées. While several uprisings against the colonialists demonstrated that the Vietnamese quality of 'patriotism' (*chu nghia yeu nuoc*) was undeniable in the region, the 'bourgeois' class character of the leaders of these uprisings resulted in their failure to achieve liberation. Their leadership not only failed to mobilise the workers and peasants, but were drawn from a class numbered among their exploiters. It was only with the founding of the Communist Party that the people obtained a leadership (the party) and a 'correct path' (socialism) certain to allow them to fulfil their aspirations.

What this work presented was a story of struggle against adversity. Identity was forged and expressed in conflict with nature, foreign threat, class oppression and degenerate traditions. This harsh context distilled grassroots heroism as the enduring quality, making it the agent of history, pitted in opposition to internal and external oppressors. This was the spirit animating the Southern Uprising:

> The spirit of the Southern Uprising is the revolutionary offensive spirit of the workers, the peasants, patriots and revolutionaries prepared to fight against imperialism and feudalism; unafraid of sacrifices for independence, the nation's freedom and an equal and happy society. The Southern Uprising is the culmination and development of our ancestors' patriotism combined with the proletarian internationalism founded by Marx and Lenin (Dang Cong San Viet Nam 1985:6).

Both the district and provincial publications described the background to the Southern Uprising in terms of a growing crisis of global imperialism leading to the increased oppressiveness of domestic rulers, increased exploitation by landlords, and the institution of the draft. Domestic and foreign oppression had reached its highest level: an intensification of exploitation that had deepened class divisions. Such had purportedly been the analysis of the Indochinese Communist Party regional committee for southern Vietnam, which grasped the initiative and correctly decided to revolt:

> Under the leadership of the southern regional party committee, the My Tho and Go Cong party chapters for the first time led the masses in the use of revolutionary violence to rise against the rule of the French colonial invaders and their lackeys, writing a glorious page of history (*trang su oanh liet*) with cadres, party members and the revolutionary masses setting examples of struggle, inexhaustible fortitude, stamina and indomitability and leaving us many precious historical experiences which our party has mobilized in the course of leading the revolution (Dang Cong San Viet Nam 1985:3).

The manifestation of the uprising in Tien Giang province was described as having been co-ordinated by the provincial committee for the uprising, based in Long Hung (Dang Cong San Viet Nam 1985:46, 53). The Chau Thanh district's account also asserted that the revolt in Chau Thanh district had been organised in Long Hung village's communal house (*dinh*), and had descended on the market area of Vinh Kim where a French garrison was located. Peasants and workers had marched in the vanguard; the account's emphasis on the use of gongs and drums in the descent on Vinh Kim underlining the role that 'tradition' played in resistance, a counterpoint to the account's central theme of 'revolutionary struggle' as tradition (Dang Bo Huyen Chau Thanh 1987:49–68).

**This memorial to Vietnam's heroic revolutionary martyrs *(anh hung liet si )* in a Cao Lanh cemetery preserves in stone the 'spirit of revolutionary struggle' that purportedly infused the fallen while in battle**

Where did my acquaintances in Vinh Kim believe the Southern Uprising (its local manifestations at any rate) to have begun? According to one elderly Vinh Kim villager the uprising had swept from Long Hung to Vinh Kim but its leadership had lain with party members who were native to, and based in, Vinh Kim. The reason, he said, was due to their high level of education. Militants and party members in Long Hung were just farmers—few were skilled in revolutionary tactics. In his view the roots of anti-colonial rebellion in the village owed much to the large numbers of Vinh Kim locals who had studied abroad in France:

> The origins of the Southern Uprising lay in the influence of
> anti-colonial patriotic intellectuals Phan Boi Chau and Phan Chu Trinh.
> From the 1930s it was difficult for anti-colonialists to move around
> and propagandise in Vietnam. Wherever people went they were tailed
> by the police. However in France it was easy to link up with the
> organisations of anti-colonial intellectuals. Study abroad in France also
> gave local intellectuals a better understanding of the weaknesses of
> French colonialism and the manner of fighting it (from fieldnotes).

This view was echoed by other elderly villagers. One said that the rebellion was organised in Vinh Kim, for that was where intellectuals were concentrated. He said that 'intellectuals found Vinh Kim more suitable for intellectual activity', which consisted, among other things, 'in determining a means to liberate the country from the French' (from fieldnotes). According to him:

> The party decided however that Vinh Kim was not a suitable place to realise (*thuc hanh*) the Southern Uprising due to it being too socially complex (*phuc tap*), with rich and poor classes, intellectuals of competing tendencies and the presence of the French garrison. Rather, they decided to stage it in Long Hung, where poor people were more numerous (from fieldnotes).

Another, a party member, who had served as a local teacher and who had led local military resistance against France in the 1945–54 period said that the poor farmers in surrounding villages followed the lead (*keo len day*) of Vinh Kim intellectuals. Local intellectuals had also played a key role in disseminating revolutionary consciousness to the masses, organising a theatrical troupe in 1928 to propagandise the Vietnamese tradition of anti-foreign resistance, by reading newspapers to surrounding villagers coming to Vinh Kim's market and by teaching in literacy education classes.

Summing up, one informant said that it was wrong to say that any one village had been responsible for the Southern Uprising:

> You have to focus on the entire region surrounding Vinh Kim as it is impossible to understand one part, one village, in isolation from the rest. The entire region acted in concert. Vinh Kim was the head, while other villages such as Long Hung were the body or limbs of the uprising. This, however, is disliked by certain big shots (*may ong bu*) from Long Hung who won't budge from their view that their home village was the cradle of the Southern Uprising (from fieldnotes).

Here a view emerged of revolution as the expression of culture, learning and intellectual cultivation, the product of an 'orchard civilisation' that had precociously developed in Vinh Kim. According to my village acquaintances, theirs was a truer version of history than that found in published texts. Such a view illustrated the role contemporary politics of identity played in the structuring of historical accounts. Villagers' concerns to 'get the facts right' about a rebellion that had occurred 53 years earlier could be seen as attempts to reclaim the past in order to mount a critique on the present.

## NARRATING VILLAGE HISTORY: A HISTORY

Locals were scathing about the manner by which the published histories had been researched. According to one villager:

> They were not the work of historians. They were researched by students under the guidance of professors from Ho Chi Minh City. Oral histories were collected and compiled with no cross-checking or

attempt to validate the information in a systematic manner (from fieldnotes).

Another said that during their brief field trip to the village, students had come to interview him at his home accompanied by a professor. He felt they were incompetent (*vo tai*), but at that time:

> I dared not say anything (*khong dam noi*), dared not be critical (*khong dam phe binh*). On the other hand, the professors heading the project did not dare say anything to me for fear of showing their ignorance!

Stung by the misrepresentation enshrined by what they saw as a process of shoddy scholarship, local villagers had pooled resources and resolved to produce their own village history. The effort began in 1987–88, the year the district party's publication had come out. A group of elderly male villagers were behind the effort. Some were party members but none were then incumbents in local administration or party chapters. One contributor was an 80-year-old former regional Viet Minh commander, a native of the village, then living in retirement in the provincial capital. Written memoirs of involvement in the Southern Uprising were sought from key players who resided away from the village. The chief compilers visited the homes of participants and elderly locals and took extensive notes. There were also many meetings held to which locals and provincial party members were invited to contribute their wider knowledge. The results, covering the years 1917–45, were typed up, while the compilation, cross-referencing of data, writing-up and typing of the manuscript for the period 1945–75 remained to be completed.

The draft manuscripts of this local history were peopled by characters frequently described in accounts of the colonial period and also found in official party histories: the oppressed poor, patriotic villagers, the leading role of the Communist Party, the handful of oppressive landlords, colonial 'lackeys' (*tay sai*) and colonial troops. Yet they also depicted revolt against colonial oppression as nested firmly within the tradition of patriotic intellectuals. This included for example the founding of the province's first party cell, in Vinh Kim village, which was described as an initiative of patriotic intellectuals. The typescript for the 1917–45 period covered the visits of noteworthy patriotic intellectuals, Phan Boi Chau, Phan Chu Trinh, Nguyen Anh Ninh and Nguyen Sinh Sac (Ho Chi Minh's father) to the village and the participation of local patriotic intellectuals in their nationwide movements. In dealing with various local protest movements, the setting up of local chapters of organisations such as the Heaven and Earth Society and Nguyen Anh Ninh Society, and the formation of the village's celebrated political theatrical troupe, the '*Ban Hat Dong Nu*' (Maidens' Theatrical Troupe), the draft account also described them as initiatives of patriotic intellectuals. Coming to the Southern Uprising, the account focused on the organisational activities of Vinh Kim locals and enshrined the view encountered in conversations with villagers, that Vinh Kim was prior to Long Hung as organisational centre of the rebellion in the district. While retaining all the formal trappings of a Communist Party local history, including nods to the organisational primacy of the party, the significance of the first raising of the gold-starred flag, the debt to Ho Chi Minh and the example of the Russian Revolution, the account placed exceptional focus on local intellectuals. In direct challenge to the official provincial and district accounts, the draft account reclaimed Vinh Kim as the centre of local revolutionary activity and explained this in terms of the village's advanced intellectual and cultural development.

The account never went to publication. In 1993 I was shown the results. The 1945–75 section remained incomplete, written, in almost illegible handwriting, in a tattered, square-ruled maths notebook: the narrative ending abruptly sometime in 1960. The 1917–45 typescript was also seen by its compilers as a draft, requiring substantial improvement. Despondent contributors told me that their project had failed to secure the support of the local administration. I immediately inferred political opposition to the project, either from party authorities disapproving of the political line taken, or from the revolutionary 'big shots' in provincial- and national-level positions reportedly behind the official histories, who did not want to see their reputations challenged.

This, my interlocutors insisted, was not the case. The explanation given was more banal although equally depressing. The problem unfortunately lay in Vinh Kim village itself. Compilers of the village's history accused their own administration of having been too selfish, irresponsible and short-sighted to lend support to publication. In the late 1980s, when the writers had gone to the village authorities seeking funds for further research, they were met by complete indifference. One contributor said he had made appointments to meet the village president several days in a row and each time had fruitlessly waited in the People's Committee offices.

According to one of the thwarted local historians, the problem lay in the fact that there had been no carry-over of local leadership from the era of the resistance wars into the post-liberation period. He said that after 1975 the village had been loaded with a series of administrators from outside the village. Two village presidents had come from a neighbouring village, the school had initially had a northern headmaster, the hamlet head's position had been taken by an individual from another district while the hamlet's party cell leader had also been an outsider to the district. These officials were criticised for not knowing or feeling sympathy for the village:

> They did not appreciate the history of the village and had no feeling of honour towards it. For example, they were not interested in erecting

a monument to the victims of the reprisal bombing following the Southern Uprising. We raised money for this by organising *cai luong* concerts. We were able to persuade a couple of big *cai luong* stars in Saigon to come down free of charge and we made a lot of money. When it was handed over to the People's Committee, the money disappeared and the monument was never constructed (from fieldnotes).

Similarly, the village's post-war officials were accused of having been 'uninterested in putting the village's history together as they had nothing personally to gain from it' (from fieldnotes).

Around this time, in the late 1980s, several villagers complained that their village had been controlled by outsiders for the past fourteen to fifteen years. One elderly man within the hamlet told me he himself had made this accusation quite bluntly at a meeting in the People's Committee offices. Whether due to such local protests or the then national policy of administrative 'renovation', a new generation of village leaders had emerged at the turn of the decade. They markedly differed from the former administrators by their youth, their mode of entry to the party (through their involvement in post-1975 'construction' rather than the pre-1975 military struggle) and by their local origins.

Yet this change was too little and too late for the revival of the history project. The new incumbents 'had an extremely low cultural level' (*trinh do van hoa rat thap*) and poor education 'like all village administrators since 1975', I was told. The villagers who had been involved in the history-writing project alleged that the new leadership did not appreciate the history of their village any more than their predecessors, nor did they possess the intellectual capacity to do research or understand the need for further work on the project. They did not fulfil their duties more responsibly than previous administrators and they were accused of exercising their functions 'according to personal gain and preference'. They were also prone to absenteeism, 'preferring to go out eating and drinking with friends rather than working in their offices' (from fieldnotes). One specific criticism was their failure to do anything to redevelop the river access to the central market hamlet where in the past, visitors had come and played music and read poetry at cafes along the river's edge.

Added to this was the march of time. The new leadership were seen as too young and out of touch with the older generation to value their concern about early resistance history. Meanwhile the older participants were passing away. The regret was more than once expressed to me that I had arrived two or three years 'too late'. Several valuable *tai lieu song* (informants, literally, 'living data') had passed away: villagers who, due to their personal involvement and high level of education, could have given me a very valuable insight into local history. The passage of time dealt its most telling blow against the realisation of a local history with the rapid deterioration of the health of the principal researchers. One had gone almost totally deaf, another had developed cataracts in his eyes. Their draft manuscripts lay at home, yellowing and incomplete, with little prospect of publication or even readership within the village.

In the course of learning about the failure of this local history-writing project, I came to view it as an event of poignant irony. Launched to counter what they saw as a distortion of history by selfish power holders, the authors sought to reclaim the centrality of their village's role in an uprising that was in turn seen as the highest expression of their village's traditions. Yet in their efforts to document this history of self-determination, they were driven to the realisation that they no longer possessed the autonomy to publish their own history. The view that their village had historically led surrounding villages in revolution failed to make it into publication, as the tables had turned. Their destiny had become controlled by imported administrators. Those who were seen to have once followed Vinh Kim's lead now ruled them at district, province and national government levels. Controlled from without and within, villagers had become powerless to represent their own past.

Displacement of agency was accompanied by a displacement of meaning. The view of revolution as an expression of Vinh Kim's developed 'orchard civilisation' had been replaced by an apparently timeless tradition of heroic struggle. Vested in poor peasants and latterly proletarians, anti-colonial rebellion was, officially at least, the expression of this tradition. It was a view which saw both the Confucian legacy and the contributions of bourgeois intellectuals as compromised and historically impotent. Official accounts downplayed and questioned the role of such figures while the local attempt to reinscribe their significance failed. In the process, the contemporary significance of intellectuals and the dubious intellectual status of the administration became a topic of wide discussion. Again it was ironic that the perceived non-intellectuality of the administration (manifested in the 'irresponsibility' and 'poor education' of village cadres and the 'incompetence' of researchers working for the district and province) had been central to the excision of intellectuals as historical agents from available published accounts of significant local events.

## SOWING REVOLT, HARVESTING WAR AND PEACE

The exclusion of local intellectuals from the history-writing process and, as protagonists, from the historical accounts themselves, contrasted sharply with the widely-felt pride of elderly male Vinh Kim villagers in their area's 'civilised' status and the nationally significant historical contributions their village had consequently made. Proud to emphasise these, all equally felt a rupture had occurred.

In explanation, one of the history project participants rued that the village had become the victim of its own precocious success:

> Due to the fact that locals were prominent in various political movements and anti-colonial uprisings, our village became well-known to the colonial police and subject to vigilant control (from fieldnotes).

He cited the Southern Uprising itself as the turning point. He argued that, due to their central role in the aborted uprising, villagers had been tailed and the village itself subject to progressively tighter policing. It was at this time, according to him, that outsiders began to be used in governing the village:

> Of those now living in the central market hamlet, perhaps 80 per cent are outsiders. This is because the subsequent Republican and communist governments continued the colonial policy of external rule (from fieldnotes).

According to this informant, local intellectuals also came under intense scrutiny in the wake of the uprising. 'From 1940 onwards, natives of Vinh Kim were not allowed to return to teach in the village school due to the central role local teachers had played in organising the revolt' (from fieldnotes).

Yet despite these developments, a new generation of idealists had been formed. Many locals were inspired by the events of 1945 and were politicised in this process. Joined by compatriots released from prison, they actively participated in resisting the return of the French and in the subsequent war of resistance (1946–54). A number spent several years fighting from bases in the neighbouring Plain of Reeds. Yet resistance was reportedly strong at home as well. A great many villagers described the anti-French resistance war as 'truly a war of the entire populace' (from fieldnotes).

The year 1954 posed a watershed in village history and in the lives of my key group of interlocutors. While virtually all of the villagers with whom I spoke said they had participated in the resistance war against the French, their activities during the period of the US-backed Republic of Vietnam (1955–75) stood in stark contrast.

Indeed I met no native of the village who had remained at home to continue the proud village tradition of resistance against the new regime. A number of villagers had presented themselves for regroupment and had travelled to the DRV regime in the North where they had worked for two decades trying to achieve the reunification of their country. However, for those who had stayed at home, continued resistance against the new regime had become impossible. One veteran of the anti-French resistance said that again it was Vinh Kim's own revolutionary precociousness that had brought this situation about. According to him, the RVN president, Ngo Dinh Diem, knew of the village's history of resistance and had it heavily controlled. He said that government officials had been posted in people's houses to monitor their activities. Tails had been put on those from well-known revolutionary families. They would have been arrested if they had re-engaged in political activities. To resist against the government, one had to leave the village. Local resistance had become increasingly organised by revolutionaries from other regions. In 1959 the government had turned up the heat by passing a law prescribing the death penalty for any involved in resistance activity. One villager called this a 'law to murder people' (*luat giet nguoi*).

Despite such draconian measures, which fanned opposition to the government and, after 1960 pushed some into the ranks of the newly formed NLF, it is clear that from 1954 villagers also saw opportunities for themselves beyond resistance. A former resistance fighter described the years 1954–60 as the 'six years of peace'. Another told me that 'from 1954 most villagers he knew were primarily concerned with 'making a living'. Yet another, a writer who had moved to Saigon in 1954 to work as a publisher said:

> It is not true that I abandoned the resistance in 1954. I fought to achieve the liberation of my country for nine years. In 1954 I felt I had fulfilled my duty and that it was time to raise a family and make a living (from fieldnotes).

From 1954 many intellectuals saw that their fortunes lay beyond the village. Saigon, the seat of the new nation, provided many opportunities for employment. Others served in provincial centres as teachers, clerks and bureaucrats. Under the colonial regime education had provided an avenue for work beyond the village and many local intellectuals had followed this path, even as many had stayed behind to farm and some to fight from their home village. The former path had been primarily restricted to families of means, some of whom had sold off their landed wealth to give their sons a good education. Under the Republic vastly increased employment opportunities swelled this trickle to a flood. This opened up chances to educated members of poorer families that had been denied them under the colonial regime. I met several villagers from poor tenant-farming families who had followed this route out of the village under the Republic. For villagers with some education, even conscription into the Army of the Republic of Vietnam (ARVN) represented a path of upward mobility. Despite joining an army engaged in one of the fiercest wars of the twentieth century, their education ensured them officer status which was seen as privileged immunity from the worst heat of conflict.

These villagers' post-1954 decisions to 'earn a living' did not necessarily imply 'war weariness' or the valuation of material above spiritual concerns. Rather, for some, the focus on work was possible as the goals of the new state were seen as consistent enough with the goals of the resistance to do so with honour. Indeed, several villagers took this one step further. Not only did they see the Republic as acceptably consistent with the values of the resistance, they saw it as a realisation of the goals of that struggle. Take the case of one elderly villager who had downed weapons in 1954 and had begun work as a mechanic on a long-distance boat, a job that he said had provided sufficient income to raise a family of seven and to construct quite a substantial home in the village. This was the self-same individual who had grimly described Ngo Dinh Diem's 1959 anti-communist law as 'a law to murder people'. Yet he told me that after the assassination of Diem in 1963 he had paid a visit to the president's grave to pay his respects. 'Perhaps no-one else in this village would have done the same,' he told me with pride. 'Ngo Dinh Diem was above all as a patriot, no matter what else people may say' (from fieldnotes). Another villager who had fought in the anti-colonial resistance war expressed similar sentiments, describing Diem as an 'intellectual', a 'patriot' and a 'defender of Vietnamese culture'. He told me, 'Under Diem, Vietnam experienced a cultural renaissance', and he cited a host of journals (for example, *Van Hoa Nguyet San* and *Bach Khoa*) and newspapers that had opened in the years of the Republic, dedicated to 'exploring new ideas and promoting Vietnamese cultural values'. This was the same individual who had described President Diem's post-1954 surveillance system in the village as having made continued resistance impossible.

One could equally trace a line of repressive continuity from the colonial to the post-colonial regime. This indeed did affect many former members of the resistance who, as suspected communists, were incapable of pursing a normal life or earning a living under the 'six years of peace' (Race 1972). The same could be said for poor farmers, dragooned into the ARVN, unable to buy exemption from military service and too poorly educated to achieve officer status. According to Hunt (1974), faced with the prospect of becoming cannon fodder, many poor villagers from this region had had little choice but to fight for the NLF. Poor villagers from Vinh Kim with whom I spoke, thought that most of the village's recruits to the NLF had been drawn from the poor. Yet they cited opportunism as a factor in the decisions of several of such people to go off to join the NLF. One member of a family of poor tenant farmers, an ex-AVRN private, said that although the rate of attrition was much higher in the NLF, promotion within the NLF was much faster than in the ARVN and the payoffs were potentially much greater if they won. Nevertheless, he admitted, only a small proportion of poor villagers had fought in the NLF.

Not all poor villagers had faced this stark choice. A number of those with whom I spoke had remained and had worked in the village throughout the war years. According to them, the village had been relatively unscathed by aerial bombardment and defoliation.[6] Some had found jobs through relatives and former landlords in the towns and cities. After several years of conscripted military service, having never experienced heated battle, one village youth from a poor sharecropper's family had been discharged and proceeded to live an uneventful life as a trader in Saigon, and said he had visited his home village on a regular basis throughout the war. He had steadily accumulated a reasonable fortune which had disappeared in several failed escape attempts after unification when his profession had been outlawed and he had been forced to return to his village. His story was typical of a great many villagers with whom I spoke, who said that they had been successful at earning a living under the sphere of the Republic of Vietnam. It was a period when the horizons of the great majority were dramatically broadened, compared with the existences they had led under the colonial regime. If they found much that had offended their sense of honour, on the balance the lives they led remained consonant with the ideals that had motivated resistance.

Idealism had been, however, a quality in dwindling supply in the village. To have continued to revolt in the village would have brought down repressive consequences. Yet to have supported the government in the village was equally suicidal. According to one villager, who had held such a position, the office of hamlet chief in the years 1954–60 became an increasingly perilous negotiation between the 'two sides' (*hai ben*). Effective performance of government dictates risked sometimes lethal retaliation from the alternative power structure of the party's local operatives, who had 'remained undercover' (*nam vung*) in 1954. Non-performance risked being branded by the regime as a communist supporter. One person who had been in this position said that throughout his brief incumbency he had been very 'scared' (*so*). He said he was relieved when, in 1960 he was told to step down by leaders of the 'liberation side' (*ben giai phong*) who had been controlling him. After 1960 polarisation had developed to the point that government agents, including armed soldiers, could only operate in the village during the day while resistance forces controlled it by night. One elderly woman from neighbouring Long Hung village described the anti-US resistance in her village as having been truly 'a war of the people' (*chien tranh cua nhan dan*), employing the phrase used by many villagers to describe the 1945–54 anti-French war. She said that many people in her village had been outraged by the bullying and coercive tactics used by the ARVN soldiers on daytime sweeps (*quet*) through her village. Yet she said the liberation troops (*giai phong quan*) had also employed coercive tactics. She said that in the late 1950s 'People's Courts' (*Toa an nhan dan*) had been staged to try those involved in village administration and punish those who had made the people suffer. During the war, if Republican soldiers from the village tried to visit their relatives, the latter would be forced to submit to 'education' (*bi giao duc*) by villagers, to convince them to renounce ties with the enemy. She said, 'very few from my village dared defect to the Republican cause. The pressure on the family would have been too intense' (from fieldnotes).

One local intellectual had become politically active during the Japanese occupation of Indochina. He had joined a non-communist nationalist party in the early 1940s and had fought against the French return to power in 1945. Among the factors motivating his resistance was the fact that his father, a village notable, had been assassinated by a group of French soldiers in the 1930s. Having fought for several years from the Plain of Reeds, he had left the resistance in the late 1940s. In his diary he wrote that the resistance movement had become hostile to intellectuals. According to his family he had furthermore disagreed with the class policies of the Viet Minh and had heard reports of repressive measures against Catholics and wealthy peasants in the North. He had worked as a journalist in Saigon until the mid-1960s when he had retired due to illness. Back in the village he had done some tutoring and, beyond passive co-operation with the NLF forces now controlling the hamlet, had stayed out of political activity. Yet his case was cited by several villagers as to the impossibility of maintaining a neutral stance in the village during the war years. According to their accounts, from time to time he had visited the Republican garrison stationed in the central market hamlet to secure the release of children from his hamlet arrested as suspected guerrilla supporters. He had proven successful at this and, my interlocutors hypothesised, this had earned him mistrust by local guerrillas suspicious of the ease with which he could influence enemy troops. To the contrary, those who recounted his story to me argued, it had been his intelligence, social skills and trustworthiness that had convinced Republican troops that he was telling the truth. Tragically, in the late 1960s he was ambushed and gunned to death on the same road where his father had been shot thirty years before. My sources had no doubt it was the liberation forces that had committed the act.

Such developments take us somewhat beyond the summation of the village intellectual, who claimed with outstanding hubris that the demise of village intellectuals as a revolutionary force was the result of their own precocious success in resistance. The escalation of violence in the countryside did remove the idealistic, consensual or neutralist middle-ground between two polarised and militarised antagonists, yet, from the material assembled here, the excision of intellectuals from locally-based resistance was the product of a complex set of factors that escape easy generalisation. Added to the escalation of coercion was the pull factor of increased opportunities for employment beyond the village and the creation of two post-colonial Vietnamese states that to varying degrees symbolised fulfilment of the anti-colonial mission, dividing the allegiance of erstwhile revolutionaries. The intensification of global cold war, the emergence of two Vietnams, the outbreak of war, and unification two decades later, were hardly the inevitable consequence of the anti-colonial path pursued by local revolutionaries five or six decades earlier. The insurgents of the 1940 'Southern Uprising' could not possibly have predicted that the intervening five decades of events would conspire to prevent their survivors from publishing a historical account of their role in village and national history. The eventuality is redolent with irony, yet in my estimation, a contingent, not inevitable, development.

Nevertheless, in seeking to publish their alternative account and in commentary on their failure, the local historians of Vinh Kim village were engaged in establishing a far more than ironic connection across the decades. In capturing the centrality of local intellectuals in past rebellions, their account was fashioned into a critical missile aimed squarely at the moral authority of the present. It was an attempted reminder that resistance was once an ideal that inspired all sectors of society, not a kind of commodity to be channelled by Communist Party incumbents for selfish political advantage. It asserted that intelligence, creativity and conscious choice were primary factors in revolutionary success, in contrast to the lack of intelligence and the incompetence widely attributed to cadres holding incumbency in post-revolutionary society. It replaced faith in the efficacy of the heroic essence of the Vietnamese and the paternalistic wisdom of the party with the agency of well-educated and conscious beings. And, perhaps dangerously, it taught that individual local citizens did once determine their own destiny in the realisation, and defence of, their own cultural accomplishments. Though the contemporary obstacles to this might be regarded as even more formidable than when the attempt to publish their account was made (not the least being the impending demise of the generation of local historians and the continued draining away from the village of the bulk of its intellectual assets), the intention of Vinh Kim's elderly historians had been clearly to fan the embers of village pride—a pre-condition for locals to snatch victory out of the jaws of irrelevance.

## ANOTHER GENERATION OF RESISTANCE?

Failure though their publication of history may have been, the generation schooled in anti-colonial resistance seemed to have been successful in transmitting the values of Vinh Kim's 'orchard civilisation' to the next generation of villagers. That generation, reaching maturity under the Republic of Vietnam, retained a commitment to education and, like their parents, used it confidently and harshly to judge the administrators based in the central market hamlet and beyond. One of these, proud of her participation as a 'patriot' (*nguoi yeu nuoc*) and an 'intellectual' (*tri thuc*) in the 'anti-American war', who had fought in a zone far from the village, confessed that on her return at war's end she no longer dared to protest or resist, although she had been shocked by the self-interest and ignorance of the new village leaders. Other members of her generational cohort were, on a private basis, equally critical in their depictions of their leaders. Their unflattering characterisations of local cadres' irresponsibility, lack of imagination and restrictive horizons were indeed similar to those voiced by their seniors.

For these villagers, in their twenties at the end of the war, peace had done nothing to contribute to restoring the prosperity and cosmopolitan reputation that, according to their parents, had distinguished their home in the past. From this generation's perspective, the most destructive period in the village's history had come in the wake of the war. Being primarily a fruit-growing village, most of its hamlets had escaped extensive collectivisation. However, the market for fruit had been extremely depressed and movement out of the village in search of work had been restricted. Meanwhile, the population was on its way to doubling within less than a generation following war's end, while the economy was becoming less productive. The new wave of administrators and co-operative bureaucrats had done little but add another load on taxation and police a more finely woven web of restrictive regulations. Two distinct groups had done better than average during the two decades following the end of the war. The first were the cadres of the new administration, whose fields mysteriously grew and multiplied, and whose houses enlarged, were renovated and became filled with new consumer products. The second group were those whose relatives had fled the country and could draw on remittances sent from abroad. For a great many young village men, the path to distinguishing oneself among peers had become how many bottles of potent rice alcohol could be consumed at a sitting.

In the post-war years, the beguiling promise of the 'civilised' world lay beyond the village and, indeed, the country's borders. For more than a decade after the war had ended, escaping the country represented the highest aspiration for a reasonably well-educated young adult villager seeking self-realisation, prosperity and honour.[7] At the end of the 1980s some slight improvements in people's economic circumstances began to be apparent. This was most notable for those who had relatives working or doing business in the city, and those with 'connections' (*quan he*) to favourably-placed officials. Poor farmers, spending days away from home hiring out their labour to the economically better-off, were able to do little more than provide their family with the basics. By 1993, several years into the era of 'reform', beyond the curious and short-lived visit of a foreign anthropologist, the promise of a reversal

**Children watching a video from Hong Kong in the house of an affluent villager**

in the village's ongoing cultural and socio-economic marginalisation was yet to become evident. For those who could in any way secure a toehold in the nation's largest city, the best solution to arresting their slide into irrelevance was to leave and relocate to Ho Chi Minh City. This was one of the few places that might allow realisation of the values which village elders had hoped to instil in village youth, by their not-entirely-unsuccessful revival of memories of their rural home's civilised past.

# Conclusion

In an interdependent world, no society is considered to lie 'beyond' the condition of modernity. But do all accept such inclusive formulations? The concept of modernity has experienced a renaissance in social theory, while simultaneously being subject to dispute in the field of identity politics. Historically, agents invoking the modern have profoundly shaped the human condition globally. Yet the challenge for those who would describe this process is to avoid repeating the exclusions enunciated in its course. Treating modernity as a subjective identity, rather than ontological condition, this work approaches the recent past in terms of one of its most important experiential categories. Arriving in many destinations as an ideology of colonial domination (although by no means exclusively in this manner), the symbolism of modernity was widely incorporated into people's self-conceptions and became a charter for diverse projects of self-actualisation. An imagined relationship to the modern informed a great variety of attempts in the colonial and post-colonial eras to enforce change, as well as to accommodate and resist it. Today, modernity is no condition which humans homogeneously share, but remains a contested category of the present.

Vietnam has had a complex history of engagements with other societies, near and far, and its place in the world is not the stuff of easy generalisation. It is one of the few countries to describe itself as an actually existing socialist society, yet the great majority of its inhabitants live in commercialised, low-technology, rural settings, deriving very little support from the state in their everyday concerns. It is a nation that was divided in a violent process of decolonisation and plunged so deeply into military conflict that its name was to become synonymous with war. Much of the history of the post-war era has been an attempt to comprehend, if not undo the legacies of those divisions. The work focuses on Vietnam's extreme South: a region incorporated relatively recently into the Vietnamese polity, with a history of intense engagement with the capitalist world. It describes attempts by the central government to eliminate and, failing that, assimilate these legacies, while trying to retain power in an era of globalised capitalism. Southern Vietnam's distinct legacies remained obvious through post-war twists and turns in the nation's orientation. Socialist restructuring in the 1970s largely failed there and, as thinking shifted, its market economy and entrepreneurial legacies came to be seen as key national resources. The region experienced the greatest uptake in foreign investment in the 1990s and was considered particularly prone to the negative effects of the market economy and 'open door' policies. By the end of that decade the nation's largest metropolis, Ho Chi Minh City, exemplified the tension between economic liberalism and authoritarian rule. Meanwhile, the southern countryside was in the grips of an extreme socio-economic crisis for which the leadership had few solutions.

Vietnamese reactions to the changes occurring in their society in the post-war years were understandably complex. This book describes dramatic shifts in the regime's approach towards the country's extreme South. After 1975, legacies of US 'modernisation' in the region such as markets and popular music were regarded by leaders of the new administration as 'poisons', harmful to thought and spirit. Much of the area below the 17th parallel was seen as dangerous terrain, strewn with the live psychological ammunition of a formidable enemy. However, many of the legacies of this era were reassessed when the commandist orientation pursued during wartime was relaxed. Fifteen years after the war had ended, the same phenomena were being reconsidered as the region of *Nam Bo*'s four-millennia-old modernist propensities. There was nothing unique about Vietnam's nineteenth- and twentieth-century engagements with the Western world, at least from the unfazed perspective of this part of the country. The same could be said for the commodity economy. Ho Chi Minh City-based social scientists were to backdate it, indigenise it, evaluate it as ancient, and ultimately naturalise it as a defining feature of the southern region.

Responses to these shifts in perspective from those living in the region were not uniform, underlining the elusive nature of 'southern' identity. Geographically, the village of Vinh Kim lay within the region championed by various state commentators as exemplifying modernity in Vietnam. This indeed accorded with the view of village history held by a cohort of its senior villagers. According to them, in the early years of the century their home village had absorbed outside influences, fostered them, improved them and re-exported them as cultural and political movements of benefit to the nation. They were proud of their village's 'civilisation': its historically cosmopolitan, inclusivist and highly educated character, which they believed had led villagers to found their province's first Communist Party cell. Such precociousness, some thought, had ironically contributed to a decline in the manifestation of those qualities in the village. In the 1990s the irresponsibility and incompetence of local cadres, the economic marginalisation of the village and its cultural stagnation were considered to be the more depressing realities. Their failure to produce a volume of village history was cited as evidence of their home's historical decline. These views were put at a time when many rural areas were sliding into irrelevance as the government's urban-centric economic liberalisation policies began to yield results.

On the other hand, while stereotyped in some renditions as worldly, cosmopolitan, pragmatic and business-oriented, many Ho Chi Minh City intellectuals were provoked by the events of the 1990s into thinking that the rate of transformation and the intensity of their encounter with the wider world had reached crisis point. In the face of rapid cultural change and commodification due to economic liberalisation, they characterised their city as a repository of threatened tradition. This contrasted with those state intellectuals who had stereotyped *Nam Bo* and, above all, Ho Chi Minh City, as a place where nothing was fixed, no tradition remained, commerce ruled and whose pragmatic inhabitants assessed all by exchange value. While many urban intellectuals recognised and were proud of southern Vietnam's legacy of intensive engagements with the outside world, they were less than eager to naturalise ceaseless fluidity as regional identity. In rebuttal of such a view some Ho Chi Minh City intellectuals placed the state itself among those alien forces that threatened the continuity of Vietnamese tradition. The regime's implication in what many saw as an ill-considered, wholesale sell-out of traditional values formed part of this critique.

The contrast between a village whose elders described themselves as precociously modern and those residents of Ho Chi Minh City, describing their home as a site of threatened traditions, illustrates the limitations of attempting to locate these social practices within frameworks that take 'tradition' and 'modernity' as objective conditions in time and space. Understanding modernity as a subjective category of identity makes the Vietnamese experience a valuable one for social theorists. The interpretive dissonance and flux which has surrounded the concept in Vietnam can be compared with the situation in other societies where time categories relating to a particular period in the expansion of European power similarly have assumed a central place in debates about cultural identity. The case of post-war southern Vietnam shows that, like the division of global space in the colonial era, national space continues to be divided according to time. This state of affairs is not an unchanging condition. The purported relation to modernity of different places or, for that matter, ethnicities, genders or religious orientations is constantly being questioned and subject to re-invention.

This insight promises to revitalise history: a discipline endangered by the stalling of time in the supposed condition of 'modernity'. Since the French annexed Cochinchina, the region of southern Vietnam has been ruled by a series of regimes, which have sought legitimisation by claiming to inaugurate 'modernity' and by displacing the preceding regime from the time of the 'modern'. This process bolstered the importance of modernity as a symbolic value by which the achievements of regimes and the fundamental goals of society were to be reckoned. It was central to the justification of the change of regime in the mid-1970s and to the policy shift in the 1980s. In the 1990s debates about the identity of popular music, meaning of the market economy, the effects of intensifying international relations on the region, and the regime's own accountability continued to be waged in these terms. Over time positions reversed, denotations changed and meanings were disclaimed. However, the multiple and contradictory significations of the concept of modernity demonstrate its relevance for Vietnamese as a term through which change has been enforced, embraced and resisted. Since Hobsbawm and Ranger (1983), historians have understood the concept of 'tradition' thus: as a symbolic resource in the configuration of contemporary power relations. Understanding 'modernity' similarly, as a contested category of the present, focuses attention appropriately on power relations and on the contemporary concerns of those employing it. This displaces categories such as modernity from a status as universal conditions and re-admits them for consideration as strategic deployments. Resistance to colonial temporalisation played a crucial early role in mapping out spaces of resistance, the success of which projects bequeathed a world of multiple temporalities. The countries of the post-colonial world are particularly rich in examples of the 'modern' adopted as a self-ascribed identity. By studying places such as southern Vietnam, where the concept of modernity was central to the establishment of colonial and successive post-colonial regimes and the defence of, and resistance to, state policy shifts, we see it deployed in the most urgent and compelling way.

This work maps out a new direction for the ethnographic study of modernity: to investigate the diverse contexts in which people objectify themselves in such terms. The momentum of this project may be easily lost in terms of a debate dominated by national elites and urban theorists. Vietnam's example illustrates the way contrasting claims about this identity were made from a number of alternative sites. It suggests that an imperative exists for anthropologists to discover what lies beyond the well-catalogued positions of socially influential leaders. In this case that search for complexity was amply rewarded. Like theorists in privileged 'Western' academic positions, many state-employed social scientists were to normalise southern Vietnam as a place of ceaseless change and commercialisation in contrast with the 'traditional' North. However not all southern Vietnamese warmed to a view of their region as a dynamic, commercial centre, nor were all able to benefit from the changes that the actualisation of such views unleashed. Equally while many members of Ho Chi Minh City's urban middle class considered themselves 'modern' in relation to a countryside described as 'traditional' or 'backward', rural intellectuals were to use a very similar dichotomy to emphasise distinctions between themselves and their local rulers. While it was not possible to find consensus on the co-ordinates of Vietnamese 'modernity', research in a number of locations confirmed its centrality as a discourse of identity in contemporary southern Vietnam. This discovery of the unexpectedly diverse displacements of the 'modern' should encourage anthropologists to persist with efforts to detect, learn from and facilitate those voices raised against the fiction of global or national unity.

# Epilogue

After nearly a decade of rapid economic growth, the widening of international relations and changes in the cultural landscape, southern Vietnam by the end of the 1990s was a very different place: its transformation driven by some of the sentiments described in this book. Nevertheless, events late in the decade demonstrated that the categories of 'tradition' and 'modernity' remained cogent to the ways these changes were understood.

Whereas news stories about Vietnam as the promising frontier of Asian capitalism were the staple fare of the first half of the 1990s, the latter half was dominated by stories of discouraged investors pulling out, complaining about excessive bureaucracy, vague laws, corruption and lack of commitment to the private sector: both domestic and foreign. Vietnam was rated as one of the most corrupt, expensive and difficult business environments in the region. The Asian financial crisis did not affect the country as rapidly and dramatically as it had countries such as Thailand and Indonesia, proving that Vietnam's integration into global economic networks was very low. However, the country was affected indirectly by the plight of its neighbours, their domestic crises choking off what had been Vietnam's most important source of foreign investment. Vietnam's boom had been a largely regional phenomenon: its fortunes tied to local developments. The country began to sink into relative obscurity, dragged down by the countries whose achievements it had hoped to emulate. In news reports at the end of the decade, Vietnam had again become a place 'beyond capitalism'. The country was 'bogged down' in debate, investment 'inflows were at the lowest levels' since 1992, business confidence was at 'rock-bottom' and investors were 'navigating a tough business climate'.[1]

Few observers credited the government with adequately responding to a deteriorating situation. Little was done in the way of making Vietnam more competitive. The government launched an anti-corruption purge within the party structure, but few Vietnamese or foreign observers expected significant gains from this. Several high-ranking party officials were expelled, a few were executed. A series of high flying southern entrepreneurs were to come crashing down, some at the centre of corruption and fraud accusations were sentenced to death. A rash of prisoners were released, including a number of prominent political prisoners. Yet many of these measures appeared cosmetic. Among the lessons that were being drawn by neighbouring countries about the Asian financial crisis were that it was necessary to increase openness. To the contrary, in Vietnam the party's response to this challenge was to continue a turn inwards that had preceded the Asian financial meltdown. Journalists were discouraged from enquiring into corruption and bank scandals, in some cases by imprisonment. A senior general critical of corruption and misrule was expelled from the party. Warnings continued to be sounded about the danger of foreign subversion and the dangers of globalisation.

In the early 1990s the leadership's buzzwords were 'openness', 'renovation' and 'market economy'. By decade's end concerns such as security, stability and secrecy were more prominent, reflecting the rise in strength of a range of conservative projects. The slowdown of the mid-decade was associated with a new slogan: 'modernisation and industrialisation by 2020'. In a climate of policy stalemate, this could be read as a fall-back to more broadly-held goals, particularly as the concrete steps for implementing this were left undefined. It was also an acknowledgment of sorts that these goals had not yet been achieved, distinct from the emphasis in the mid-1980s when *doi moi* had been advanced as the perfection of the world's highest human achievement: socialism. Yet it could also be regarded as the slogan of ascendant conservatives, who, by mid-decade, were concerned to re-emphasise the goals of national security and political control.[2] While some had held out hopes that the effervescent economy of the early 1990s would translate into political change, by decade's end it appeared to many that the consolidation of power was being pursued even at the expense of economic benefit.

Southern Vietnam challenged this bleak view of the nation's prospects by continuing to buck national trends. Growth remained relatively high, especially in the southern metropolis. Industrial parks in the outskirts of Ho Chi Minh City continued to expand. Remittances, smuggled goods, electronic communications and visits by relatives bringing gifts and news kept the population attuned to the wider world. Taiwanese investment continued to flow in as the capital reserves of other countries dried up. Personal relations with Taiwanese and other foreign sojourners, education and work abroad were pursued by many southerners as a path to upward and transnational mobility. The southern region also continued to be a place offering challenges to the regime. Riots greeted the 300th anniversary of the founding of Saigon in 1998. A resistance group, the People's Action Party, was successful in infiltrating the South. The Hoa Hao religion was legalised in 1999 after many years of suppression and its leaders immediately called for greater freedoms. Critics such as Thich Quang Do of the Unified Buddhist Church and former prisoner of conscience, Nguyen Dan Que, made vocal appeals for similar goals. The number of Internet sites published by individuals and groups critical of the current regime increased and continued to project bleak news, disseminate dissident critiques and attempt to mobilise resistance, many keeping the virtual Republic alive as a symbolic reference point by which to evaluate events of the post-1975 South.

The economic slowdown in some ways satisfied the conservative aspirations espoused by a number of Ho Chi Minh City residents in the early 1990s. As the decade drew to a close, many urban intellectuals were to find their worst fears of foreign cultural inundation unfounded. Instead, one malaise was replaced by another. Foreign investment and trade, a major source of employment in the city, dwindled. Urbanites were gripped by concerns more akin to the late 1980s. Unemployment rose relentlessly, consumers complained of rising prices, businesspeople complained of high taxes and a lack of government comprehension of the requirements of doing business. Some urbanites complained that they had been conned by the government's reform rhetoric: that a decade of sacrifices such as clearances, re-zonings, tax hikes, financial contributions to the countryside, and the purchasing of bonds and donations for disaster relief had yielded no positive returns. An outpouring of solicited contributions had only left schools and hospitals in a more precarious state with both education and health increasingly prerogatives of the rich. Many middle class urbanites in the late 1990s complained vociferously about the deterioration of what they asserted was once a prosperous and orderly city, due to crime, prostitution, pavement dwellers, shantytowns and peddlers clogging the streets. Some pinned the blame on rural migrants and on a government too 'backward' to manage the needs of what they recalled was a once thriving, modern urban centre.[3]

Nevertheless, by the end of the decade a shift in urban middle class consciousness had occurred vis-à-vis the countryside. As the pace of urban life appeared to some to reach new levels,[4] those who were established residents of Ho Chi Minh City were increasingly inclined to be romantic about the countryside as a place where traditions had been preserved. Many continued to visit their homes in the delta or elsewhere on Tet holiday or to take part in commemorative family occasions. Otherwise they would visit the city outskirts, where a variety of new tourist attractions offered a controlled taste of the countryside. This move towards consuming a romanticised countryside coincided with the fashion for coarse silk clothing, highland people's textiles, rough-cut paper decorations and bamboo and handicraft furniture, as the emerging middle class distinguished themselves by reference to culturally essentialist motifs. *Cai luong* re-emerged as a pursuit of the southern Vietnamese elite. *Cai luong* idol Hoai Thanh set up a bar in District One to give his protégés performance practice, which, in contrast to the situation in the city's big *cai luong* theatres, was patronised mainly by men: bankers, company directors and diplomats, given to ostentatious tips equal to the monthly wage of an urban labourer. Many of these new ways of consuming tradition were driven by overseas Vietnamese nostalgia and their huge disposable incomes, but by decade's end had well and truly taken hold among the urban middle class. This group increasingly took part in pilgrimages to renovate pagodas and shrines in remote rural destinations. As a yawning disparity emerged between urban comfort and rural desperation, the development of a wealthy, urban middle class consuming marginalised rural areas as signifiers of 'tradition' was a disconsolate feature of the social landscape.

The countryside became the scene of important protests against the regime in the late 1990s. The most newsworthy were those which occurred in the northern province of Thai Binh, however they were scattered through the countryside. The foci of protest were very much the types of issues that plagued the villagers of Vinh Kim: corruption, abuse of power, administrative incompetence and a lack of attention to rural development. The Asian financial crisis exacerbated the suffering of the countryside, already experiencing a dearth of private investment. Provincial capitals across the Mekong delta were slugged by the withdrawal of Thai, Malaysian and Korean capital. Meanwhile opportunities for employment in the cities and industrial zones were drying up as investment shrank. In response, the government was to request aid donors to redirect aid to the countryside. A comprehensive rural development strategy was crafted and this provided the framework for lending by international aid agencies. By the end of the decade, aid donors were the most significant foreign group continuing to back the government. They were key props for a relatively urban-focused government whose rhetorical commitment to realising prosperity for the majority of its population was not matched by practical solutions. Aid was indeed welcome wherever it arrived; however designated beneficiaries commonly claimed that it was 'eaten' (*an*) by the upper echelons of political administration. By the end of the decade, thoughtful residents of Vinh Kim could not imagine how an injection of aid would fundamentally change their conditions of life. It was considered unlikely to induce improvements in the provincial administration. It was not thought calculated to make local leaders better disposed towards private initiatives, or teach them how to adjust policy to encourage investment. An even greater problem for many was the slowdown in the cities. A valuable place of employment for villagers earlier in the decade, work opportunities there were decreasing.

At the end of the decade, southern Vietnam remained a place where the categorisation of a world having attained the condition of 'modernity' was challenged in a complex fashion. The central government defiantly maintained that the world was moving in the direction of socialism and that the Communist Party was the best qualified organisation to negotiate a viable place for the Vietnamese nation in a world of deregulated trade and rapid information flows. Yet in tandem with elsewhere in the nation and abroad, the 'revival of the past' (Kleinen 1999) was proceeding apace and throwing up 'tradition' as an essentialised identity. In southern Vietnam, the return to the past threw up as many symbols of former modernist projects as it did 'tradition'. The relative dynamism of parts of the southern region offered continued cues for contrasting the 'modern' South with the 'backward' North, while the relative decline of many rural areas kept alive the use of this distinction between the city and the country. Overseas Vietnamese signified both the promising and the threatening faces of intensified links with the world beyond Vietnam and at the same time continued to bring new ways of thinking about cultural identity and imagining the past. A quarter of a century after peace came to the region, there was little to indicate that the cultural complexity of this region would subside as national integration or global 'normalisation' proceeded. In all likelihood changes would continue to be conceptualised in diverse ways, making southern Vietnam a place where one could continue to find fruitful ways of thinking about places and their times.

# Notes

## INTRODUCTION

1 The remarkable title of an economic study of this period, 'Vietnam joins the World', framed the 1990s as the dawn of Vietnam's global integration, (Morley and Nishihara 1997).

2 For example, when theorists began to refer to the contemporary era as 'postmodern', Smart (1990:28) and Friedman (1992) discovered that 'modernity' had 'moved' east to Asia.

3 For a discussion of the intersection of this politicised identity with issues of class, gender, space and memory in one Vietnamese Diasporic community, see Mandy Thomas, *Dreams in the Shadows* (1999).

4 See for example, the views discussed in Scigliano (1964) and Bernard Fall (1967). US 'modernization theory' placed the US struggle for influence over the process of global political decolonisation within the context of modernisation and nation-building, situating US society, as it was in the 1950s, at the end point of this process.

5 Certain foreign observers were to celebrate the Vietnamese regime's embrace of the market economy as the triumphant vindication of the irrepressible South. 'The North won the war but the South won the peace' (*FEER* 4 May 1995:5), was typical of the headlines greeting the twentieth anniversary of the 'fall' of Saigon. Such a view sourced capitalist tendencies in the present regime to 'the South', as if the font of capitalism were indigenous to South Vietnam. Odd it was to hear 'the South' accorded the vigour, not to mention coherence necessary to remain irrepressibly potent for two decades, when it was once widely viewed as a fragile construct of US foreign policy. For some journalists, this also meant that the blemishes of contemporary Vietnamese society equally flowed from a font of sleaze in the South. Speaking of the northwards spread of 'social ills' such as prostitution, Henry Kamm wrote: 'what is a return to the norm in Saigon, however negative some of its symptoms,

is new to Hanoi, a city that has always reflected the more traditionalist character of the North Vietnamese' (Kamm 1996:65).

6 Paul Mus was particularly influential, seeing Vietnam as a traditional nation which had been put 'off balance' by the depredations of colonial modernity (McAlister and Mus 1970). According to Guy Gran, such a case against France was at its strongest in Cochinchina. With traditions most intensively uprooted and the imposition of capitalist social relations more complete than elsewhere in Vietnam, village Cochinchina had been rapidly stripped of the traditional social and moral fabric that had provided villagers with ontological security since time immemorial (Gran 1975).

7 Frances Fitzgerald (1972) accused the US in South Vietnam of decimating what she portrayed as a traditional society. According to David Hess (1979), who shared this time frame, traditional Vietnamese culture met its nemesis in refugee-swollen Saigon of the 1960s and 1970s.

8 In this work I make the somewhat idiosyncratic but necessary distinction between 'modernity', a purportedly objective condition, and 'modernist', discourses which frame identity in such terms.

9 Just as the 'fragmentation' or multiplication of time is evident when nations are imagined as ancient, each nation-state producing its own temporal referents (Furet 1982:70), such is also the case in a world of contending assertions of modernity.

10 In *Modernity and its Malcontents*, the Comaroffs (1993:xiv) describe modernity as 'always an imaginary construction of the present in terms of a mythic past'.

11 Robertson argues that ideas such as 'tradition', 'nostalgia' and the 'nation' were subject to a process of 'modern', global diffusion. This insight could be extended to the 'modern' and indeed the 'global': surely subject to the same process (1992:153).

12 I translate the term *van minh* interchangeably as 'modern' or 'civilised'. Current usage of the noun *nen van minh* closely approximates nineteenth-century European usage of the term 'civilisation' (denoting inter alia progress, industrialisation, order, science). The term *van minh* is readily given as a synonym of *hien dai*, and, as they share many of the same referents, I translate them somewhat interchangeably as 'modern'. The term *can dai* is used by historians to refer to the 'modern era'.

13 This is not to say that time (*thoi gian*) as a category did not exist. Heterogeneous conceptualisations of time as cyclical, pendulum-like (as in the concept of yin-yang or *am-duong*), evanescent, inalterable, regular or intermittent, and dependent on astrological relationships, Heaven's will, karmic burden, skills at negotiating with the living and the dead, or with the 'natural' and 'supernatural' worlds, co-existed with recognition of the effect on people of singular events from wars to floods, conceptualised as determined by some underlying reality (principles/agents/forces), which, if grasped, could enable one to improve one's condition.

14 Nola Cooke has persuasively argued that neo-Confucianism was less central to Vietnam's nineteenth-century Nguyen Dynasty's cosmology than Woodside and others have emphasised. Just as important as such 'Sinic' legacies were Southeast Asian-influenced ideas of receiving protection from the spirits of royal forebears, reliance on a host of efficacious spirits

and syncretistic Buddhism, which she attributes to this pre-colonial dynasty's geographic origins in the southern parts of the country (Cooke 1997).

15 The Enlightenment notion of historical time as unilineal and progressive (Xiaobing 1996:28).

16 This exploited constructions of the world shared by most nineteenth-century European thinkers, foremostly Hegel, who, in the *Philosophy of History*, wrote: 'The History of the World travels from East to West, for Europe is absolutely the end of history, Asia the beginning' (Hegel 1956 [1899]:103).

17 *Duy Tan* is today translated as 'modernisation' (Dang Chan Lieu et al. 1997). Woodside (1976:37) illuminatingly translated it as 'renovation': a Vietnamese version of the Japanese Meiji Restoration, remembering that for the Vietnamese, the Japanese exemplified successful acquisition of the military, technological and scientific power that brought them equivalence with Europe. In the pamphlet *Tan Viet Nam* (*The New Vietnam* 1907), as cited by Shiraishi Masaya, Phan depicted an image of Vietnam after *Duy Tan*: 'the country would be rich and strong and the people would enjoy democracy and a developed civilization' (Shiraishi Masaya 1988:63).

18 Duara 1995 illustrates the parallel adoption in China of what he calls 'Enlightenment History'.

19 An influential activist who, in his early twenties, was to galvanise popular protest against the French with brilliant oratory and arresting images.

20 The pen name of novelist, publisher and activist, Nguyen Tuong Tam.

21 A political party founded in 1917, centred in Saigon and representing wealthy indigenous commercial interests over colonial monopolies.

22 Southern Vietnam, otherwise known as *Nam Bo* or *Nam Ky* and, in colonial times as *Cochinchine*, lies in the extreme south of the country, and is to be distinguished from the area below the 17th parallel, formerly under the Republic of Vietnam (1955–75), which is referred to here as South Vietnam, and in Vietnamese (usually) as *Mien Nam*.

23 Their typical designation as anti-colonialists shouldn't obscure that in practice much of their rhetorical heat was directed against the domestic beneficiaries of colonialism: uneducated pretenders, political opportunists, corrupt mandarins and outmoded traditionalists, who most vividly illustrated the deficit between France's civilisational ideals and its colonial reality.

24 The Vietnamese Nationalist Party (Viet Nam Quoc Dan Dang), established in 1927 and among the ICP's most serious contenders for power, was an almost uniquely northern phenomenon and similar to other movements originating from this region, it was to derive prestige from appropriating the symbols of distant power centres, in this case, the nationalism of the Chinese Guomindang.

25 The Cao Dai religion, founded in 1926 and Hoa Hao Buddhism, founded in 1939, are two of Vietnam's most important indigenous religions, originating in, and remaining most popular in, the southern Vietnamese plain.

26 Conceptualised as the third and final era of global history, in which the divinity speaks to humanity directly through spirits, which for the Cao Dai included the spirit of Victor Hugo.

27 This approach can be put alongside studies into the uses of 'tradition' in

political projects of self-definition in Vietnam, studied for example by Pelly 1995, Vasavakul 1994 and Giebel 1995. I have adopted a different approach, for the concept of modernity occupies as much attention, and is used with great self-assurance in Vietnam as elsewhere, yet there are few tools in social theory with which to address this.

## CHAPTER 1—NEO-COLONIALISM AS POISON

1 The Vietnamese Communist Party was founded in 1930 as the 'Indochinese Communist Party' (ICP). Between 1951 and 1976, this party went under the name of the 'Vietnam Workers' Party'. After formal unification it took the name of the 'Vietnamese Communist Party' (abbreviated to 'the party' in the text).

2 During the war years, the party projected its alternative vision through the framework of the RVN's rival for post-colonial, modern statehood, the Democratic Republic of Vietnam (DRV) in North Vietnam and, south of the 17th parallel, the National Liberation Front for South Vietnam (NLF) and the Provisional Revolutionary Government for South Vietnam (PRG).

3 The regime's use of military images, songs and language recalled an observation by Bourdieu: 'Every social order systematically takes advantage of the disposition of the body and language to function as depositories of deferred thoughts that can be triggered off at a distance in space and time by the simple effect of re-placing the body in an overall posture which recalls the associated thoughts and feelings, in one of the inductive states of the body which, as actors know, give rise to states of mind . . . Bodily hexis is political mythology realized, embodied, turned into a permanent disposition, a durable way of standing, speaking, walking and thereby of feeling and thinking' (Bourdieu 1990:70). The difficulty faced by the unifying regime was to go beyond the representation of ideal citizens to the embodiment of its vision in the dispositions of its new subjects.

4 In this group, Giap included the 'petty bourgeoisie', 'national bourgeoisie', the 'ethnic minorities', the 'religions' and even members of the 'puppet army' and 'refugees from the North'.

5 Such a line was maintained at a time when many southerners who, during the war, had participated in party-sponsored frameworks such as the PRG, were being sidelined from influential positions in the post-war regime (Truong Nhu Tang 1985; Porter 1993).

6 The editorial's title was: 'Based on recorded achievements, put your strength into struggle to forcefully advance the southern revolution' (*Tren co so nhung thanh tich da dat duoc, ra suc phan dau dua su nghiep cach mang mien nam tien len manh me*).

7 According to one author, 'The American culture of neocolonialism [is] a kind of venom (*noc doc*) disseminated by American imperialism across our South during the years of occupation. It is necessary to understand its reactionary essence (*ban chat phan dong*) and its vestigial presence in the newly liberated areas, to know how to fight and cleanse it' (Tran Quang 1976:10).

8 The sense of disorientation experienced by a cadre of the new regime on

his first visit to Ho Chi Minh City is described in the short story 'City Life' by Nguyen Ngoc Ngan (1988).

9 Published in Hanoi by the Arts Institute of Vietnam under the Ministry of Culture.

10 According to Hanoi culture critic, Le Anh Tra, artistic works that relied on appeals to the senses were dangerous, for such appeals might mask pernicious content, or end up being goals in themselves: 'With respect to tastes in literature and art, many persons are unable to evaluate correctly a poem, novel, work of theatrical art, film, song, painting and so forth. Some persons only like excitement in art, such as colourful lines of literature, "rock and roll" music and "romantic" songs, styles of perform-ing on stage that bring "cheap" laughs, scenes of spectacular violence in films and so forth but never give attention to whether their content is progressive or backward' (Le Anh Tra 1977:65).

## CHAPTER 2—RENUNCIATIONS OF SOCIALISM

1 The term can be found to describe becoming a party member—a process of maturation—in the politicised world view of many party histories and autobiographies.

2 Do Muoi went on to serve as Party Secretary-General until late 1997, the last year of his tenure marked by policy drift, economic stagnation and serious rural protests.

3 In 1998, Prime Minister Phan Van Khai asserted that 'disastrous and prolonged mistakes' in economic management in the post-war era had been due to the residual wartime mentality that everything could be accomplished by willpower alone (*duy y chi*), a view he and others retrospectively referred to as a 'subjective malady' (*benh chu quan*) (Phan Van Khai 1998: 40).

4 Throughout the 1990s, socialism retained its status as the unquestionable official world view. In May 1997, the party marked the 179th birthday of Karl Marx, with commentaries in the state-controlled media praising both Marx and Lenin. According to *Reuters*, the *People's Army Daily* (*Quan Doi Nhan Dan*) wrote that 'Marxism and Leninism remain a shining beacon for the proletarian class and working people in the world in their struggle for the noblest goal of the times' (*Reuters* 1997b).

5 The article provided biographical details. 'Born in Hai Duong province, Pham grew up in North Vietnam and in 1977 went to Germany to study at Humboldt University. She returned to Vietnam 1983 to live in Hanoi where she worked as an archivist and began to write seriously when she was 23. In 1993, the German translation of *Crystal Messenger* won the Frankfurt Liberaturpreis for the best foreign novel.'

6 Lu Phuong was born Le Van Phuong in 1938 in Ha Nam Ninh province. He graduated from the Saigon University in 1960 and worked for the *Tin Van* magazine. In 1968 he joined the National Front for the Liberation of South Vietnam and served as Cultural Deputy Minister of its Provisional Revolutionary Government. After the war he worked for a few years at the Culture Ministry in Hanoi and retired to Saigon, earning his living by tutoring and writing (Free Vietnam Alliance 1997).

7 Nguyen Xuan Tu, who received his postgraduate biology degree in Czechoslovakia, thereafter worked at the Science Institute in Da Lat.

8 In November 1995 Ha Si Phu returned from Da Lat to Hanoi to visit his family and was arrested for allegedly 'stealing state secrets'.

9 Nguyen Ho was a veteran party member. He fought the French and Americans and held several high ranking positions within the Vietnamese Communist Party. He helped inaugurate the Club of Former Resistance fighters as the club's president. Due to its intense attacks on corruption and 'negative' conduct within the party ranks, the club was eventually forced to disband and some of its members including Nguyen Ho arrested. Following the release of this paper 'My View and Life', Nguyen Ho was rearrested in 1994.

10 A soldier with at least ten years of active service, Duong Thu Huong's novel came out in 1988. It sold rapidly before being banned the following year. In 1990 the author was expelled from the party for 'indiscipline' (Hue Tam Ho Tai 1993:83) and was imprisoned the next year for 'revealing state secrets' and 'violating national security' (Bui Tin 1995:181).

11 Then President of the National Committee of Social Sciences.

12 Since its inception in the late 1970s, the Ho Chi Minh City Institute of Social Sciences, part of the National Institute for Social Sciences, was headed by senior Soviet and PRC-trained academics—party members— dispatched from the North after unification in 1975. Nguyen Cong Binh was among the earliest of these imported academic administrators.

13 Unless special usage is pointed out, the term '*Mien Nam*', translated as 'the South' or 'South Vietnam', refers to the region below the 17th parallel.

14 Rostow saw the Republic of Vietnam as participating in a process of 'modernisation', which he held was happening, 'throughout Latin America, Africa, the Middle East and Asia . . . Old societies are changing their ways in order to create and maintain a national personality on the world scene and to bring to their peoples the benefits modern technology can offer. This process is truly revolutionary. It touches every aspect of the traditional life—economic, social and political. The introduction of modern technology brings about not merely new methods of production but a new style of family life, new links between the villages and the cities, the beginnings of national politics and a new relationship to the world outside' (Rostow 1961:109).

15 Party dissident Nguyen Ho also considered the countryside a refuge from the party's mental confinement.

16 In 1994 I was quizzed by an officer of the People's Army, a northerner, who was visiting relatives in the Mekong delta after an absence of ten years, as to whom the credit was due for the changes that had taken place in the last decade. I replied, citing the factors many of my southern acquaintances would have given: 'Foreign investment and overseas Vietnamese money.' 'Incorrect,' he adjudicated. 'The changes are due to the wisdom of our party in having the foresight to create policies that will allow Vietnam to develop into a strong nation and wealthy people.'

17 Gareth Porter reported that the initiative proved enormously successful,

doubling and then trebling agricultural production in the province (Porter 1993:123).

18 For those interested in exploring the pedigree of '*doi moi*', this 'defence' of existing relations contrasts with the image of 'fence-breaking' state enterprises or the way the contract system in the northern port town of Haiphong has been characterised as an 'experimental' predecessor to the full-blown policies of the mid-1980s.

19 This view was parodied by mercurial southern historian, folklorist, novelist, and journalist Son Nam. 'Southerners are socialists' he insisted, gesticulating with his breakfast, a 'Saigon 333' beer. 'Take the overseas Vietnamese returning to visit his homeland. He's brought back a pile of hard-earned money to help his family construct a beautiful new house. First he meets his old ARVN army buddies whom he is obliged to treat. Then it's his ex-neighbours, old classmates and other friends. He invites them all to a "hugging bar"', a *bia om*. More than enough food and drinks are laid on for everyone, plus tips for the hostesses, waiters and *cyclo* drivers. By the time he makes it back to his home in the provinces, he's planning a more modest house. That's what socialism means in the South' (from fieldnotes).

20 The southern Sino–Vietnamese entrepreneur, Tang Minh Phung, a success symbol of the early 1990s, was sentenced to death in the late 1990s for involvement in massive debts and fraud activities.

21 'Pragmatic' and 'practical' are commonly used to describe the former southern-based party leaders associated with the *doi moi* reforms, Nguyen Van Linh, and Vo Van Kiet (for example, Duiker 1996:371).

22 Both rival post-colonial regimes had employed the image of resistance as a tradition to buttress their claims to legitimate post-colonial status. Pelly (1995) for instance, has written about the DRV's ideological use of Vietnam's 'history of resistance'.

23 In a commemorative volume on southern women, Nguyen Thi Ba, former head of the Ho Chi Minh City Food Trading Corporation, was described in this vein as a 'hero' (*anh hung*) and as a 'pioneer' (*nguoi khai pha*) for her role in the purchase of food on the free market in the South in the late 1970s, when the bureaucratic system still prevailed. For 'daring to take charge of such a risky and unstable assignment, sure to meet difficulties and obstacles', she was described as 'in the front line of those contributing their intellect, sweat and tears to enable the country to achieve something so miraculously ordinary' (Bao Tang Phu Nu Nam Bo 1993: 118).

24 It might be noted that from different historiographic concerns, the campaign to eliminate bourgeois commerce began only in March 1978 (Thayer and Marr 1982; Duiker 1989:50; Vo Nhan Tri 1990). In addition, several writers have noted that less than 50 per cent of industry and commerce was ever nationalised in the South: the socialist sector never assumed the monopolistic role planned for it (Thayer and Marr 1982; Beresford 1993:222). Even within the socialist sector, black marketing was rife and much nationalisation and collectivisation was in form rather than substance (Porter 1990:73).

25 This comment reflected the self-perception of former party secretary

Nguyen Van Linh, who, in an interview with Neil Sheehan (1992), described his own opposition to post-war commandism and his pioneering leadership of the *doi moi* policies as the acts of an enlightened and humanitarian rationalist.

26 Most of the air traffic through Saigon in the 1960s and 1970s comprised American military aircraft, there to shore up the existence of the South Vietnamese regime.

27 French colonialism had been in full swing for many decades prior to this and Saigon had been the major focal point for the export economy of the colony of Cochinchina. The subsequent nine years of French colonial presence was not a favourable time for export agriculture, as much of the Mekong delta was at war and under partial economic blockade. Meanwhile, through nearby Haiphong, Hanoi had had significant commerce with the rest of the world.

28 Factors omitted include ongoing French control of Saigon until 1954, US support of a rival post-colonial state in Saigon until 1975 and the location of large and influential anti-communist political movements in the Mekong delta.

29 For many southerners as well, the 'Revolution' (as the post-war administration came to be known) was the antithesis of the idea of modernity they embraced. Their new leaders were seen to have brought an end to the relative prosperity and cosmopolitan culture formerly typifying their region.

## CHAPTER 3—INDIGENISING MODERNITY IN *NAM BO*

1 *Nam Bo*, literally, the 'southern administrative division', comprises about one-quarter of the nation's land mass and includes the lower Mekong delta, Ho Chi Minh City and several provinces to that city's north and east.

2 The territory under RVN administration comprised the southern half of the former colonial Protectorate of Annam and the entirety of the former colony of Cochinchina.

3 Son Nam had been a party member, based in the Mekong delta during the 1945–54 Resistance War. Although imprisoned for a period by the Republican regime, he was not under formal party supervision during the 1955–75 period.

4 Although Nguyen Cong Binh here used the term '*Mien Nam*' which I have translated as 'South Vietnam', the content and the context showed that he was referring to the more limited region which he refers to elsewhere as *Nam Bo*.

5 Some accounts of Vietnam's encounter with the West, in the form of French colonialism, cast it in terms of a clash between a 'traditional' and a 'modern' socio-cultural system with often drastic implications for traditional social relations and categories such as the person (McAlister and Mus 1970:38, 95; Fitzgerald 1972:263). Such accounts assume the 'pre-modern' Vietnamese to have moved in an undifferentiated Maussian world of roles, personages and masks. A world of communal solidarity is sketched, where individuals were subservient to the collective, children in

life-long debt to their parents and the living in debt to the dead. Women found recognition only through practice of the three obediences and the four virtues. Notions such as individual autonomy and self responsibility were alien. One's fortune was dependent on the virtue of the King, on the deeds of the extended family, living and dead, on one's actions in past lives, on the whims of denizens of the densely populated spirit world, on the movement of astrological bodies, on the geomantic context of one's acts in both space and time.

6 Hoang Thieu Khang used the terms '*Mien Nam*' and '*Nam Bo*' interchangeably, in reference to the region discussed in this chapter. Son Nam (1992) used '*Mien Nam*' in the same way, in his classic study of 'southern' Vietnamese personhood: *Ca Tinh Cua Mien Nam.*

7 This claim contrasted sharply with that of Phan Thi Dac (1966) who, in *Situation de la Personne au Vietnam*, argued that 'despite the political, economic, social and spiritual upheavals of the last century, Vietnamese society still sinks all its roots into an ancient system of order and of values which leaves scarcely a space for the "me" (*moi*) of the individual and small latitude for its expression. On the contrary, social pressure is strong and continuous throughout one's life and in all domains.'

8 This 'indigenous modernity' is not to be confused with a 'world-system' type argument—that societies such as Vietnam's were transformed by the global expansion of capitalism.

9 An example of this historiographic convention can be found in Tran Van Giau's (1987) contribution to *Dia Chi Thanh Pho Ho Chi Minh* (Ho Chi Minh City Cultural Monograph). Tran Van Giau wrote that Vietnamese settlers in the region now covered by Ho Chi Minh City had to contend with tigers, and that the land in which they settled was a wilderness (*dai hoang*) (Tran Van Giau 1987:236).

10 One of the notable exceptions was Phan Quang (1967).

11 Many members of Vietnam's Cambodian minority refer to Vietnam's lower Mekong delta as *Kampuchea Krom* (South Cambodia).

12 By 'South Vietnam' (*Mien Nam Viet Nam*), Le Xuan Diem referred to the southern half of the country, and extended this concluding observation to the area which was home to the Sa Huynh and Cham cultures as well.

13 In fact he was one of its editors and a member of its 36-member authorial collective.

14 '*Nam Bo*' is used interchangeably with 'Mekong delta' throughout the book.

15 The historical accuracy of this comparison may be doubtful but the explanation given for it draws on widely-held views about the ecological differences between these two regions.

16 Fabian (1983) argued that anthropology similarly employs an 'allochronic' distancing device, 'denying coevality', that is excluding from the time frame of the observer, any society considered as 'the Other'.

## CHAPTER 4—REINVESTING MODERNITY AS THREAT

1 This sense of witnessing a historic transition applied especially to those whose view of Vietnam was derived primarily from exposure to the north.

2 The vulnerability of cadres to these hostile external forces was purportedly extended to their children. Paul Quinn-Judge, writing in the *Far Eastern Economic Review*, cited an article in the party journal *Tap Chi Cong San* that alleged that the PRC was trying to subvert the children of party leaders and revolutionary families to bring the revolution into further disrepute (Quinn-Judge 1982:28).

3 Vietnam Electronic Import-Export Company.

4 This term designated 'degenerate' (*doi truy*) or culturally 'inappropriate' (*khong thich hop*) items, including pornographic or violent movies, sex manuals, playing cards, 'outmoded feudal romances', occult manuals and music videos.

5 In the heyday of Vietnamese socialist realism, whose voluntarist aesthetic equated realism with optimism, the euphemistic term 'negative phenomenon' was the most graphic term used to assess shortcomings of the revolutionary administration. This was a time when the term '*chua tot*' (not yet good) represented harsh criticism. The term 'negative phenomena' was reserved for endemic problems in the administration itself. Its referents included bureaucratism, theft of state property, smuggling and corruption.

6 The crisis, as reported in both Vietnamese official press organs and by foreign observers, was usually expressed in terms of a deterioration in the moral standards of an administration once renowned for its austerity and integrity. For example, in 1991 the labour union newspaper *Lao Dong* reported that in the DRV, during the war, the courts tried only five to seven cases of corruption each year (*FEER* 1992b:13). 'But by 1985— when the party launched reforms to move the country to a free-market economy—the number of cases had increased by 1,800% over 1976; by 1988 they had soared by 2,230%' (1992b:13). In the same *FEER* article, Hiebert reported that: '[a]lthough Hanoi mounted a campaign in June 1990 to combat corruption, many Vietnamese claim the problem has worsened in the past two years. Hanoi residents say it is now virtually impossible to find a job, get a licence to build a house, receive treatment in a hospital, get a child into nursery school, obtain a visa to travel abroad, or secure a business or import-export licence without paying bribes' (1992b:13). In 1994 and 1995 respectively, Kerkvliet and Marr argued that corruption and smuggling were perceived to be dramatically on the rise (Kerkvliet 1995b:20–28; Marr 1995:12–13). Changes in the number of cases of corruption as Kerkvliet argued, may have been due to changes in the way they were tallied 'hence the contrasts are not meaningful' (Kerkvliet 1995b:22). However it was clear that these issues had become an increasingly explicit topic of concern. Reporting was becoming more detailed, illustration more specific and evidence that the problem was endemic was impossible to ignore.

7 Economic liberalisation and political decentralisation forced schools, culture houses and artists to adjust their activities to a market-driven common denominator and open up to a flood of cheap and profitable cultural imports. According to a 1990 report in the Ho Chi Minh City newspaper *Saigon Giai Phong*, 'quite a few artistic groups had to discard song and dance numbers full of folkloric and ethnic values and replace them with

"new and exciting" ones' (*Saigon Giai Phong* 1990:2). The report warned that traditional folk cultural (*van hoa gian dan*) and ethnic (*dan toc thieu so*) performances were facing 'a great and alarming danger of becoming hybridized or lost' (*Saigon Giai Phong* 1990:2).

8 In 1993, the emergence of the market economy was only one of several factors identified by the new Minister of the Interior as behind the spread of crime and social problems such as prostitition in the country: 'The country's social disorder and degradation are side effects of the market-driven economy coupled with poor experience in economic and social management, and the fact that our policies and legal stipulations have lagged behind reality and contain many loopholes, thus creating favourable conditions for the development of crime, social ills and illegal activities' (Bui Thien Ngo 1993:3).

9 Describing this as 'a term borrowed directly from Chinese Communist Party propaganda', David Marr characterised the campaign against 'peaceful evolution' as 'designed to warn all citizens of an insidious plot conducted by international human rights campaigners, overseas Vietnamese and American pop stars to destabilise Vietnam and extinguish socialism in yet another country.' He saw the campaign as representing: 'the current alliance between security officials, political commissars in the army and party "ideas and culture" barons' (Marr 1995:20).

10 The timing coincided with the national *Tet* holiday—a time of heightened consumption and festive participation in many of the activities labelled as social 'evils'. One can thus also see this campaign as something of a pre-emptive strike aimed at preventing such indulgence from reaching excessive proportions.

11 In an article published in *Nhan Dan* newspaper in August 1997, Nguyen Duc Binh, a member of Vietnam's politburo warned against 'dangerous manifestations' of a 'Western press perspective' unduly influencing domestic journalists. Formulating the issue as one of 'cultural and political trespassing' by foreign views, he argued that such influences 'destroy the boundaries of social order and national sovereignty in press and information activities' and decreed that 'these manifestations are strange and unacceptable for our news publications'. Nguyen Duc Binh reportedly suggested an alternative role for the press, not as a medium of transmission but as a line of defence: 'The press should not just contribute to a correct political orientation, but also prevent and eliminate from social life the harmful germs and poisonous weeds which are trespassing into our country through information channels' (*Reuters* 26 August 1997c).

12 A life of 'urgency, pragmatism and existentialism' as one official critic from Hanoi had put it (Nguyen Kien Phuoc 1990:21).

13 This criticism was made notwithstanding Gerard Hickey's observations of this pattern in the southern plain in the late 1950s (Hickey 1964).

14 A brunt of suspicion among ethnic Vietnamese intellectuals were overseas Chinese investors, exploiting cross-border ties of kinship and seen as masters of the under-the-table contract. Here the anxiety of loss of sovereignty was at its shrillest. Allegedly complicit in this invisible recolonisation were state power holders, seen as capable of doing anything for a price. The corruption and covert selling out of Vietnamese values in

the Chinese–cadre nexus was a criticism commonly voiced by urban intellectuals.

## CHAPTER 5—CIVILISATION IN THE ORCHARD

1 In *After Sorrow* (Borton 1995), an account of her post-war visit to the neighbouring village of Ban Long, Lady Borton recorded an identical claim, that indeed it was Ban Long that had been the centre of the Southern Uprising.

2 (Dang Cong San Viet Nam 1985.)

3 (Dang Bo Huyen Chau Thanh 1987.)

4 This part of Tien Giang province had formerly lain within My Tho province.

5 Long Hung native, Nguyen Thi Thap, commemorated in the provincial party history of the uprising with two photographs, was, at the time of writing these accounts, national president of the Vietnamese Women's Association.

6 The provincial party school director, his secretary, the village president and hamlet party cell leader, of roughly equivalent age, all saw the war with the US as the biggest challenge the village had faced. Villagers in the same generation as them (40–50 years old) were quick to remind me that not one of these, who claimed that the war had defoliated and blackened the village, had actually resided in the village during the war. The hamlet cell leader, village president and the provincial party school director had all resided in Saigon during the war. School secretary Brother Hiep had fought, but in a different locality. I got a very different story from several people who had resided in the hamlet during the war. Locals claimed that defoliation had not taken place. Apart from sporadic shelling when guerilla operations were detected in the area, they said that the only aerial bombardment of the village had come in retaliation against a guerilla offensive launched in 1972. This had been confined to some of the other hamlets in the village and was not of the same scale as witnessed elsewhere. They conceded that their village had been most fortunate in this. Parts of many of the surrounding villages had been virtually flattened by extraordinarily heavy bombing.

7 One 44-year-old female villager who had fought in the NLF for eight years called the boat people exodus 'the movement of escape' (*phong trao vuot bien*), using the party's own term for its attempts to mobilise the population in political 'movements'. She said she would have herself joined in, had it not been for family responsibilities.

## EPILOGUE

1 *Reuters* Dec 13 1999 'Vietnam investors paint gloomy picture'.

2 For example, Greg Torode, 'Vietnam feels sharp pain of modernisation', *South China Morning Post*, Thursday, December 31, 1998.

3 'They have no clear policy and are totally incompetent before the storm of radical changes in the world,' Nguyen Dan Que interviewed by Dean Yates Hanoi, Jan 28 2000 (*Reuters*) 'Challenges cloud Vietnam party anniversary'.

4 See references to the debate on 'speed culture' (*van hoa toc do*) in David Marr's 'Vietnamese youth in the 1990s' (1997).

# Bibliography

AP-Dow Jones News Service 1997, 'Vietnam's government clamps down on cultural evils' (December 12), posted on Internet (URL http://wwwvinsightorg/1997news/1212htm)

Bao Tang Phu Nu Nam Bo 1993, *Phu Nu Nam Bo* (*The Southern Vietnamese Woman*), Bao Tang Phu Nu Nam Bo, Ho Chi Minh City

Bauman, Zygmunt 1992, *Intimations of Postmodernity*, Routledge, London

Beresford, Melanie 1989, *National Unification and Economic Development in Vietnam*, Macmillan, London

——1993, 'The political economy of dismantling the "bureaucratic centralism and subsidy system" in Vietnam', in Kevin Hewison et al. (eds), *Southeast Asia in the 1990s: Authoritarianism, democracy and capitalism*, Allen & Unwin, Sydney, pp. 215–36

——1995, 'Interpretation of the Vietnamese economic reforms: 1979–85', in Adam Fforde (ed), *Researching the Vietnamese Economic Reforms 1979–86*. Australia-Vietnam Research Project, School of Economic and Financial Studies, Macquarie University, Sydney, pp. 1–16

Berman, Marshall 1983, *All That is Solid Melts into Air: The experience of modernity*, Verso, London

——1990, 'Why modernism still matters', in Scott Lash and Jonathan Friedman (eds), *Modernity and Identity*, Blackwell, Oxford, pp. 33–58

Borton, Lady 1995, *After Sorrow: An American among the Vietnamese*, Viking, New York

Bourdieu, Pierre 1990, *The Logic of Practice*, Polity, Oxford

Breckenridge, Carol A. (ed.) 1995, *Consuming Modernity: Public culture in a South Asian world*, University of Minnesota Press, Minneapolis

Brocheux, Pierre 1995, *The Mekong Delta: Ecology, economy and revolution, 1860–1960*, Center for Southeast Asian Studies, University of Wisconsin-Madison, Madison WI

Bui Dinh Nguyen 1990, 'Reader's letter', *Quan Doi Nhan Dan*, (15 March, p. 3), JPRS-SEA–90–016:22

Bui Thien Ngo 1993, '*Lam tot cong tac giu gin trat an ninh xa hoi*' ('Do well in the task of maintaining social order and security'), *Tap Chi Cong San*, (10), pp. 3–6

Bui Tin 1995, *Following Ho Chi Minh: Memoirs of a North Vietnamese colonel*, Crawford House Publishing, Bathurst

Central Committee of the Communist Party of Vietnam 1996, 'Draft political report to the seventh Party congress' (abridged transcript), *Social Sciences* (3), pp. 100–1

Chalmers, John 1996, 'Xenophobia creeps into Hanoi's new culture drive', *Reuters* (February 2), posted on Internet (URL http://www.vinsight.org/1996news/0202.htm)

Chanda, Nayan 1986, *Brother Enemy: The war after the war*, Collier, New York

Clammer, John 1995, *Difference and Modernity: Social theory and contemporary Japanese society*, Kegan Paul, London

Comaroff, Jean and John Comaroff (eds) 1993, *Modernity and its Malcontents: Ritual and power in postcolonial Africa*, University of Chicago Press, Chicago

Cooke, Nola 1997, 'The myth of the restoration: Dang Trong influences in the spiritual life of the early Nguyen Dynasty (1802–47)', in Anthony Reid (ed.), *The Last Stand of Asian Autonomies: Responses to modernity in the diverse states of Southeast Asia and Korea, 1750–1900*, Macmillan, London, pp. 269–95

Cuu Long Giang 1976, '*Am nhac phan dong*' ('Reactionary music'), *Van Hoa Nghe Thuat*, (10), pp. 42–4

——1977, '*Thuc chat cua cai goi la nghe thuat am nhac Saigon cu*' ('The essence of what is termed the musical art of former Saigon'), *Van Hoa Nghe Thuat*, (6), pp. 37–9

*Dai Doan Ket* 1977, 'Letters from readers' (16 April 1977:6), JPRS-VN–1893:80

——1989, 'Interview with Interior Minister Mai Chi Tho' (11–17 July 1989:1, 6), JPRS-SEA–89–034:41

Dang Bo Huyen Chau Thanh 1987, *Lich Su Truyen Thong Dau Tranh Cach Mang Cua Nhan Dan Huyen Chau Thanh* (*1930–54*) (History of the Revolutionary Struggle Tradition of the People of Chau Thanh District), Communist Party of Vietnam, Chau Thanh District Chapter, My Tho

Dang Canh Khanh 1996, 'Some views about the prevention of the influence of pornographic cultural products on teen-agers and adolescents', *Social Sciences* (6), pp. 70–8

Dang Chan Lieu et al. (eds) 1997, *Tu Dien Viet Anh Vietnamese English Dictionary*, Ho Chi Minh City Publishing House, Ho Chi Minh City

Dang Cong San Viet Nam 1985, *Tien Giang Trong Cuoc Khoi Nghia Nam Ky* (Tien Giang in the Southern Uprising), Ban Nghien Cuu Lich Su Dang Tien Giang, Ho Chi Minh City

Dang Phong 1995, 'The Vietnamese reforms viewed horizontally and vertically', in Adam Fforde (ed.), *Researching the Vietnamese Economic Reforms, 1979–86: Vietnam's transition to a market economy—an introduction to theoretical and empirical issues*, School of Economic and Financial Studies, Macquarie University, Sydney

Dao Duy Tung 1989, 'On Renovation of Thinking', *Vietnamese Studies* (New Series), (20), pp. 21–32

Dao Trong Tu 1977, 'Renaissance of Vietnamese Music', in Dao Trung Tu et al. (eds), *Essays on Vietnamese Music*, Red River, Hanoi, pp. 96–161

De Francis, John 1977, *Colonialism and Language Policy in Vietnam*, Mouton, The Hague

Dinh Gia Khanh 1990, 'Tradition and modernity in Culture', *Social Sciences* (2), pp. 30–4

Do Duc Dinh 1991, 'The public sector of Vietnam' in Dean K. Forbes et al. (eds), *Doi Moi: Vietnam's renovation policy and performance*, Monograph 14, Department of Political and Social Change, Australian National University, Canberra, pp. 54–67

Do Huy 1989, 'Identifying Vietnamese Culture', *Tap Chi Cong San* (5 May), JPRS-ATC–89–009, 10 October 1989, pp. 15–18

Do Thai Dong 1993, 'Economic opening and social reform (*Mo cua kinh te va cai cach xa hoi*), Report on project KX0110'. Unpublished paper submitted to Professor Nguyen Duy Quy and members of research program KX01 of the National Institute of Social Sciences

——1997, 'The impact of transformation on rural women in South Vietnam', *Vietnam Social Sciences* 2 (58), p. 77

Duara, Prasenjit 1995, *Rescuing History From the Nation: Questioning narratives of modern China*, University of Chicago Press, Chicago; London

Duiker, William 1976, *The Rise of Nationalism in Vietnam 1900–1941*, Cornell University Press, Ithaca

——1989, *Vietnam Since the Fall of Saigon* (updated edn), Ohio University Centre for International Studies, Athens, Ohio

——1996 (2nd edn), *The Communist Road to Power in Vietnam*, Westview, Colorado

Duong Thong 1991, 'Increased ideological work needed', *Quan Doi Nhan Dan* (3 May), JPRS-SEA–91–019, pp. 41–3

Duong Thu Huong 1994, *Paradise of the Blind*, Penguin, New York

Fabian, Johannes 1983, *Time and the Other: How anthropology makes its object*, Columbia University Press, New York

Fall, Bernard 1967, *The Two Viet-Nams: A political and military analysis* (2nd rev. edn), Pall Hall, London

*Far Eastern Economic Review* 1988, 'Socialist stagnation: Vietnam faces deepening economic and political problems' (28 July), pp. 20–2

——1989, 'Against the tide: the communists fear political reforms in East Bloc' (14 September), pp. 29–30

——1991, 'ASEAN investment helps to buoy Vietnam's economy' (27 June), pp. 52–3

——1992a, 'The tilling fields: rice glut worries Vietnamese farmers' (14 May), pp. 57–8

——1992b, 'No dong no deal: corruption spreading rapidly in the north' (25 June), p. 13

——1995, 'The South Rises: Old Saigon wins the peace' (4 May 1995), p. 5

Fforde, Adam 1991, 'The successful commercialisation of a neo-Stalinist economic system—Vietnam 1979–89 with a postscript', in Dean K. Forbes et al. (eds), *Doi Moi: Vietnam's renovation policy and performance*, Monograph 14,

Department of Political and Social Change, Australian National University, Canberra, pp. 95–117

Fitzgerald, Frances 1972, *Fire in the Lake: The Vietnamese and the Americans in Vietnam*, Vintage Books, New York

Free Vietnam Alliance 1997, 'Biography of dissident Lu Phuong', posted on FVA website, the Internet (URL http://www.fva.org/bios/luphuong.htm)

Friedman, Jonathan 1992, 'Narcissism, roots and postmodernity: the constitution of selfhood in the global crisis', in Scott Lash and Jonathan Friedman (eds), *Modernity and Identity*, Blackwell, Oxford

Furet, Francois (trans John Mandelbaum) 1982, *In the Workshop of History*, University of Chicago Press, Chicago

Giddens, Anthony 1990, *The Consequences of Modernity*, Polity, Cambridge

Giebel, Christoph 1995, 'Telling life: an approach to the official biography of Ton Duc Thang', in K.W. Taylor and John K. Whitmore (eds), *Essays into Vietnamese Pasts*, Southeast Asia Program, Cornell University, Ithaca

Gran, Guy 1975, *Vietnam and the Capitalist Route to Modernity: Village Cochinchina 1880–1940*, PhD thesis, University of Wisconsin-Madison, Madison

Habermas, Jurgen 1987, *The Philosophical Discourse of Modernity*, MIT Press, Cambridge, Massachusetts

Ha Huy Giap 1978, 'Fostering new socialist men and women', *Vietnamese Studies*, (52), pp. 16–22

Ha Si Phu 1996, 'Farewell to ideology' (excerpt), *Vietnam Insight* (May 1996), (URL http://www.vinsight.org/0596/hsphu.htm)

Ha Xuan Truong 1977, '*Cuoc dau tranh chong anh huong cua van hoa nghe thuat tu san*' ('The struggle against the influence of bourgeois culture and art'), *Nghien Cuu Nghe Thuat*, (1), p. 15

——1978a, '*Tiep tuc dau tranh xoa bo tan du "van hoa" thuc dan moi*' ('Continue to struggle against the vestiges of neo-colonial "culture" '), *Nghien Cuu Lich Su*, (180), pp. 66–75

——1978b, 'Socialist fatherland: ideals and realities', *Vietnamese Studies*, (52), pp. 9–15

Hegel, Georg Wilhelm Friedrich (trans J. Sibree) 1956, *The Philosophy of History*, Dover, New York

Hemery, Daniel 1992, 'Saigon Le Rouge', in Philippe Francini (ed.), *Saigon 1925–1945: De la belle colonie a l'eclosion revolutionnaire ou la fin des dieux blancs*, Editions Autrement, Paris

Hess, David Lazear 1979, *The Educated Vietnamese Middle Class of Metropolitan Saigon and their Legacy of Confucian Authority, 1954–1975*. PhD thesis, New York University, New York

Hickey, Gerald C. 1964, *Village in Vietnam*, Yale University Press, New Haven

Hiebert, Murray 1989, 'The Joy of Marx: no sex please, we're Vietnamese communists', *Far Eastern Economic Review* (31 August), p. 31

——1993, 'Dissenting voices: criticisms ahead of party conference anger government', *Far Eastern Economic Review* (2 December), p. 26

——1994, *Vietnam Notebook* (revised edn), Review Publishing Company Limited, Hong Kong

Ho Phuong 1991, 'On culture literature and the arts', *Tap Chi Cong San*, March, JPRS-ATC-91-007, pp. 10–11

Hoang Ngoc Nguyen 1991, 'Economic renovation in southern Vietnam: challenges-responses-prospects', in Dean K. Forbes et al. (eds), *Doi Moi: Vietnam's renovation policy and performance*, Monograph 14, Department of Political and Social Change, Australian National University, Canberra, pp. 34–45

Hoang Ngoc Thanh 1991, *Vietnam's Social and Political Development as Seen Through the Modern Novel*, P. Lang, New York

Hoang Nhu Ma 1976, 'The strangle of neocolonialism is being broken in South Vietnam', *Doc Lap* (20 Oct 1976, pp. 1, 6), in JPRS-VN–1887, pp. 19–24

Hoang Nhu Mai 1987, 'Cai Luong', *Vietnamese Studies*, (17), pp. 17–32

Hoanh Thieu Khang 1990, '*Tu diem xuat phat di len chu nghia xa hoi nhin co che nhan cach con nguoi Mien Nam*' ('Embarking on socialism—regarding the Southern Vietnamese personality structure'), in Nguyen Quang Vinh et al. (eds), *Mien Nam Trong Su Nghiep Doi Moi Cua Ca Nuoc*, Social Sciences Publishing House, Ho Chi Minh City, pp. 307–20

Hobsbawm, Eric and Terence Ranger (eds) 1983, *The Invention of Tradition*, Cambridge University Press, Cambridge

*Hoc Tap* 1976, '*Tren co so nhung thanh tich da dat duoc, ra suc phan dau dua su nghiep cach mang mien nam tien len manh me*' ('Based on recorded achievements, strenuously struggle to advance the southern revolution'), (4), pp. 1–9

Hue Tam Ho Tai 1992, *Radicalism and the Origins of the Vietnamese Revolution*, Harvard University Press, Cambridge, Massachusetts

——1993, 'Duong Thu Huong and the Literature of Disenchantment', *Vietnam Forum*, (14), pp. 82–91

Hunt, David 1974, 'Organising for revolution in Vietnam: study of a Mekong delta province', *Radical America*, (8): entire volume

——1982, 'Village culture and the Vietnamese revolution', *Past and Present*, (94), pp. 131–57

Huntington, Samuel 1968, 'The bases of accommodation', *Foreign Affairs* (July), pp. 642–56

Huynh Lua 1982, '*Cong cuoc khai pha vung Dong Nai-Gia Dinh trong the ky 17–18*' ('Settlement of the Dong Nai-Gia Dinh region in the 17th and 18th centuries'), in Nguyen Khanh Toan et al. (eds), *Mot so Van De Khoa Hoc Xa Hoi ve Dong Bang Song Cuu Long*, Social Sciences Publishing House, Hanoi, pp. 85–94

Huynh Ngoc Trang 1992, '*Tong quan ve van hoa Nam Bo*' ('A synopsis of *Nam Bo* culture'), *Social Sciences Review*, (11), pp. 59–70

Hy Van Luong 1992, *Revolution in the Village: Tradition and transformation in North Vietnam 1925–1988*, University of Hawaii Press, Honolulu

Jamieson, Neil 1993, *Understanding Vietnam*, University of California Press, Berkeley

Kamm, Henry 1996, *Dragon Ascending: Vietnam and the Vietnamese*, Arcade, New York

Kerkvliet, Benedict J. Tria 1995a, 'Dilemmas of development: an introduction', in Benedict J. Tria Kerkvliet (ed.), *Dilemmas of Development: Vietnam update 1994*, Monograph 22, Department of Political and Social Change, Australian National University, Canberra, pp. 1–4

——1995b 'Politics of society in the mid 1990s', in Benedict J. Tria Kerkvliet (ed.), *Dilemmas of Development: Vietnam update 1994*, Monograph 22, Department of Political and Social Change, Australian National University, Canberra, pp. 5–43

Kerkvliet, Benedict Tria J. and Doug J. Porter (eds) 1995, *Vietnam's Rural Transformation*, Westview Press, Boulder, CO

Kim Ngoc Bao Ninh 1996, *Revolution, Politics and Culture in Socialist Vietnam, 1945–1965*, PhD thesis, Yale University

Kimura, Tetsusaburo 1989, *The Vietnamese Economy, 1975–86: Reforms and international relations*, Institute of Developing Economies, Tokyo

Kleinen, John 1999, *Facing the Future, Reviving the Past: A study of social change in a northern Vietnamese village*, Institute of Southeast Asian Studies, Singapore

Kolko, Gabriel 1985, *Anatomy of a War: Vietnam, the United States and the modern experience*, Pantheon, New York

——1995, 'Vietnam Since 1975: Winning a war and losing the peace', *Journal of Contemporary Asia*, (25), pp. 3–49

——1997, *Vietnam: Anatomy of a peace*, Routledge, London

Kroker, Arthur and David Cook 1988, *The Postmodern Scene: Excremental culture and hyper-aesthetics*, 2nd edn, Macmillan Education Edition, Basingstoke

Le Anh Tra 1977, *'Giao duc tham my trong cach mang tu tuong va van hoa'* ('Teaching aesthetics in the ideological and cultural revolution'), *Tap Chi Cong San*, (9), pp. 55–60

Le Duc Thuy 1990, 'Economic reforms in Vietnam: contents, achievements and prospects', in Tran Van Tho (ed.), *The Economic Development of Vietnam in an Asian Pacific Perspective*, Japan Centre for Economic Research, Tokyo

Le Duc Thuy et al. 1991, 'The market mechanism in the new economic management system in Vietnam, in Per Ronnas and Orjan Sjoberg (eds), *Socio-Economic Development in Vietnam: The agenda for the 1990s*, SIDA, Stockholm

Le Hong Phuc 1990, 'Vietnam's agriculture and industry on the path of renewal: initial achievements and issues for the nineties', in Tran Van Tho (ed.), *The Economic Development of Vietnam in an Asian Pacific Perspective*, Japan Centre for Economic Research, Tokyo

Le Hong Quang, Major-General 1993, 'Transition to socialism in Vietnam—thoroughly understanding the seventh Party congress resolution: fighting opportunism and revisionism, an urgent task in today's ideological struggle', *Tap Chi Quoc Phong*, (September), JPRS-SEA–94–001, pp. 28–30

Le Huyen Thong 1990, 'Party reorganisation in a large city', *Nhan Dan* (7 September, p. 3), JPRS-SEA–90–030, pp. 8–11

Le Xuan Diem 1990, *'Mien Nam Viet Nam, mot vung van hoa-lich su song dong'* ('South Vietnam, a lively cultural-historical region'), in Nguyen Quang Vinh et al. (eds), *Mien Nam Trong Su Nghiep Doi Moi Cua Ca Nuoc*, Social Sciences Publishing House, Ho Chi Minh City, pp. 297–306

Lefebvre, Henri (trans John Moore) 1995, *Introduction to Modernity: Twelve preludes September 1959–May 1961*, Verso, New York

Li Tana and Anthony Reid 1993, *Southern Vietnam under the Nguyen: Documents on the economic history of Cochinchina (Dang Trong), 1602–1777*, Institute of Southeast Asian Studies, Singapore

Lockhart, Greg 1996, 'Introduction', in Greg Lockhart and Monique Lockhart,

*The Light of the Capital: Three modern Vietnamese classics*, Oxford University Press, Kuala Lumpur; New York

Long, Nguyen and Harry Kendall 1981, *After Saigon Fell: Daily life under the Vietnamese Communists*, Institute of East Asian Studies, Berkeley

Lu Phuong 1993, 'Questions and answers about Marxist Socialism', *Dien Dan*, (24)

——1994 'Civil society: from annulment to restoration', paper presented at *Vietnam Update 1994*, Australian National University, Canberra

Mai Chi Tho 1988, '*May van de cap bach ve cong tac bao ve an ninh, trat tu va xay dung luc luong cong an nhan dan*' ('Some urgent problems concerning security, order and building the people's public security force'), *Tap Chi Cong San*, (12), pp. 12–19

——1989, 'We are facing not only a socio-economic crisis, but also a moral crisis' (interview), *Dai Doan Ket* 11–17 July, JPRS-SEA–89–034, p. 41

Marcus, G. 1986, 'Contemporary problems of ethnography in the modern world system', in James Clifford and George E. Marcus, *Writing Culture: The poetics and politics of ethnography*, University of California Press, Berkeley

Marr, David G. 1971, *Vietnamese Anticolonialism 1885–1925*, University of California Press, Berkeley

——1981, *Vietnamese Tradition on Trial 1920–1945*, University of California Press, Berkeley

——1995, *Vietnam Strives to Catch Up*, The Asia Society, New York

——1997, 'Vietnamese Youth in the 1990s', *The Vietnam Review* (No. 2 Spring-Summer), pp. 288–354

McAlister, John and Paul Mus 1970, *The Vietnamese and their Revolution*, Harper, New York

Miller, Daniel 1994, *Modernity, an Ethnographic Approach: Dualism and mass consumption in Trinidad*, Berg, Oxford; Providence, RI

Miller, Daniel (ed.) 1995, *Worlds Apart: Modernity through the prism of the local*, Routledge, London; New York

Minh Bui 1997, 'Fire's out but Hanoi still hot', *The Sydney Morning Herald* (28 October)

Morley, James and Masashi Nishihara (eds) 1997, *Vietnam Joins the World*, ME Sharpe, New York

Murray, Martin J. 1980, *The Development of Capitalism in Colonial Indochina (1870–1940)*, University of California Press, Berkeley

Nguyen Cong Binh 1989a, '*Thu tong bien tap*' (letter from the editor), *Tap Chi Khoa Hoc Xa Hoi*, (1), p. 1

——1989b, '*Mot so dac diem xuat phat cua Mien Nam di len chu nghia xa hoi*' ('Some starting points of the South on its way to socialism'), *Khoa Hoc Xa Hoi*, (2), pp. 3–12

——1990, '*Mot so dac diem xuat phat cua Mien Nam di len chu nghia xa hoi*' ('Some starting points of the South on its way to socialism'), in Nguyen Quang Vinh et al. (eds), *Mien Nam Trong Su Nghiep Doi Moi* (South Vietnam in the Renovation task), Social Sciences Publishing House, Ho Chi Minh City, pp. 21–34

——1991, '*May khia canh xa hoi qua cuoc dieu tra kinh te-xa hoi nong nghiep Dong Bang Song Cuu Long*' ('Some social aspects through the agricultural-social-economic survey of the Mekong delta'), *Tap Chi Khoa Hoc Xa Hoi*, (9), pp. 10–20

Nguyen Cong Binh et al. (eds) 1990, *Van Hoa va Cu Dan Dong Bang Song Cuu Long* (The Culture and Population of the Mekong delta), Social Sciences Publishing House, Ho Chi Minh City

Nguyen Cong Binh et al. 1991, 'Ve co cau xa hoi va chinh sach xa hoi o Nam Bo' ('On social structure and social policy in *Nam Bo*'), *Tap Chi Khoa Hoc Xa Hoi*, (7), pp. 28–40

Nguyen Ho 1988, 'Conscience and loyalty', *Truyen Thong Khang Chien* (special issue), (December 1988, p. 9), JPRS-SEA–90–007, pp. 12–14

——1994, '*Quan diem va cuoc song*' ('My views and life'), Vietnam Insight (June 1994), (URL http://www.vinsight.org/0694/party.html)

Nguyen Khac Vien 1974, *Tradition and Revolution in Vietnam*, Indochina Resource Centre, Berkeley

——1977, 'From one delta to another', in Nguyen Khac Vien (ed.), *Southern Vietnam 1975–1985*, Foreign Languages Publishing House, Hanoi, pp. 279–325

——1981, 'Ho Chi Minh City: a turning point', in Nguyen Khac Vien (ed.), *Southern Vietnam 1975–1985*, Foreign Languages Publishing House, Hanoi, pp. 178–89

——1983, 'The Mekong delta: socio-historical survey', in Nguyen Khac Vien (ed.), *Southern Vietnam 1975–1985*, Foreign Languages Publishing House, Hanoi, pp. 338–61

——1985, *Southern Vietnam 1975–1985, Foreign Languages Publishing House, Hanoi*

——1987, *Vietnam: a long history*, Foreign Languages Publishing House, Hanoi

Nguyen Khac Vien and Phong Hien 1974, 'The other war', *Vietnamese Studies*, (19), pp. 151–87

——1982, 'American neocolonialism in South Vietnam 1954–1975: socio-cultural aspects', *Vietnamese Studies*, (69), pp. 1–122

Nguyen Kien Phuoc 1990, 'Ho Chi Minh City resolving three major problems to advance', *Nhan Dan*, (15 June, p. 3), JPRS-SEA–90–22, pp. 20–2

Nguyen Ngoc Ngan 1988, 'City Life', in Huynh Sanh Thong (ed. and trans), *To Be Made Over: Tales of socialist reeducation in Vietnam*, Yale Center for International and Area Studies, New Haven, CT, pp. 147–63

Nguyen Quang Vinh et al. (eds) 1990, *Mien Nam Trong Su Nghiep Doi Moi* (South Vietnam in the Renovation task), Social Sciences Publishing House, Ho Chi Minh City

Nguyen Sinh Huy 1996, 'Some manifestations of the conflict of values in the areas of ethics and social life', *Social Sciences*, (4), pp. 87–92

Nguyen Thi Dieu 1999, *The Mekong River and the Struggle for Indochina: Water, war and peace*, Praeger, Westport, Conn

Nguyen Thu Sa 1991, '*Ve nhan vat trung tam o nong thon Nam Bo: nguoi trung nong*' ('On the main character in rural *Nam Bo*: the middle peasant'), *Tap Chi Khoa Hoc Xa Hoi*, (9), pp. 30–3

Nguyen Van Huyen 1996, 'Some criteria for priority values when the country shifts to the market economy', *Social Sciences*, (4), pp. 82–7

Nguyen Van Linh 1988, *Vietnam, Urgent Problems*, Foreign Languages Publishing House, Hanoi

Nguyen Van Trung 1998, 'Luc Chau Hoc', in *Nhan Dinh X*, self-published manuscript, Montreal

Nguyen Vinh Long 1978, 'Changes in Saigon's Stage and Cinema', *Vietnamese Studies* (52), pp. 120–8

Nhan Dan 1977, 'Press forward with the offensive on the agricultural front', (8 February 1977), JPRS-VN–1893, 25 February 1977, pp. 7–8

——1985, 'Editorial' (16 July 1985), in Kimura Tetsusaburo 1989, *The Vietnamese Economy, 1975–86: Reforms and international relations*, Institute of Developing Economies, Tokyo, p. 56

——1990, 'Smuggling continues, despite severe penalties', (6 July, p. 3), JPRS–90–024, p. 53

Nhi Phu 1976, 'Brazen chaps!', *Saigon Giai Phong* (8 October, p. 3), JPRS-VN–1880, pp. 34–6

Nhieu tac gia 1972, *Trang Su Oai Hung cua Xa Vinh Kim* (A formidable page in the history of Vinh Kim village), Chanh Duc An Quan, My Tho

Pelly, Patricia 1995, 'The history of resistance and the resistance to history in post-colonial constructions of the past', in K.W. Taylor and John K. Whitmore (eds), *Essays into Vietnamese Pasts*, Southeast Asia Program, Cornell University, Ithaca

Pham Cuong 1970, 'In the liberated areas', *Vietnamese Studies*, (23), pp. 102–44

Pham Nhu Cuong 1990, '*Doi moi nhan thuc ve chu nghia xa hoi, mot yeu cau cap bach trong su nghiep doi moi cua chung ta*' ('Renovate perceptions of socialism, a pressing requirement in our task of renovation'), in Nguyen Quang Vinh et al. (eds), *Mien Nam Trong Su Nghiep Doi Moi* (South Vietnam in the Renovation task), Social Sciences Publishing House, Ho Chi Minh City, pp. 11–19

Phan Huy Le 1989, 'Tradition and Revolution', *Vietnamese Studies* (new series), (24), pp. 81–9

Phan Quang 1967, *Viet Su: Xu Dang Trong 1558–1777 Cuoc Nam Tien cua Dan Toc Viet Nam* (History of The Inner Region 1558–1777: The southward advance of the Vietnamese people), Nha Sach Khai Tri, Saigon

Phan Thi Dac 1966, *Situation de la Personne au Vietnam*, Editions du Centre National de la Recherche Scientifique, Paris

Phan Van Khai 1985, 'Ten years of socialist transformation and building in Ho Chi Minh City (1975–1985)', *Social Sciences*, (3), pp. 14–23

——1998, 'Kinh Te Viet Nam qua muoi nam doi moi' ('Vietnam's economy after ten years of renovation'), in Tra Nham (ed.), *Co Mot Vietnam Nhu The*, Nha Xuat Ban Chinh Tri, Hanoi, pp. 34–101

Phong Le 1991, 'Heading toward a new stage of development of culture, literature and art', *Tap Chi Cong San* (February), JPRS-ATC–91–008, pp. 16–18

Piot, Charles 1999, *Remotely Global: Village modernity in West Africa*, University of Chicago Press, Chicago

Popkin, Samuel 1979, *The Rational Peasant: The political economy of rural society in Vietnam*, University of California Press, Berkeley

Porter, Gareth 1990, 'The politics of "renovation" in Vietnam', *Problems of Communism*, (39), pp. 72–88

——1993, *Vietnam: The politics of bureaucratic socialism*, Cornell University Press, Ithaca

Pred, Allen 1995, *Recognizing European Modernities: A montage of the present*, Routledge, London

*Quan Doi Nhan Dan* 1977a, 'Silent bullets' (14 August, p. 4), in JPRS-VN–1976, p. 75

——1977b, 'Eliminate the poisonous cultural vestiges' (14 August 1977 p. 4), in JPRS-VN–1976, p. 76

Quinn-Judge, Paul 1982, 'Combat fatigue sets in', *Far Eastern Economic Review* (28 May), pp. 26–8

Rabinow, Paul 1989, *French Modern: Norms and forms of the social environment*, MIT Press, Cambridge, Mass

——1992, 'A modern tour in Brazil', in Scott Lash and Johnathon Friedman (eds), *Modernity and Identity*, Blackwell, Oxford

Race, Jeffrey 1972, *War Comes to Long An: Revolutionary conflict in a Vietnamese Province*, University of California Press, Berkeley

Reid, Anthony (ed.) 1997, *The Last Stand of Asian Autonomies: Responses to modernity in the diverse states of Southeast Asia and Korea, 1750–1900*, Macmillan, London

*Reuters* 1996, 'Vietnam's Muoi warns old Saigon a city at risk' (Hanoi: 18 June), posted 25 June 1996 on Internet (URL http://www.saigon.com/vnforum.html)

——1997a, ' "Social evils" to be purged in Ho Chi Minh City' (Hanoi: 15 April), (URL http://www.vinsight.org/1997news/0415a.htm)

——1997b, 'Vietnam hails Marx as shining beacon for oppressed' (Hanoi: 5 May), (URL http://www.vinsight.org/1997news/0505b.htm)

——1997c, 'Vietnam launches broadside at Western press ideals' (Hanoi: 26 August 1997), (URL http://www.vinsight.org/1997news/0826.htm)

Robequain, Charles 1941, *The Economic Development of French Indochina*, Oxford University Press, London

Robertson, Roland 1992, *Globalization: Social theory and global culture*, Sage, London

Rostow, W. 1961, 'Guerilla warfare in underdeveloped areas' (Address to the graduating class at the US Army Special Warfare School, Fort Bragg, June 1961, in Marcus Raskin and Bernard Fall (eds) 1965, *The Viet-Nam Reader: Articles and documents on American foreign policy and the Vietnam crisis*, Vintage Books, New York

Sahlins, Marshall 1993, 'Goodbye to tristes tropes: ethnography in the context of modern world history', *Journal of Modern History* 65, p. 21

Said, Edward W. 1978, *Orientalism*, Routledge and Kegan Paul, London

*Saigon Giai Phong* 1976a, 'Saigon's many faces' (5 August p. 4), JPRS-VN–1856, p. 49

——1976b, 'Comrade Mai Chi Tho attends national day celebration at Cu Chi' (4 September, p. 4), in JPRS-VN–1852:14–7

——1976c, 'Great rice crops' (13 October), JPRS-VN–1859, pp. 19–20

——1976d, ' "Researching" yellow music' (23 September, p. 4), JPRS-VN–1868, p. 92

——1976e, 'Saigon's many faces' (24 September, p. 4), JPRS-VN–1868, p. 4

——1977a, 'Think correctly and have a correct attitude' (Editorial, 21 April, p. 1), JPRS-VN–1948, pp. 68–70

——1977b, 'Letter to Saigon people's forum column' (19 January, p. 1)

——1990, 'Efforts needed to improve ethnic cultural life' (30 August, p. 2), JPRS-SEA–90–031, pp. 39–40

(The) Saigonese 1997, 'Just Wait [Regarding the serious illness of President Le Duc Anh]', *Vietnam Democracy Newsletter* (February) (URL http://www.fva.org/)

Schwartz, Adam 1996, 'Bonfire of the Vanities', *Far Eastern Economic Review* (7 March), pp. 14–15

Scigliano, Robert G. 1964, *South Vietnam: Nation under stress*, Houghton Mifflin, Boston

Scott, James C. 1976, *The Moral Economy of the Peasant: Rebellion and subsistence in Southeast Asia*, Yale University Press, New Haven

Sheehan, Neil 1992, *Two Cities: Hanoi and Saigon*, Picador, London

Shiraishi Masaya 1988, 'Phan Boi Chau in Japan', in Vinh Sinh (ed.), *Phan Boi Chau and the Dong Du Movement*, Yale Southeast Asia Studies, New Haven

Smart, Barry 1990, 'Modernity, postmodernity and the present', in Bryan Turner (ed.), *Theories of Modernity and Postmodernity*, Sage, London

Son Nam 1992, *Ca Tinh Cua Mien Nam* (The Southern Personality), Nha Xuat Ban Van Hoa, Ho Chi Minh City

*Sydney Morning Herald* 1977 (23 April), p. 1

*Tap Chi Cong San* 1983, '*Nang cao tinh to chuc va ky luat cua can bo, dang vien*' ('Raise the organisational and legal spirit of cadres and Party members'), (2), pp. 1–6

Thach Phuong and Tran Huu Ta 1977, '*Nhung noc doc van nghe thuc dan moi o mien nam*' ('Neocolonial cultural poisons in the South'), *Tap Chi Cong San*, (8), pp. 43–50

Thayer, Carlyle A. and David G. Marr 1982, *Vietnam Since 1975: Two views from Australia*, Griffith University Centre for the study of Australian–Asian Relations, Nathan, Qld

Thomas, Mandy 1999, *Dreams in the Shadows: Vietnamese-Australian lives in transition*, Allen & Unwin, St Leonards

*Tin Sang* 1977, 'A guideline for providing small merchants with a livelihood', (20 October, p. 1), JPRS-VN–1999, pp. 19–20

To Vu 1976, '*Nhac vang la gi?*' ('What is yellow music?'), *Van Hoa Nghe Thuat*, (5), pp. 43–6

Tran Dao 1993, 'Economic crimes in our country in recent years', *Tap Chi Cong San* (7 July, pp. 51–3), JPRS-ATC–93–009, pp. 8–11

Tran Do 1977, '*Mot so quan diem ve van hoa nghe thuat trong tinh hinh cach mang moi*' ('Some basic viewpoints regarding culture and art in the new revolutionary situation'), *Van Nghe*, 20 August, pp. 1–3

Tran Du Lich 1989, '*Dac diem san xuat hang hoa o mien nam Viet Nam nhin duoi khia canh phat trien*' ('Characteristics of commodity production in South Vietnam from a developmental perspective'), *Tap Chi Khoa Hoc Xa Hoi*, (1), pp. 13–21

Tran Duc Nguyen 1991, 'Vietnam's socio-economic development to the year 2000: approaches and objectives', in Per Ronnas and Orjan Sjoberg (eds), *Socio-Economic Development in Vietnam: The agenda for the 1990s*, SIDA, Stockholm

Tran Hoang Kim et al. 1991, *Dong Bang Song Cuu Long: Vi tri va tiem nang*

(The Mekong Delta: Its location and potentialities), Statistical Publishing House, Hanoi

Tran Huy Quang 1993, '*Linh Nghiem*' ('The prophecy fulfilled'), *Vietnam Forum* (14), pp. 55–60

Tran Ngoc Dinh 1978, '"*Vien tro*" *My*—*nhan to quyet dinh su ton tai cua che do nguy quyen Saigon*' ('US "aid"—the decisive factor in the survival of the puppet regime'), *Nghien Cuu Lich Su* (177), pp. 46–52

Tran Quang 1976, '*Vai suy nghi ve tan du van hoa thuc dan moi o Mien Nam hien nay*' ('Several reflections on the vestiges of neo-colonial culture in the South today'), *Van Hoa Nghe Thuat* 1976, (1), pp. 10–17

Tran Tan 1977, '*Em oi doi tan*', *Van Hoa Nghe Thuat*, (6), p. 38

Tran Thanh 1977, '*Thanh pho Ho Chi Minh sau ngay giai phong*' ('Ho Chi Minh City after liberation'), *Tap Chi Cong San*, (3), pp. 63–70

Tran Tho 1981, '*Tu lieu ve dot truy quet van hoa pham phan dong doi truy vua qua*' ('Some data on the recent phase of wiping out reactionary and decadent cultural products'), *Tap Chi Cong San*, (10), pp. 62–3

Tran Van Giau 1982, '*May dac tinh cua nong dan Dong Bang Song Cuu Long-Dong Nai*' ('Several features of the Mekong-Dong Nai peasants'), in Nguyen Khanh Toan et al. (eds), *Mot so Van De Khoa Hoc Xa Hoi ve Dong Bang Song Cuu Long*, Social Sciences Publishing House, Hanoi

——1987, '*Luoc su Thanh Pho Ho Chi Minh*' ('History of Ho Chi Minh City'), in Tran Van Giau et al. (eds), *Dia Chi Thanh Pho Ho Chi Minh*, Ho Chi Minh City Publishing House, Ho Chi Minh City

——1993a, *He Y Thuc Phong Kien: va su that bai cua no truoc cac nhiem vu lich su* (Feudal ideology and its failure in the face of historical responsibilities), Nha Xuat Ban Thanh Pho Ho Chi Minh, Ho Chi Minh City

——1993b, *He Y Thuc Tu San: va su bat luc cua no truoc cac nhiem vu lich su* (Bourgeois ideology and its impotence in the face of historical responsibilities), Nha Xuat Ban Thanh Pho Ho Chi Minh, Ho Chi Minh City

Truong Chinh 1976, 'Towards realisation of national unification on the state level', *Vietnam Quarterly*, (Spring), pp. 31–5

——1989, 'Reflections On the Spiritual Values of the Vietnamese', *Vietnamese Studies*, (24), pp. 20–7

Truong Nhu Tang 1985, *A Viet Cong Memoir*, Harcourt Brace and Jovanovitch, San Diego

Tu Wei-ming (ed.) 1996, *Confucian Traditions in East Asian Modernity: Moral education and economic culture in Japan and the four mini-dragons*, Harvard University Press, Cambridge, MA

Turley, William 1993, 'Political renovation in Vietnam: renewal and adaptation', in Borje Ljunggren (ed.), *The Challenge of Reform in Indochina*, Harvard Institute for International Development, Harvard University, Cambridge, MA

Turley, William and Mark Seldon (eds) 1993, *Reinventing Vietnamese Socialism: Doi Moi in comparative perspective*, Westview Press, Boulder

Uy Ban Khoa Hoc Xa Hoi Viet Nam 1982, *Mot So Van de Khoa Hoc Xa Hoi Ve Dong Bang Song Cuu Long*, Social Sciences Publishing House, Hanoi

Van Tao 1976, '*Xay dung mot nen thong nhat Viet Nam vinh cuu*' ('Establishing the permanent reunification of Vietnam'), *Hoc Tap*, (248), pp. 30–7, 65

Van Thanh 1976, '*Tinh ta sau dau*', *Van Hoa Nghe Thuat*, (5), p. 44

Vasavakul, Thaveeporn 1994, *Schools and Politics in South and North Vietnam: A comparative study of state apparatus, state policy and state power: 1945–1965*, PhD thesis, Cornell University

——1995, 'Vietnam: the changing models of legitimation', in Muthiah Alagappa (ed.), *Political Legitimacy in Southeast Asia: The quest for moral authority*, Stanford University Press, Stanford

Vinh Sinh 1988, 'Phan Boi Chau and Fukuzawa Yukichi: Perceptions of National Independence', in Vinh Sinh (ed.), *Phan Boi Chau and the Dong Du Movement*, Yale Southeast Asia Studies, New Haven

Vo Nguyen Giap 1966, 'The liberation war in South Vietnam: its essential characteristics', *Vietnamese Studies*, (8), pp. 5–36

Vo Nhan Tri 1990, *Vietnam's Economic Policy Since 1975*, ASEAN Economic Research Unit, Institute of Southeast Asian Studies, Singapore

Vo Phien (trans by Vo Dinh Mai) 1992, *Literature in South Vietnam 1954–1975*, Vietnamese Language & Culture Publications, Melbourne

Vo Van Kiet 1981, 'The cultural and ideological front in Ho Chi Minh City', *Vietnamese Studies*, (69), pp. 130–50

Wolf, Eric 1969, *Peasant Wars of the Twentieth Century*, Harper and Row, New York

Woodside, Alexander 1971, *Vietnam and the Chinese Model*, Harvard University Press, Cambridge, MA

——1976, *Community and Revolution in Modern Vietnam*, Houghton Mifflin, Boston

Xiaobing Tang 1996, *Global Space and the Nationalist Discourse of Modernity: The historical thinking of Liang Qichao*, Stanford University Press, Stanford

## VIETNAMESE LANGUAGE NEWSPAPERS AND JOURNALS CITED

*Dai Doan Ket*
*Hoc Tap*
*Nhan Dan*
*Nghien Cuu Lich Su*
*Nghien Cuu Nghe Thuat*
*Quan Doi Nhan Dan*
*Saigon Giai Phong*

*Tap Chi Cong San*
*Tap Chi Khoa Hoc Xa Hoi*
*Tin Sang*
*Truyen Thong Khang Chien*
*Van Hoa Nghe Thuat*
*Van Nghe*
*Xa Hoi Hoc*

# Index